Psychosis
Understanding and Treatment

Edited by Jane Ellwood

Jessica Kingsley Publishers
London and Bristol, Pennsylvania

'Learning to Think About Schizoid Thinking' by Murray Jackson was first published in *Psychoanalytic Psychotherapy 6*, 3, pp.191–203 (1992). Reproduced by kind permission.

'Working with Psychotic Processes in Art Therapy' by Katherine Killick was first published in *Psychoanalytic Psychotherapy 7*, 1, pp.25–36 (1993). Reproduced by kind permission. A slightly amended version appears in this volume.

'Psychotic Interventions at the Arbours Crisis Centre' by Joseph H. Berke was first published in *Sanctuary: The Arbours Experience of Alternative Community Care* edited by Joseph H. Berke, Chandra Masoliver and Thomas J. Ryan (Process Press, London, 1995). Reproduced by kind permission.

'Individual Psychoanalytic Psychotherapy with Severely and Profoundly Mentally Handicapped Patients' by Valerie Sinason was originally published in *Treatment of Mental Illness and Behavioural Disorder in the Mentally Retarded: Proceedings of the International Congress, May 3–4, 1990, Amsterdam, the Netherlands*, edited by Anton Dosen, Adriaan van Gennep and Gosewijn J Zwanikken (Logon Publications, Leiden, Netherlands, 1990). Reproduced by kind permission.

The 1992 Psychosis Conference, held at the University of Essex, Colchester, on which this book is based, was underwritten by the North East Essex Mental Health Services Trust.

First published in the United Kingdom in 1995 by
Jessica Kingsley Publishers Ltd
116 Pentonville Road
London N1 9JB, England
and
1900 Frost Road, Suite 101
Bristol, PA 19007, U S A

Copyright © 1995 The contributors and the publisher

Library of Congress Cataloging in Publication Data
Psychosis : understanding and treatment / edited by Jane Ellwood.
p.   cm.
Includes bibliographical references and index.
ISBN 1-85302-265-9
1. Psychoses.   2. Schizophrenia.   I. Ellwood, Jane, 1937–
RC512.P76 1995
616.89--dc20
95-6606
CIP

British Library Cataloguing in Publication Data
Psychosis:Understanding and Treatment
I. Ellwood, Jane
616.89

ISBN 1-85302-265-9

Printed and Bound in Great Britain by
Biddles Ltd, Guildford and King's Lynn

Psychosis

Understanding and Treatment

of related interest

Forensic Psychotherapy
Crime, Psychodynamics and the Offender Patient
Edited by Christopher Cordess and Murray Cox
ISBN 1 85302 240 3

The Cradle of Violence
Essays on Psychiatry, Psychoanalysis and Literature
Stephen Wilson
ISBN 1 85302 306 X

Shakespeare as Prompter
The Amending Imagination and the Therapeutic Process
Murray Cox and Alice Theilgaard
ISBN 1 85302 159 8

Contents

Part Two Treatment

Introduction

Jane Ellwood

Primitive and irrational processes are central to human nature and persist despite our attempts to outlaw them. Without acknowledging their existence, many human behaviours can scarcely be understood. Yet most of our present society is based on the premise that the basic state of affairs is logicality and rationality and that the only logical and rational way of carrying on is to ignore or discount the irrational. Such cut and dried perceptions can often lead to a dead end where all we can say is – things don't make sense.

Psychosis is the irrational writ large. In its extreme form it is a massive projection of primitive and frightening parts of the self into the external world (for the purpose of this book this would mean into the hospital or community where the person suffering this illness lived, or into the person of the therapist). Thus the world that the person suffering from this illness lives in is frightening, persecuting and/or meaningless.

This volume springs from a conviction that psychosis should be central to our understanding of mental illness in all its shapes and should not be pushed to the remoter shores of our history, society and work; in other words: as far from our own lives as possible. The way a society treats its most puzzling and disturbing members is an indication at one level of its maturity and of its ability to tolerate the anxiety generated by psychotic disturbance. The first part of the book seeks to establish the processes by which psychosis, and people called psychotics, come to be scapegoated and treated as alien from ordinary human beings. This section then goes on to set out the meaning that can be found in psychotic communication, and why a mind in the grip of psychosis tries so vigorously to destroy all sense and to create a world seemingly totally other to the one you and I experience most of the time.

How threatening and difficult it is to treat the primitive and irrational behaviour and communication of psychosis as anything other than irrelevant nonsense which ultimately has to be medicated away, shut away or variously disowned, is evident not only from Peter Barham's and Richard Marshall's chapters, but also from the experience of Christopher Cordess, whose paper delineates the difficulties of working with young offenders whose crimes defy common sense. Cordess quotes Glover (1944): 'Crime and Common Sense are refractory bed-fellows: So long as the existence of unconscious motives is disregarded we cannot learn any more about crime than an apparent common sense dictates.'

As a child psychotherapist, I spent time working with young patients whose behaviour and communications are every bit as strange and unpredictable and every bit as full of potential meaning as an adult suffering from psychosis.

I remember working with a little boy whose psychotic mother had run away with a fellow patient when the boy was nine months old, leaving her young son with the father. The father had remarried, to a woman with children of her own. The little boy dealt with this trauma by being a little angel at school, whilst at home he was considered a demon and locked in his room. It was incomprehensible to school why the parents should behave so cruelly and it was equally incomprehensible to his parents how their demon could transform into an angel at school. This was the paranoid schizoid world of the adult psychotic, and it is similar to the Jekyll-and-Hyde world inhabited by the murderers described by Arthur Hyatt Williams, where the focus of their projective processes split their world into two parts: good and bad. It was interesting that the course of this boy's recovery was seen as a failure both by school and home. At school, he gradually lost his angelic status and became more ordinarily naughty; the school was not happy with this. At home he began by changing from total refusal to eat his step-mother's food but sneaking down in the middle of the night to eat food direct from the freezer, to sneaking down in the night and attempting to cook the food – this was seen as 'worsening'. He followed this by relinquishing the behaviour pattern of sneaking down at night and stealing food and began to pillage neighbours' gardens for fruit and vegetables – the parents saw this as a further deterioration, since now his bad behaviour, which had been shut up in the house, had become public knowledge. What I saw happening with the young boy was two unreal worlds ameliorating into the very difficult real world that he unfortunately lived in.

One particular incident in his therapy proved a turning-point in my under-standing of him. One day when he was, for once, sitting quietly, very high up on the lockers looking down on me – this made a pleasant change from his usual wild rampaging around in the room so I was feeling more friendly than usual towards him – he began to plead with me to fetch him a beaker of water. I thought I would. I reached up to him, offering him the full beaker; he took it, and then threw it full in my face, laughing uncontrollably. Strangely enough at that moment I was overcome with a feeling of intense sadness which I was able to understand, and to put into words that he understood, and as a result our relationship changed. What it seemed to me had happened was that he had re-enacted a scene with his mother. He had become the mad mother on high, and I was the child hopefully seeking a drink (ultimately the breast), but instead teased and tormented. This gave me a vivid picture of his internal world where he had never, in a meaningful sense, been fed, and of his relationship with his mother as a part object which he had lived out so intensely with me.

One would have no trouble labelling this behaviour psychotic in an adult but in the world of the child, or rather of the child with acute difficulties, such behaviour could almost be described as normal. In the consulting rooms of child psychotherapists throughout the United Kingdom, children such as the one I described or often with more bizarre behaviour are commonplace. Valerie Sinason, also a child psychotherapist, in her chapter in clinical section, takes up the incredibly difficult task of working with mental or physical handicap and psychosis, but she makes it very clear that if the therapist can bear the pain, the young person can certainly use the intervention, which is appreciated like water in the desert. The point I wish to make here and which is made throughout the book is that psychosis is part of all of us. It is at the beginning of our humanity and at the roots of our dreams and creativity.

In itself it is a rejecting, dehumanising and distancing process to label someone, whether it be 'the liver' in bed eight or 'the psychotic' in ward nine. A verbal shift which transforms the perception is from the psychotic...to...the person with psychosis. Menzies Lyth (1988), among others, has shown us the need there is in hospitals for the staff to find ways of protecting themselves from the anxieties that the work causes, that is, working with people in physical and/or mental pain. The way society, we, often behave towards people with psychosis is an indication of how much we need to protect and defend ourselves against mad parts of ourselves. The children that manage to get themselves into individual child psychotherapy are children where the early developmental processes occurring in the first months or years of life have gone awry, so these children are still saddled with the intense world of the baby, who can only make sense of her world in omnipotent ways but who is yet so fragile and dependent. Up to the ages of seven, eight or nine it is, on the whole, acceptable for children to have imaginary friends, to hear voices, to talk to parts of their body or inanimate objects and to behave in an inexplicable way, according to the 'objective' canons of everyday life. It is when this behaviour becomes more extreme and unacceptable to the parents, such as in the case of the boy I saw, that the lucky children are seen in therapy; others may go on, possibly learning to live with and disguise the more worrying symptoms, until external or internal pressures become too much and a psychotic breakdown occurs, sometimes in adolescence but more often in adulthood. The person suffering from psychosis relates not to the real world but – like a baby needing desperately to hold onto good experiences, good memories (the good objects), and succeeding in so doing only by getting rid of (projecting) the bad and frightening feelings into the outside world – he or she constructs his or her own world by omnipotently imposing his or her own unreal inner structure on the real outside world which has, perforce, to contain all the terrifying thoughts and objects which had never previously in infancy been contained and assimilated. Considered in this way, psychosis is part of our very early developmental process, most of us know it is still there and keep in touch with it through dreams, and others – the poets, artists, musicians – have access to it in the painful process of creation.

The first half of this book, then, looks at the history of psychosis and how theories have affected practice, and goes on to present current psychoanalytical thinking relating to various aspects of the illness. The second half of the book is more concerned with the clinical work with the patient, the to and fro of projective identification. Katherine Killick takes us through the work she did in a big art therapy department in a large mental hospital. She warns the reader not to read too much into the paintings and communications of people suffering from psychosis; or rather that the vivid symbols are there for us alone, not for the sufferer who lives in a concrete world of 'symbolic equations' from which meaning is unremittingly expunged. I was reminded of the well-known poem by Stevie Smith, 'Not Waving But Drowning': 'I was too far out all my life/And not waving but drowning', which points not only to the precariously 'normal' world of those people described as borderline. Robert Young cites Meltzer and says: 'desperate defences against schizophrenic breakdown account for much of the psychology and behaviour of competitive and dramatically successful execu-tives and leaders', but also for our own wish to normalise and to read (comforting) meanings which are not there for the sender. Killick describes patient work over years before verbal contact can be made. This involves establishing a setting (a container) and a beginning and an ending. If beginnings and endings are non-existent, there is no moment when the therapist is not there, or here for that matter, nor is there any possibility for the development of symbolisation; there is no experienced need for symbols. Thinking, seeing and learning all depend on an ability to differentiate. Gregory in *Eye and Brain* (1966) describes the effect on a blind man who gained his sight in mid life. He describes his new found sighted world as a jumble of shapes and colours, blurring into one another. He was unable to differentiate one thing from another, finally gave up and became chronically depressed. In contrast, how quickly the baby learns to differentiate its mother's face and how quickly the baby learns to differentiate sounds. Another crucial differentiation is between the inner world of phantasy and the outer world of reality. When I listen to an unknown foreign language I cannot differentiate separate words and find it hard to imagine that the jumble of sounds I am hearing has a structure and separate words. The world of the person suffering from psychosis can turn into this meaningless confusion consequent on a failure to differentiate inner and outer reality. David Bell in his paper describes the superimposition of false knowledge on a reality that is otherwise unbearable. False knowledge stands in the way of learning.

The clinical papers all illustrate the intense difficulties of working with people living in a psychotic world, and although their reality is dramatically at variance with their therapist's, they nevertheless come through in these papers as having a great wish and determination to work in therapy.

Joseph Berke gives us a picture of psychosis as a communicable illness, where the professional members of the Arbours communities, no matter how they might pride themselves on their sanity and insight, can find themselves acting in ways they subsequently cannot describe rationally. He shows how workers in such a community can, with support, hold on to mad projections, think about their feelings and sometimes thus enable their guests to bear the pain themselves that they were projecting out into the community. Bell also talks about the possibilities of working with people suffering from psychosis in a community. I find myself wondering how one therapist could carry all the feelings that a person deep in the throes of a psychotic breakdown would need to project. Fakhry Davids talks of his feelings of isolation working on a one-to-one basis with someone who could possibly be described as borderline. Kenneth Sanders also describes individual psychoanalytic work with a borderline patient who was able to dream but whose life and work were terribly damaged. The advantage of working with psychosis in a community is that the therapists can support one another and can be made aware of and share what might happen to them as a result of the very powerful projective processes that are constantly at work evacuating feeling and, with it, meaning. The patient as well is possibly helped by not having to put all his or her eggs in one basket, so to speak. There is a selection of people into which various past objects, aspects of the self, can be projected, and some members of staff might even find themselves giving a home to the more hopeful aspects of the patient which can thus be better preserved and later reintegrated. One-to-one therapy could be seen as potentially dangerous for a very damaged person, for whom the most threatening thing in the world would be to relate to one other human being, who would represent the dreaded other into whom all their worst fears and most hated aspects of themselves would be projected. Thus one-to-one therapy would be likely to bring out all their resistances in a very extreme way, which could easily result in the therapy being broken off and destroyed. The roots of the work of the Arbours association go back to Laing and his pioneering work in the 1960s, when he worked with the families of people suffering from psychosis and thereby unlocked what seemed then a totally new way of working with and thinking about psychosis. Looking at Barham's chapter, however, we can see that in the last century in Switzerland Bleuler's community enabled people suffering from schizophrenia to live a life with meaning in the context of their families and their friends.

One thing that this book shows is that people suffering from psychosis do not all paint the same picture – we move from Killick's 'incomprehensible' communications to the dreams of Sanders and the surprising kindness of Berk's guests. The people suffering from this illness are as various as any other group of people. Some may recover, some may not and most may have intermittent episodes of varying severity. The more theoretical half of the book attempts to give us frameworks – more than one – for thinking about this illness and also to put it in a social and historical context; the clinical part perhaps gives more questions than answers. To end I return to Smith's poem 'Not waving but drowning' and the world of signs and signals. Signs and symbols represent a link between the world of the child and the world of the adult suffering from psychosis, and point to the work of differentiating the concrete from the symbolic. Editing this book has given me added conviction both that the dangers and difficulties of working with young children should not be underestimated, but also that the difficulties in the way of making contact with someone suffering from psychosis should not be overestimated.

References

Glover, E. (1944) *The Roots of Crime: Selected Papers on Psychoanalysis,* Vol.2. New York: International Universities Press.

Gregory, R.L. (1966) *Eye and Brain.* London: Weidenfeld and Nicholson.

Menzies Lyth, I. (1988) *Containing Anxiety in Institutions.* London: Free Association Books.

Smith, S. (1957) 'Not Waving but Drowning.' In the *Collected Poems of Stevie Smith.* London: Penguin (1985).

Part One

Understanding

CHAPTER 1

Learning to Think About Schizoid Thinking

Murray Jackson

INTRODUCTION

Psychoanalytic knowledge has much to contribute to the understanding and treatment of the seriously mentally ill. It can make apparently bizarre manifestations comprehensible, can facilitate the formulation and implementation of a psychotherapeutically-oriented treatment plan and can allow the selection of those individuals suitable for psychological treatments in general and psychoanalytic psychotherapy in particular.

All staff working with psychotic patients can be helped by acquiring some understanding of the nature of psychotic communication, and learning to think about schizoid and schizophrenic thinking could be regarded as a most important activity. It requires a hospital milieu where there is an interest in psychodynamics, staff who are actually wanting to undertake psychotherapeutic work with psychotic patients, and opportunity for supervision and discussion. Appropriate theoretical concepts are essential, and those of Klein and Bion are particularly helpful.

The author describes experience of such work in hospital settings in Scandinavia. All those participating learned how to begin to think about schizoid thinking, and to understand the nature of psychotic communication in greater depth. Ward staff appreciated the approach, and psychotherapists improved their skills, learning of the dangers of poor work with inappropriate patients, and of the benefit of careful work within a properly supportive context. Many patients who would not normally have been regarded as suitable for psychotherapy have been helped by this approach.

I begin with some abbreviated clinical material.

COMING AND GOING

A psychotic patient, attending for twice-weekly psychotherapy, enters the room, sits down, and remarks that when he comes in a bird lands on his head and when he leaves it flies away.

Another such patient, aware that the session is about to end, looks out of the window at a tree where birds are singing and anxiously announces that it is a blackbird that is singing, and that it is wicked and evil.

A third patient brings into the therapist's room a small jar containing a strange fluid and a ball-point pen. He says that the fluid is a mixture of semen, saliva, and urine, and explains that by keeping this jar with him he can feel safe and stay alive.

MEANING

Those of us who have long listened to psychotic and schizophrenic communication with interest, and sometimes with baffled incomprehension, will recognise that these vignettes are meaningful statements. I use the term 'meaningful' in a simple everyday sense of being a communication of significance and perhaps of importance, both emotionally and cognitively, in the mental life of the speaker. Some would regard these examples as typical of schizophrenic talk, and since we are liable to become confused in the attempt to understand the statements we would feel justified in regarding the talk as a reflection of schizophrenic thought disorder. When further enquiry reveals evidence of disturbed emotional development in childhood in each of these three patients, subsequent interest may take very different lines. depending on the professional role and frame of reference of the worker.

LISTENING

At this point the questions might be asked 'Who is it who is listening to the patient, and what models and concepts has he at his disposal? What credentials of experience and training does he have? What is he trying to do – to, for, or with the patient? What are the likely consequences of any response or intervention he might make on the patient, on the professional staff, and on himself, in the short and long term?'

PSYCHOANALYTIC PSYCHIATRY

The psychiatrist whose perspective is more neurobiological than psychoanalytic may be primarily concerned with matters of diagnostic classification, and the procedures for investigating disturbed cerebral function and of stabilising possibly defective cerebral metabolism with modern neuropharmacological preparations. If he regards early environmental experience as merely pathoplastic, rather than pathogenic, he may consider that modern techniques of stress management of the patient within the family, and of psycho-educational methods in general, will provide all the understanding that is necessary. The outcome for the patient may largely depend on the dynamic psychopathology of his disorder and on the experience and sensitivity of the practitioner. In some patients this may amount to the best possible treatment; in others a bad experience of not being listened to or understood (Jackson 1991).

Psychoanalysts rarely have the opportunity for extensive experience of psychotic patients which is available to the general psychiatrist (see Freeman 1985), but a small number of them have made investigations in depth that have revolutionised our understanding and psychotherapeutic potential.

Psychiatrists may criticise psychoanalysts on the grounds that much of their writing about schizophrenia does not concern 'true' schizophrenia, but rather deals with atypical psychoses such as reactive, cycloid, or paranoid states (Cutting 1985), and that they ignore the growing evidence of genetically determined predisposition in serious mental disorder. Psychoanalysts may dismiss the biomedical approach and the priority given to neuropharmacology and brain disturbance as merely defensive activities aimed at keeping the patient quiet and reducing the painful impact of the patient on the practitioner. However much justification there may sometimes be in these criticisms, it is the patient who is likely to suffer from the failure of the professionals to achieve an integrated approach where mutual learning can take place.

'SCHIZOPHRENIA' OR 'SMD'?

The patient may also suffer from the promiscuous use by professionals and public of the term 'schizophrenia', which has powerful implications of a disease of exclusively biological nature, of poor prognosis, chronicity, unsuitability for psychotherapy, and of the necessity of exclusively biomedical attention. The psychoanalytic view of ego dysfunction associated with a wide range of psychodynamic mental organisations (internal part- and whole-object relations) with various degrees of rigidity of destructive and constructive motivations, and various degrees of accessibility to change and growth, helps to resolve many diagnostic and procedural difficulties. The terms 'Psychotic Conditions' and 'Serious Mental Disorder' (SMD) are less vulnerable to such unfortunate connotations than is the term 'Schizophrenia'. The conclusive evidence of brain abnormality, such as ventricular enlargement and hypofrontality, in some cases is a welcome addition to our knowledge and a pointer to better treatment of some patients. The explosion of new knowledge about genetic transmission is leading to greater understanding of cerebral function and dysfunction. However, such advances in knowledge, impressive though they be, do not alter the fact that every individual's capacity to live in the world of reality depends on his success in developing a stable ego, and an unstable brain, and an unfavourable early environment at sensitive periods of his development provide independent or joint pathogenic factors.

PSYCHOANALYTIC THEORIES OF PSYCHOSIS

It has often been pointed out that psychoanalysts may not be very good at communicating with psychiatrists, and insofar as this is true it is not surprising. Psychoanalytic theories of psychosis are complex, constantly evolving and dealing with material that is extremely difficult to conceptualise in simple terms. Much psychoanalytic work deals with internal reality and unconscious phantasy, and these are essential basic concepts that may be very difficult to grasp or use in a helpful manner. Without some experience of personal psychotherapy, it may require exceptional qualities of the individual worker to begin to realise the profound significance of this perspective. Without some supervised psychotherapeutic contact with individual psychotic patients, learning to understand psychotic communication and to respond helpfully to it may be very difficult indeed.

Psychoanalytic theories of psychosis are complex and sometimes conflicting (see Arieti 1974, Benedetti 1987), and may present the learner with a conceptual jungle in which he may easily become lost in confusion and abandon the enterprise. One such conflict within psychoanalysis concerns the concept of ego boundary and its impairment in schizophrenia. Following the original work of Federn (1952), many analysts working in the 'ego-psychology' framework regard this phenomenon as a reflection of psychological deficit, a view that tends to lead to a supportive, ego-strengthening approach. By sharp contrast, the Kleinian theorists regard such ego weakness as the expression of powerful defensive activities.

KLEINIAN CONTRIBUTIONS

The work of Melanie Klein and the 'post-Kleinians' (of whom the best known are Rosenfeld, Segal, Bion, Joseph, Money-Kryle, Meltzer, Rey) takes a new path from the base of classical psychoanalytic theory (see Spillius 1989). Springing from a deep-seated dread of destructiveness, a force that is innate in its origins, the potential schizophrenic, in this view, makes excessive use of primitive defence mechanisms in order to protect and preserve his primary object, the nurturing mother. This represents an exaggeration of the normal developmental sequences in which idealisation, splitting, projective and introjective identification structure the inner world and developing ego of the infant and lead to transition from the paranoid-schizoid position to the depressive position, where whole-object relations and constructive reparative guilt begin to emerge.

When things go wrong, especially in the earliest relation with the mother, these primitive mechanisms persist and predispose to subsequent psychotic developments. Excessive use of projective identification distorts the perceptual world, leads to confusion between self and object, internal and external reality, predisposes to concrete thinking and disturbance of symbolic thinking, and weakens the ego. Successful psychotherapy at any stage of life reduces the use of projective identification, strengthens the ego, and leads to a more realistic view of the world and the self. The life-long use of excessive projective identification for defensive purposes (rather than for purposes of empathy and communication) constitutes a very real psychological deficit. In this view, the defence-deficit controversy is no longer of great significance.

THE PSYCHOTIC SELF

More recent work develops the concept of narcissism, of the pathology of thought and of thinking, and casts new light on subtle and hidden processes deriving from what Bion (1957) called the psychotic part of the personality. Motivated by destructive envy and the attempt to avoid the inevitable pain of relating to separate objects, the psychotic self launches an attack on any mental process that might threaten to bring awareness of human need and potentially healthy dependency. Such thoughts that have been thus rejected, or in some cases have never achieved mental representation, may be encountered by the subject in the form of a wide variety of environmental intrusions, such as hallucinations, illusory perceptions, or paranoid experiences.

Such processes, originally recognised by Tausk (1919) have been vividly exemplified in the writings of Searles (1965). They have been investigated in detail by Bion (1957) who employed the term 'proto-thoughts' for those mental elements seeking for recognition and representation, and 'bizarre objects' for the confused conglomerates that may result from the conflict of forces attempting to achieve recognition with those opposing it (see Ogden 1990, Lucas 1992). These damaged residues of 'stillborn' thoughts may often contribute to schizophrenic delusional experience.

USE OF THESE CONCEPTS

Some of these ideas represent a revolutionary departure from classical psycho-analytic theorising. They may prove difficult to grasp, and their usefulness in situations other than classical psychoanalysis may not be obvious. The extension of classical psychoanalytic concepts to the field of psychoanalytically-oriented psychotherapy and milieu therapy has long been established (see Sandler, Dare and Holder 1973) and such basic concepts as unconscious conflict and defence, transference, countertransference, repetition-compulsion, interpretation, and working-through, are straightforward enough and are the reliable tools of all psychoanalytically-oriented psychotherapists. It is not difficult to follow how the term 'schizoid' has been extended far beyond the intentions of Kretschmer (1936) and Bleuler (1978), to understand those formulations of Fairbairn (1952) which Klein adopted, and to appreciate Winnicott's (1960) popular macroscopic model of 'true' and 'false' self. It can be much more difficult to comprehend fully the Kleinian microscopy of psychotic mental processes, and some of the developments of Bion, such as his concept of maternal alpha-function and of 'container and contained'.

Klein's 'schizoid', for example, is a category of mental organisation encountered in all mental states, from the normal to the severely psychotic, and as such cuts across the familiar classifications of borderline, narcissistic, psychotic, schizophrenic, and manic-depressive. 'Notes on some Schizoid Mechanisms' (Klein 1946) is a crucial text, but makes difficult reading.

These considerations bring me back to the questions implied in my title. What are the characteristics of schizoid thinking? Who should learn about them, and why? What should be done with the new knowledge? Following Bion's injunction that the best learning is that deriving from experience I think that thorough personal analysis of one's own schizoid components of personality and supervised psychoanalytic psychotherapy of carefully chosen non-chronic psychotic patients, within a supportive and dynamically-oriented ward milieu, provide the ideal learning situation (see Jackson 1992). However, in the real world of mental-health care today, these conditions are a luxury available only in active psychoanalytic centres, and professionals must do their best with what is available. Despite this handicap, important work takes place in some 'peripheral' centres.

LEARNING BY EXPERIENCE: DANGERS AND OPPORTUNITIES

Having had the unusual opportunity of conducting on-going clinical seminars in several centres in Scandinavia, both with small groups of psychotherapists and larger groups of ward-milieu staff, I have been profoundly impressed by the enthusiasm of participants, their willingness to become involved psychotherapeutically with psychotic patients, and their determination to learn. Enthusiasm and zeal, however, may have adverse consequences if they are not guided and supported by sufficient knowledge. Rosenfeld sounded the warning that

'unskilled psychotherapy of the psychoses is a danger to the therapist's personality because it inevitably stimulates his feelings of omnipotence and helplessness.' (Rosenfeld 1987, p.8)

The British aphorism 'a little knowledge is a dangerous thing' may lead on to the recommendation that 'ignorance is bliss', which, if followed, would mark the end of new understanding. The dangers of 'wild' therapy are well known. They can, however, be minimised by recognising the fact that although it is a good experience to acquire a deeper understanding of your patient's inner world and methods of communication, and although in the course of your activity you may have given the patient a good experience of being listened to and accepted at his own concrete level of thinking, conveying your understanding to the patient and working through is another matter.

In actual practice, however, fears that participants would dilute the knowledge and behave omnipotently with their patients, interpreting symbolic material in an inappropriate or dangerous way, were very rarely realised. Several of the participants had been working psychotherapeutically with psychotic patients for many years, with encouraging results. Psychotic transferences have inevitably appeared, but where the supportive environment was strong these proved manageable, and the profound therapeutic opportunity of attempting to work these through became obvious. There was no evidence of patients or therapists being harmed by therapy, and considerable evidence that some patients have been greatly helped.

Some therapists came to realise that although they thought they were practising psychoanalytic psychotherapy what they were really doing was in fact psychoanalytically-oriented supportive therapy, albeit often of high quality. For these therapists, deepening their understanding, and moving gradually towards a more actively exploratory and interpretive mode where appropriate, proved to be a difficult but rewarding experience.

Although effective contact with a psychotic patient is an emotional matter for both parties, dedication and empathy alone are not enough. We need to learn the mental mechanisms that the patient is using, and the fears he is trying to control, in as much detail as possible; to talk to his sane and intelligent self as much as possible; and to provide him with a cognitive framework within which to understand his experience in a new way. The earlier in the patient's psychiatric career the attempt can be made the greater are the chances of helping him.

We need to learn to talk to our patients in as clear and simple a manner as we can, at the level that they can understand and use. Introducing parameters, such as touching or holding, or easy 'sharing' of our countertransference feelings, is alien to the Kleinian tradition, which considers that the patient feels sufficiently 'held' psychologically when he is being understood, and that the therapist's function is to try to understand and to convey this understanding verbally wherever possible. In this view, holding, touching, and sharing intense emotions, which is at times an essential part of the nursing staff's function, is not an appropriate technique for the psychoanalytic psychotherapist.

Episodes of regression are common in the course of therapy, and regressive revival of the infantile dependent transference may sometimes be a prerequisite for psychological growth. However, the use of regression as a deliberate technique is a dynamically complex procedure best left in the hands of the few highly experienced people qualified to do such experimental work. The learner should at least start his career in a more pedestrian and less ambitious manner.

I have been surprised at how often a patient appears to be asked to be understood and to be helped to understand his confused experience. One patient said 'Rocky Marciano is inside Rocky Stallone and Rocky Stallone is inside Per, and I am Per! This is true but it can't be!' The therapist had become aware of the space-centred nature of much schizoid thinking, and of the concrete nature of psychotic wishful identifications (in this case wishing to be hard, big, and strong, and not small and weak like a little boy) and was able to explore the patient's current fears. Another male patient said 'People are inside me and I am inside people. I am pregnant but I'm not! Why do I have these crazy thoughts?'

Some patients may reach a point where they can be offered an answer to such questions. Such an answer might be 'Because for you there are two realities, and two modes of thinking when you are awake, whereas for most other people the second reality is only obvious in infancy or when dreaming, or sometimes in creative activity.' Although such a response may sound unduly didactic, it addresses a profound truth about some aspects of schizophrenic thinking. Freud's conceptualisation of the 'primary processes' of thought has been amplified by the work of Matte-Blanco (1988) on symmetrical thinking and bi-logic, and it is possible that many patients can be helped by the acquisition of such knowledge.

A SWEDISH ENTERPRISE

Theory without experience is of limited use. Experience without theory may be hard to communicate. A judicious combination of theory and practice optimises learning. Obvious though these statements may be, it is much less obvious how to follow this counsel in the interests of the psychotic patient. One such attempt has been taking place in Sweden on a small, but significant, scale.

In the Falun Hospital in Kopparberg County, in the district of Darlana, one psychotherapist's interest in the work of Klein and Bion led him to set up a study group which met at fortnightly intervals. His successor, a senior psychotherapy supervisor, continued the tradition. Major works were systematically and care-fully studied, and tests of level of understanding were regularly undertaken. For several years I have visited this 'PPSG' (Psychotherapy of Psychotics Study Group) every three months, and conducted a work discussion seminar focused on the use of these psychoanalytic ideas in understanding the psychotic patients whom they had in therapy. Typical of the generosity of provision for mental-health services in Sweden, all the particpants had access to regular supervision with experienced psychoanalytically oriented psychotherapists.

Clinical work at such long intervals could not qualify as supervision, so much as an on-going experiment in the acquisition of knowledge about schizoid and schizophrenic thinking, and an attempt to create a culture where the highest priority is given to listening to the patient and trying to understand him. Many of the examples given above derive from this working group, and illustrations of the characteristics of schizoid thinking were a central feature of the activity. A practical consequence of this group's activity has been the decision to inaugurate a small unit for the 'integrated' approach to the treatment of first-attack psychotic patients.

SCHIZOID THINKING

I shall mention and exemplify some characteristics of schizoid thinking in summary form, drawing on the formulations of Rey (1988).

The schizoid individual has failed to transform certain sensori-motor experiences into representations, images, symbols and memories, a transformation that is essential for the construction of a normal apparatus for thinking. Schizoid elements of thought have a concrete character and tend to be space- and action-centred.

A patient violently pounds on the wall of a restaurant where, as he later explains to his therapist, 'the white blues were coming through the wall of the restaurant with pistols shooting electricity waves at me!' The 'white blues' are small figures coming through the wall, glaring at him, and trying to make him do things he does not want to do. At first he found them bad and frightening, but has since begun to feel extremely confused because he sometimes thinks they are good. He cannot bear the confusion and he screams and yells and asks the staff for more medication. The therapist expresses sympathetic interest in his frightening experience and learns that blue is associated with the lights of police cars, and that the lights allow the police to see inside him, where there is a woman trying to humiliate him by making him masturbate.

His associations continue, and the therapist begins to think that something has happened to stimulate intolerable thoughts and wishes. Evacuated from his mind, they return in the form of electricity waves and bizarre objects – the small figures composed of a confused conglomerate of parts of the self, condemned by primitive superego elements as bad, or maybe good, sexual wishes. Further exploration might reveal more of the nature of these guilty sexual feelings and their likely connection with the transference, and the therapist, from his knowledge of the patient is now in a position to give useful thought to the matter, and may have enough contact with the patient to be able to talk with him about it. He may not get very far, but he may give the patient the experience of being listened to by someone who seems to consider that his bizarre and terrifying experience may become understandable in a different and less confusing way.

The schizoid individual thinks, not in terms of persons, but of objects (or parts of objects) situated somewhere in a container. As Rey puts it, thoughts tend to be experienced as material objects or processes contained somewhere, expelled into something or other (often into the mental representation of the subject's own body), and even the containing object is itself contained somewhere. Nothing is not inside something.

One young woman explained that when she walks into the woods it prevents the animals from having babies. She had no conscious awareness of the destructive quality of her unresolved jealousy of younger siblings, but the therapist had. However, this familiar Oedipal theme may be less important than its possible meaning as a transference communication. Rosenfeld advised the therapist to pay the closest attention to what a patient is saying. He was convinced that

> '...the psychotic patient's speech and behaviour (particularly in sessions) invariably makes a statement about his relationships to the therapist.' (Rosenfeld 1987, p.3)

Looked at in this perspective, the therapist would need to consider that his creative work is going to be attacked from the moment the session begins, and that the sane part of the patient has some awareness of this.

A young schizophrenic man had, in a state of confusion, killed his mother. He was referred from a forensic unit for psychotherapy where he made strenuous efforts to convince his therapist that he had a large lump protruding visibly from his head. This, he said, was caused by an editing machine inside his head. It could alter and edit stories and had proved for him that his mother was not dead at all. When the therapist expressed interest the patient asked if this could really be true. The therapist, quietly and kindly, said he did not think so. The patient responded by saying that the lump had now disappeared and that he felt a little better.

The schizoid person thinks in terms of an 'inside' and an 'outside', of invasion and being invaded. So powerful is the unresolved infantile dread of separation, separateness, and loss of a symbiotic or parasitical existence, that claustrophobic and agoraphobic panic is an ever-present threat. He cannot acquire a stable ego, because of his invasive-projective impulses, which distort the object, rendering it dangerous, collapsed, or invasive. His mental life is often a claustrophilic one, seeking to maintain an omnipotent phantasy of living safely inside his objects. The most extreme cases enact this in real life, with varying degrees of concreteness, such as transsexualism, or in living as a misanthropic hermit in a hut or cave, both instances representing (in unconscious phantasy) the invasion and colonisation of the maternal space (Rey 1988, p.218). In such a state of profound narcissism, he attempts to obliterate any recognition of his isolation and need for others, and the dangers of associated aggressive feelings which he fears might destroy them.

SCHIZOPHRENIFORM, BORDERLINE, SCHIZOPHRENIC, MANIC-DEPRESSIVE

An individual may find himself assigned to one or more of the conventional psychiatric diagnostic syndromes at various times during the course of his psychiatric 'career'. These diagnoses may be perfectly correct and appropriate, but may not necessarily be stable, in that the patient may change to a different mental state, better or less well integrated, requiring a revision of diagnosis. The concepts of 'psychotic part of the personality' and of progress from the paranoid-schizoid to the depressive position, help to make these not-uncommon shifts more understandable. Although genetic and neurochemical factors may sometimes be important, it is the shifting of defensive organisations and their relative degrees of flexibility or rigidity that can at times be discerned on retrospective anamnestic examination, or observed directly during the course of therapy. Evidence of schizoid mechanisms may be found in a wide variety of non-psychotic states, such as character disorders, sexual perversion, anorexia nervosa, homosexuality, and personality disorder; but it may require the action of many other factors, such as the intra-psychic activation of destructive processes, disappointment in attempts at object-relating, trauma, deprivation, genetic vulnerability alone or in combination, to promote the fateful step from schizoid to the severe loss of reality contact that characterises schizophrenia. It is often the case that the individual who has regressed to a schizophrenic level in the face of depression is more suitable for psychotherapy than the one who has never achieved such an integrated level of response to object-relating.

The manic-depressive, by contrast, has achieved a higher development level, and may swing like a pendulum between triumphantly identifying with an omnipotent ego-ideal and masochistically submitting to its demands. Evidence of reparative wishes tend to be more clearly discernible and some patients are suitable subjects for psychotherapy provided that a supportive inpatient hospital context is available (Jackson 1989).

PSYCHOTHERAPY

Progress in psychotherapy into the beginnings of a healthy dependence is likely to be painfully slow. If the psychoanalytically-oriented therapist succeeds in making real contact with his patient he should be prepared for a commitment of five years or more, with one-, two-, or three-times-weekly sessions. Not all therapists are capable of such a commitment; nor should they be pressed to undertake such work. Although all patients can benefit from a psychoanalytic attitude, the selection of patients suitable for psychoanalytically-oriented psychotherapy is a crucial and complex matter. Undue analytic optimism about unsuitable patients can be damaging for all concerned, but psychotherapy undertaken with suitable patients in an institution offering competent treatment can have impressive results (see Cullberg 1991, Cullberg and Levander 1991).

Even in the best circumstances, progress is likely to be punctuated by crises of acting-in and acting-out. The therapist must be prepared to tolerate the fact that he will often not know exactly what is going on, particularly during the in-patient phase of treatment, where complex transference processes may involve staff members in a way that may be difficult or impossible to identify and manage. On the other hand, without the 'containing' function of a well organised ward milieu, therapy may prove impossible, whereas support of the therapist can greatly reduce the personal stress on him or her.

CONCLUSION

Work of this kind provides an unlimited source of illustrations of schizoid thinking and those who become involved in it will be rewarded for their efforts by increased understanding of basic mental processes, normal and abnormal, and the possibility of using psychoanalytic ideas constructively in the attempt to help a much-neglected section of the psychiatric population.

The therapist must often be content with possible or probable meanings of obscure psychotic communications, but occasionally may achieve a more clear understanding. The cases quoted at the beginning of this paper can now be considered in the light of our excursion into the field of psychoanalytic knowledge.

The patient who was frightened by the blackbird at the end of the session was disturbed by the awareness that he is leaving the session, and that departing matters to him. The therapist has perhaps become a new transference figure for him, arousing thoughts and wishes prohibited by his primitive and punitive superego. Splitting and projection of his 'evil' feelings into the image of the blackbird resulted in a sudden paranoid experience which he is unable to recognise as the consequence of his own thoughts.

The patient with the jar of mixed-up body fluids is making a complex statement to his therapist, and possible meanings may be discerned. The ball-point pen may refer to his penis, its functions and incapacities, associated with memories and perhaps of a dream of the previous night. However, it may also have a symbolic phallic meaning, unknown by his conscious self. A ball-point pen has many possible symbolic references, and its characteristics may be classified in a variety of ways, an obvious one being to the category of written, and thus verbal thinking and discourse. As a reference to thinking and knowledge, the pen may represent a sane possibility in an insane world where part-substances and processes are being equated in an undifferentiated way to create a narcissistic illusion of masturbatory self-sufficiency (see Segal 1957, Hinshelwood 1989, p.342).

The patient may even be trying to communicate to the therapist that he will be safe so long as he can regain control of his own mental processes and not be interfered with by the therapist, who may regard him as being mad. Since the patient 'knows' in his psychotic self that he is sane, such interference would be equivalent to the mad therapist trying to drive him crazy.

As therapy proceeded with the patient preoccupied with the bird on his head, the meaning became slowly clear. It became apparent that the bird represented a thought about coming and going, a transient recognition that the therapist exists and is important for him, and that being inside the session is different from being outside, As therapy progressed the bird ceased to be mentioned, but a 'heavy feeling' took its place. This, in turn, came to be recognised as a 'tension'. At this point the patient brought to the session a cartoon of a patient with a cloud over his head, and a psychiatrist was unravelling it by a thread which he put in his pocket as the cloud diminished in size. The patient was now able to recognise that he was acknowledging that the therapist brought him relief, a recognition of the metaphorical significance of the experience which originally had a concrete and near-delusional quality.

Presented with communications such as these, the therapist can expand his capacity for discerning possible meanings, with the aim of conveying something to the patient that will have a useful meaning for him. It is this refined listening to the patient and searching for meanings, with a psychodynamic hospital milieu where a high level of integrated psychiatry is practised and where the aims are understood and supported, that offers the best hope for new learning and for help for psychotic patients.

ACKNOWLEDGEMENT

I am indebted to the many participants in this work for their enthusiastic contributions, and also for their willingness to allow me to use suitably anonymised illustrative case material.

REFERENCES

Arieti, S. (1974) *Interpretation of Schizophrenia.* New York: Basic Books

Benedetti, G. (1987) *Psychotherapy of Schizophrenia.* London: New York University Press.

Bion, W.R. (1957) 'Differentiation of the psychotic from the non-psychotic personalities.' *International Journal of Psychoanalysis 38,* 266–75. Reprinted in W.R. Bion (1967) *Second Thoughts.* London: Heinemann. Also in E.B. Spillius (1989) Vol.1.

Bleuler, M. (1978) *The Schizophrenic Disorders.* New Haven, CT: Yale University Press.

Cullberg, J. (1991) 'Recovered versus non-recovered schizophrenic patients among those who have had intensive psychotherapy.' *Acta Psychiatrica Scandinavica 84,* 242–245.

Cullberg, J. and Levander, S. (1991) 'Fully recovered schizophrenic patients who received intensive psychotherapy.' *Nordic Journal of Psychiatry 45*, 235–262.

Cutting, J. (1985) *The Psychology of Schizophrenia*. London: Churchill Livingstone.

Federn, P. (1952) *Ego Psychology and the Psychoses*. New York: Basic Books.

Freeman, T. (1985) 'Nosography and the theory of the schizophrenias' *International Journal of Psycho-Analysis 66*, 237–243.

Hinshelwood, R.D. (1989) *A Dictionary of Kleinian Thinking*. London: Free Association Books.

Jackson, M. (1989) 'Manic-depressive psychosis: psychopathology and psychotherapy in a psychodynamic milieu.' In S. Gilbert, S. Haugsjerd and H. Hjort (eds) *Lines of Life, Psychiatry and Humanism*. Oslo: Tano.

Jackson, M. (1991) 'Psychotic disorders.' In J. Holmes (ed) *A Textbook of Psychotherapy in Psychiatric Disorders*. Edinburgh: Churchill Livingstone.

Jackson, M. (1992) 'Psychodynamics and psychotherapy on an acute psychiatric ward: an experimental unit.' *British Journal of Psychiatry 160*, 41–50.

Klein, M. (1946) 'Notes on some schizoid mechanisms.' In R. Money-Kyrle (ed) *The Writings of Melanie Klein* Vol. 3. London: Hogarth (1975).

Kretschmer, E. (1936) *Physique and Character* 2nd edition (ed Miller). London.

Lucas, R. (1992) 'The Psychotic personality: a psychoanalytic theory and its application in clinical practice.' *Psychoanalytic Psychotherapy 6*, 73–79.

Matte-Blanco, I. (1988) *Thinking, Feeling and Being*. London: Routledge.

Ogden, T.H. (1990) 'On the structure of experience.' In L.B. Boyer and P.L. Giovacchini (eds) *Master Clinicians on Treating the Regressed Patient*. London: Aronson.

Rey, J.H. (1988) 'Schizoid phenomena in the borderline.' In E.B. Spillius (1989) *op. cit.*

Rosenfeld, H. (1987) *Impasse and Interpretation*. London: Tavistock.

Sandler, J., Dare, C., and Holder, A. (1973) *The Patient and the Analyst*. London: Allen and Unwin.

Searles, H.F. (1965) *Collected Papers on Schizophrenia and Related Subjects*. London: Hogarth.

Segal, H. (1957) 'Notes on symbol formation.' *International Journal of Psycho-analysis 38*, 391–7. Republished in H. Segal (ed) (1981) *The Work of Hanna Segal*. New York: Aronson.

Spillius, E.B. (1989) *Melanie Klein Today*. London: Routledge.

Tausk, V. (1919) 'On the origin of the influencing machine in schizophrenia.' *Psychoanalytic Quarterly 2*, 519–556.

Winnicott, D.W. (1960) 'Ego distortion in terms of true and false self.' In *The Maturational Process and the Facilitating Environment*. London: Hogarth. (Republished 1990, London: Karnac.)

CHAPTER 2

Manfred Bleuler and the Understanding of Psychosis

Peter Barham

In essence, in my own work, the questions that have interested and concerned me are quite simple ones. They all converge around the problem of the social worth or value of the mentally ill in modern societies. I have tried to examine this problem on different fronts. For example, in terms of the social history of responses to insanity over the past 150 years or so; in terms also of the history and development of the intellectual frameworks that have underpinned distinctive practices towards the insane; and lastly, and more immediately, in the exploration of the demoralisation of former mental patients, their enforced powerlessness, in our contemporary society. It seems useful to try and address some of these issues through a discussion of the work of the great Swiss psychiatrist Manfred Bleuler, the son of Eugen Bleuler.

Manfred Bleuler's personal and professional history is intertwined with key developments in the social and intellectual history of late nineteenth and early twentieth century psychiatry. His writings, and in particular his reflections on the history of which he found himself part, his struggles to negotiate an alternative stance to the dominant one he encountered, provide an instructive link between the late nineteenth century and the present day. Through them we can, I believe, understand more deeply the nature and force of the legacy that is still very much part of our contemporary situation.

I will say a little about the work of Manfred Bleuler and the context in which his work has developed. I will not attempt anything like an overview of his writings, but will merely point to some aspects that I think particularly important.

The term 'psychosis' was originally used by alienists in the first half of the nineteenth century. Some nineteenth century authorities, such as Griesinger (1861), regarded all types of psychotic experience as expressions of different stages of a single mental disorder (*Einheitspsychose*), seen as a disease process.

Griesinger, for example, thought that there was an underlying cerebral dysfunction which provided the common somatic basis for the psychoses. In the late nineteenth century and early twentieth century there appeared a great flurry of neuropathological theories of a pre-somatic basis of psychoses, for example, those of Meynert (1884), Wernicke (1881–3) and Kleist (1908), to mention only three authorities.

Kraepelin (1899) pulled together earlier descriptions by Kahlbaum (1874) (catatonia), Morel (1852, 1860) (*démence précoce*) and Hecker (1871) (hebephrenia) into a single category, which he called *dementia praecox*. Although heredity played a part in his theories, Kraepelin was not strictly speaking a degenerationist. He was, however, less than sanguine about the outcome of dementia praecox, the meaning of which he took quite literally.

Manfred Bleuler's father, Eugen Bleuler (1857–1939), who served for many years as director of the Burghölzli Clinic, Zürich, where Jung also worked for a time, first introduced the term schizophrenia in an article in the *Allgemeine Zeitschrift für Psychiatrie* (E. Bleuler 1908), in which he argued that Kraepelin's dementia praecox was not necessarily a form of dementia, and that what had been called dementia was in the main a secondary symptom, arising from the patient's reactions to the way in which the primary disturbance had been responded to and treated. The word 'schizophrenia' – splitting of the mind – stresses the dissociation of psychic functions (associations), which to Bleuler was the feature common to a group of heterogeneous psychoses. Bleuler was one of the first clinical psychiatrists to pay serious attention to Freud's theories.

Manfred Bleuler was born in 1903 in his parents' apartment in the Burghölzli Clinic, and subsequently became director of the Clinic himself, a post he held from 1942 to 1969. He has described how he never needed to study the history of the concept of schizophrenia in books, as he had lively memories from his early childhood of the development of the concept. As a child he listened to many discussions about schizophrenic psychoses between his father, Kraepelin, Jung, and others. 'Dementia praecox' was the first Latin expression with which he became acquainted, but he did not merely learn the word, for in the clinical community in which he grew up he came to know many people who were regarded as having dementia praecox, and learned to recognise at an early age that they required particular empathy and attention. Manfred Bleuler describes how he spent his entire childhood and adolescence in close contact with patients. He and his siblings were taught to engage in many of the patients' activities, for example to take part in theatricals with them (M. Bleuler 1982 and personal communication 1983).

Eugen Bleuler was brought up in Zollikon, near Zürich, which until the beginning of this century was a small country village with a farming population. According to his son, Eugen Bleuler was greatly influenced by his rural background and acquired from his local community a sense of mission to demonstrate a more immediate and empathic understanding of the mentally sick than was typical of the aristocratic city doctors of his time, or of the German professors in the new psychiatric clinic of Burghölzli which had been established in 1870. At that time Zürich had no academic tradition in psychiatry, so professors from Germany, such as von Gudden and Hitzig, had to be recruited. The rural population in the neighbourhood of the Clinic, Manfred Bleuler reports, felt that these men were more interested in laboratory studies than in getting to know their patients. Furthermore, they only spoke to their patients in German, and not in the local Zürich dialect.

In Manfred Bleuler's view, his father's main contribution to the problem of schizophrenia was to favour the study of what was going on psychodynamically in a schizophrenic patient, and so to create a basis for a psychotherapeutic and psychosocial approach. This constituted a real break from Kraepelin, who had no serious interest in any form of therapy. There is, however, an important dimension of Eugen Bleuler's professional history which his son does not recount. In an interesting article, Helm Stierlin (1967) has discussed the confusing heritage of Eugen Bleuler. Most American or British readers are familiar only with Bleuler's monograph *Dementia Praecox or the Group of Schizophrenias* (E. Bleuler 1950). Originally published in 1911 (as a volume of Aschaffenburg's *Handbuch*), an English translation appeared in 1950. In Germany, however, the monograph was never reprinted and Bleuler's ideas became known through his textbook of psychiatry (E. Bleuler 1924), of which six editions were published in his lifetime. The interesting thing here is that the accounts of schizophrenia in the textbooks suggest a very different perspective from that in the original monograph. Overwhelming criticism, Stierlin (1967) tells us, had been directed against Bleuler's psychological theory of the psychoses in which he had applied the ideas of Freud. Authorities such as Gruhle, Bumke and Hoch repudiated it in whole or in major part. Not only had psychoanalysis been allowed to creep into the domain, but Bleuler had implicitly questioned the assumptions on which psychiatry rested. We can identify, Stierlin writes, 'bitter emotional undertones in the criticism launched at him' (1967). As a consequence, from 1913 onwards Bleuler began to move away from Freud and closer to organic psychiatry. He became more interested in claiming organic causes for the disturbances of schizophrenia. As Stierlin concludes, though, 'in a sense he never seems to have given up on the task of reconciling the two psychiatric traditions...this task clearly overtaxed him.'

However, although Manfred Bleuler may have been silent on what happened to his father in this conflict between traditions, the conflict itself is one that he fully recognised and provides in a sense the key to his life's work. He, perhaps, showed more stamina for it than his father. Indeed, one way of characterising Manfred Bleuler's project over almost half a century is to say that he has tried to make amends for the inadequacies in his father's very partial critique of Kraepelin's theory. I would summarise this by saying that throughout his career he has set himself resolutely against a view of the schizophrenic patient as someone who can only be discussed in the language of pathology, beyond the pale of ordinary human recognition and understanding, as an incurable lunatic in the dogma of the period.

We need of course to understand Bleuler's endeavour in terms of the social history that had produced the late nineteenth century asylum in Britain and Germany, as elsewhere. Early nineteenth century asylums, such as the Retreat in York, had been founded on rehabilitative ideals. Many of them were in effect country houses; intimacy of scale was a crucial consideration, and the aim was always to maintain channels of communication between the asylum and society. There is not the space to discuss this history here, but by the late nineteenth century, the 1870s or thereabouts, the asylums had become vast warehouses for the chronically insane. From being the 'instrument of regeneration' the asylum had become the 'dustbin of the incurable'. This development was not, of course, created by the psychiatric profession, but nonetheless psychiatry came to play an important part in ratifying and legitimising what was taking place. Confronted by a 'motley crowd of persons of weak minds or low spirits', psychiatry delivered the final sentence upon them. In the last decades of the century, psychiatric perceptions and judgements became increasingly inflexible. The idea that insanity was largely incurable was divested of its controversial or contestable aspect and taken very much for granted. The locus of psychiatric exclusion was reproduced in the scientific frameworks in which insane people were classified and analysed; they were abandoned both to an asylum and to an intellectual framework which declared them incomprehensible.

The psychiatric construction of the dementia praecox patient, it has been suggested, was informed by a stigmatising political discourse about the urban poor and drew on a number of representative preoccupations of the period: 'psychological weakness', 'psychic degeneration', 'deterioration', and above all the constitutional basis of the 'socially unfit'. The late nineteenth century asylum thus became a 'site in which stigmatising symbols were concentrated, refined and applied to those who could not or did not engage in productive social relations' (Barrett 1988, p.373). The pauper lunatic was conceptualised as the converse of Darwinian man. We can therefore understand the category of dementia praecox as (Barrett 1988):

'...the product of a clinically accurate but politically saturated discourse generated by an emerging European professional class in dialogue with the insane of a pauper class, a discourse which was inclined to characterize the latter in terms of an endogenous biological flaw which leads to a failure of the capacity to be productive, to compete and adapt, and ultimately to an evolutionary decline.' (p374)

However, unlike Britain and Germany, Switzerland was a more unified society that did not exhibit the same degree of class tension and conflict. For that reason, perhaps, the emerging professional class did not lose touch with traditional roots and allegiances to the same extent as in Britain and Germany and permitted in Manfred Bleuler's case the creation of a much more accommodating discourse in his dialogue with the mentally disturbed. Bleuler's portrait of his father, particularly in its populist and pastoral emphasis, gives us, I think, a sense of his own mission. 'Only late in life,' he wrote in 1980 (Bleuler 1982), 'did I realise how much a calling rooted in the minds of my ancestors' community, has also influenced the course of my own development.'

In his major work, *The Schizophrenic Disorders: Long-Term Patient and Family Studies* (M. Bleuler 1978a, first published in German in 1972), Bleuler has given us the most incisive and critical account that we have to date of the history of schizophrenia. What we find in this study are really three parallel and interconnected narrative histories: a history of the scientific project of schizophrenia; a history of the lives of a large group of schizophrenic patients; and the history of Bleuler's own relationship to, and within, each of these.

In the following quotation, Bleuler (1978a) provides a gripping account of the ideological force field in which the whole problem of schizophrenia was entrapped:

'All suspicions and assertions to the effect that schizophrenias are the manifestation of organic idiocy, a brain atrophy, a progressive process, or of an event that continues to propagate its own development, that defies understanding or perception by the emotions, have created unfavourable presuppositions for the scientific exploitation of clinical experience with chronic schizophrenics. The clinician who discovered after years of observation that there was an improvement, and who found an abundance of inner life, of emotional perception, of human rationale in his chronic schizophrenic patient – rather than the expected inexorable progression of the disease – during certain periods of history almost had to be ashamed of his discoveries. On the other hand he felt secure and in concert with the accepted hypotheses if he was able to record an increasingly severe state of idiocy and dehumanization of the patient... At certain times, researchers were even in danger of being reproached for having an unscientific, uncritical mentality, of being insulted and ostracized, if they did not conform by "admitting" that there were physical explanations for schizophrenia... In a peculiar reversal of otherwise valid norms, assumptions used to be declared "scientific" that resulted from poor speculation or emotional needs, and any attempt to consider only information that could be proved was rejected as "unscientific".' (p.447)

Bleuler describes the dogma of 'incurability in principle' that governed psychiatric thinking in the years after Kraepelin introduced the concept of dementia praecox, and remarks on the bitterness of psychiatrists of this epoch at their inability to discover a brain disease as an explanation for schizophrenia. So firmly entrenched was 'faith in the incurability of the disease', that what looked to be a recovery was made subject to reinterpretation. So for example, 'if a patient was released after a schizophrenic psychosis, and if he remained socially well integrated for many years, and finally died, it was suspected that he would eventually have become schizophrenically demented again, if he had only lived long enough'.

I think it is apposite to remark here that Bleuler's argument with certain dominant traditions in Germany psychiatry has evidently been a lasting one. In a personal communication in 1985, for example, he describes how: 'I have been recently much attacked by some German authors, who state that describing late improvements and recoveries of schizophrenic psychoses only proves that such an author is too silly to make a proper diagnosis.'

What especially interests Bleuler is what happened to the patient, and in particular to the relationship between patient and doctor, under these conditions. He wants to show that if there has been a problem about how to characterise what is happening with a schizophrenic patient, there has also been a closely connected problem around the kind of self-understanding possessed by the typical scientist. This comes out in the following quotation (M. Bleuler 1978a). The schizophrenic was conceived as suffering from 'a final and irrevocable loss of his mental existence':

> 'So it happened that the clinician became increasingly accustomed to seeing in his schizophrenic dementia cases an autistic attitude on the part of the patient. The patient and those who were healthy had ceased to understand one another. The patient gives up, in abject resignation or total embitterment, any effort to make himself understood. He either no longer says anything or says nothing intelligible. In so doing the naive observer declares, out of hand, that the patient has lost his reasoning powers.' (p.417)

In Bleuler's study we have, as Edward Hare (1979) has put it, 'a historical record, perhaps unique in its thoroughness and probably now unrepeatable, of what schizophrenia was like in a particular place and time'. As Bleuler (1978a) describes in his preface, his intention was 'to depict the life vicissitudes of 208 schizophrenics and their families' as he has 'personally experienced these, together with them, over a period of more than 20 years'. The trouble with previous studies was that they had described the long-term courses only of hospitalised patients. In consequence, 'nothing was really known about the fates of the great number of patients with whom, after their release, the doctor lost contact', and it was the life histories of these people in particular that Bleuler wanted to draw into his account.

Bleuler was able to show that contrary to old notions of a progressive worsening of the disease, after an average duration of five years the condition does not deteriorate any further but may improve. Of the 208 patients in the study about 25 per cent achieved full recoveries and about 10 per cent remained permanently hospitalised as severe chronic psychotics. Between these two extremes there was a large group of people who never achieved a stable outcome but of whom many experienced intermittent recoveries. However the interest of Bleuler's study lies not merely in the facts about outcome – important though they certainly are – but more especially in what he is able to show about the nature of the interaction between the schizophrenic person and the world in which he lives (M. Bleuler 1978b):

> 'The closer we live together with patients, even the most chronic ones, the more astonished we are at fluctuations in their condition. The great majority of the alterations in the course of many years after the onset of the psychosis are clearly in the direction of improvement. The improvements are manifold in nature. Some of the patients who have hardly ever uttered coherent sentences start to speak or behave as if they were healthy on certain occasions, for instance, when on leave, at hospital festivities, or on the occasion of a catastrophe such as exploding bombs in wartime. I have seen improvements after 40 years' duration of a severe chronic psychosis. And, what is even more amazing, a schizophrenic may recover after having been psychotic and hospitalized for decades. Such a late, complete recovery is rare, but it occurs.' (p.633)

In certain obvious respects, Bleuler gives us a much more optimistic account of the outcome of a schizophrenic illness than the traditional view had allowed for, but, taken overall, what he does, perhaps, is complicate our understanding of the life histories of schizophrenic patients. The lives of schizophrenic patients clearly cannot be assimilated to the sort of predictive apparatus which psychiatrists of the late nineteenth century had constructed; they are instead replete with surprises, some of them for the better, others again for the worse.

Perhaps one of the strongest things that comes through is Bleuler's modesty, his awareness of the vulnerability of his judgements. He does not theorise about the social sciences, indeed it is likely that he was not widely read in the philosophy of the social sciences. But just for that reason his often understated remarks are all the more compelling. For example he says (M. Bleuler 1978a):

> 'Naturally a person in my position finds it easy to emulate what many other investigators have done, namely, at the end, to render a decision after a lengthy interview with a patient or a member of his family, to the effect that his mother was "domineering" or that his father remained apart from the rest of the family. But in the end I am not convinced that I have captured the entire truth of the situation in stating a summary judgement of that sort. And if I carefully allow the patient to speak freely in a relaxed atmosphere, I find time and again that he himself begins, quietly or vehemently, to shake the carefully erected structure of every summary

judgement, even though I had earlier skilfully obtained his complete
agreement.' (p.116)

An important part of Bleuler's concern is to forge a concept of schizophrenic
illness not as a discrete and encapsulated aberration but as 'staged in the same
general spheres of life where the neuroses are formed, and in which the human
personality is shaped in a constant interplay between hereditary developmental
tendencies and environmental experience' (1978a, p.457). 'According to our
present day concept,' he writes, 'schizophrenics founder under the same difficulties with which all of us struggle all our lives' (ibid., p.502).

(I am reminded here of a remark of Winnicott's (1971): 'While we recognize
the hereditary factor in schizophrenia and while we are willing to see the
contributions made in individual cases by physical disorders, we look with
suspicion on any theory of schizophrenia that divorces the subject from the
problems of ordinary living, and the universals of individual development, in a
given environment.)

Bleuler, I believe, helps us to take seriously the idea of a more complex and
intricate interweaving between schizophrenic and 'normal' forms of life than has
generally been assumed. He has worked in relative isolation but we can see how,
unawares, he arrives at formulations and conclusions that are in keeping with
much of what theorists of the human sciences have been arguing in recent years.
His intellectual struggle is twofold: first to try to understand his patients, to
fashion a satisfactory language for discussing these strange and perturbing modes
of existence; and second – and equally important – to contend with the problems
of an intellectual legacy, with the plethora of dogma and mistaken biases in which
the lives of schizophrenics have become entangled. At points in his writing he
debates with himself whether he is not half-clinician and half-scientist, not fully
reconciled to his purposes. However, we should, I think, see in Bleuler's repeated
conflicts of adjustment and presentation not a set of personal foibles but an
attempt to sort out what a scientific assay on this field can achieve. These are not
sundered voices, they are both of them the expressions and equivocations of a
scientist debating with himself and his material over what is to be said and how.
And in his work, Bleuler provides us, through the imaginative effort of single
scientist, with a conception of how scientific study in this field ought to look.

Most of all perhaps, he succeeds in giving substance to a conception of the
schizophrenic person not as someone 'who has become unintelligible in his
thinking and feeling and in principle a creature different from ourselves', but as
'a brother whom we can judge according to our own nature' (M. Bleuler 1963,
p.952). To me, what is really important about Bleuler is his relentless commitment
to the ethical standpoint, to retaining a view of his patients as fellow human
subjects.

It is no accident that the German psychiatrist Alfred Hoche was one of those
who most vociferously attacked Eugen Bleuler's psychodynamic account of

schizophrenia. In 1920 Hoche promoted the concept of 'life unworthy of life', whereby mental patients were deemed to be nothing but 'human ballast' and 'empty shells of human beings' (Binding and Hoche 1920, quoted in Lifton 1986, p.47). Putting such people to death, he wrote, 'is not to be equated with other types of killing...but is an allowable, useful act'. As Robert Lifton has remarked, Hoche was in effect saying that the mentally ill are already dead (1986, p.47).

So far as a group of people ceases to figure within the human picture that we have of a society, it then becomes difficult to recognise them as people and to identify with them. The closing decades of the nineteenth century, and the early decades of the present one, are littered with ideologies of 'social waste', efforts to comprehend and find solutions to the problem of the 'socially unfit', '*die Gemeinschaftsunfähigen*' (see Dörner 1989). Hoche's proposals were especially drastic, but the social and ideological conditions in which they could be given a hearing and taken in earnest were not of his own making. The name which Klaus Dörner (1989) has recently given to the attitude which made the killing of mental patients possible is '*tödliches Mitleid*' (deadly compassion). Many psychiatrists and their staff, he said, were against the transportation and murder of their patients. But their resistance had crucially been weakened. The medicalisation of 'inferior' people had worked to good effect and psychiatrists and others came to see it as their social and professional duty to help restore the social body to good health. The value of mental patients had already been reduced in the professionals' own eyes, so that when it came to the critical moment they were unable to identify with their patients or to defend them. Echoing Manfred Bleuler's discussion, Robert Lifton tells us that most German psychiatrists, in common with the majority of their counterparts elsewhere, were 'committed to the idea of schizophrenia as an organic, incurable disease, whose natural course was deterioration. Indeed, for many, professional pride depended on that view. Any effort to penetrate the psyche of a schizophrenic patient as a means of understanding and a form of treatment was viewed by these psychiatrists as "unscientific" and therefore a professional and personal threat' (1986, pp.112–113). The extermination programme was officially halted in 1941 (although in fact of course it continued), so Lifton tells us, not in response to protests from psychiatrists and other physicians, but in response to pressure from a few Church leaders 'who gave voice to the grief and rage of victimized families with ethical passions stemming from their own religious traditions' (p.95). In the encounter with their patients, psychiatrists saw themselves only as taking part in a suffering which was not their own. The communal meaning of suffering had been erased and the psychiatrist had ceased to be a partner with the suffering patient. Powered by a characteristically modern but ethically moribund understanding of rationality and scientific inquiry, psychiatry had assisted in lending authority to the depersonalisation and debasement of the mental patient.

It would of course be comforting to suppose that this was just a disgraceful little episode, a nasty little deviation in the development of more promising social prospects for the long-term mentally ill. But as James Birley (1991) has recently reminded us in a courageous address as President of the Royal College of Psychiatrists, we cannot permit ourselves such comfort. There is not the space in which to develop this argument here, but social and cultural conditions do presently exist in which the doctrine of the hopeless case can be reproduced both in the real world of outcomes and in our own perceptions and reflexes. The identities of former mental patients in the community are insecurely grounded. They are therefore inevitably vulnerable both in themselves and, just as important, to misrecognition by others. What must compel our attention, however, is not so much natural inadequacy as an understanding of structurally produced inadequacy, the social forces that conspire to render the person with a history of mental illness incompetent and demoralised.

My real concern, as I have recently tried to argue (Barham 1992), is about the political grounding of hope. Hopes for improved prospects for the mentally ill are certainly clinically well enough grounded, but whether they are politically securely grounded – that is, grounded in an accurate recognition of the type of outcome that is at all likely within the antagonistic processes of a modern society – is quite a different question. Manfred Bleuler is, I believe, helpful in stating the vantage point that we need to occupy but as to the solutions, these we must grapple with for ourselves.

NOTE

This chapter is a slightly modified version of the talk I gave at the International Conference on Psychosis (1992), based on discussions in two works of my own (Barham 1992, 1993). For additional information on Bleuler and the Burghölzli tradition see also Bleuler (1979) and Rihner (1982). The psychiatric traditions referred to are also usefully discussed in Bynum (1983) and Scharfetter (1983a, b).

REFERENCES

Barham, P. (1992) *Closing the Asylum*. London: Penguin Books.

Barham, P. (1993) *Schizophrenia and Human Value*. London: Free Association Books. (Originally published in 1984 by Basil Blackwell, Oxford.)

Barrett, R. (1988) 'Interpretations of schizophrenia.' *Culture, Medicine, and Psychiatry, 12*, 357–88.

Binding, K. and Hoche, A.E. (1920) *Die Freigabe der Vernichtung Lebensunwerten Lebens.* Leipzig: Meiner.

Birley, J.L.T. (1991) 'Psychiatrists and citizens.' *British Journal of Psychiatry 159*, 1–6.

Bleuler, E. (1908) 'Die Prognose der Dementia Praecox.' *Allgemeine Zeitschrift für Psychiatrie 65*, 436–64. (Reprinted in M. Bleuler 1979.)

Bleuler, E. (1924) *Textbook of Psychiatry.* Authorised English version, edited by A.A. Brill. New York: Macmillan. (Translation of *Lehrbuch der Psychiatrie* (1918). Berlin: Julius Springer.)

Bleuler, E. (1950) *Dementia Praecox or the Group of Schizophrenias.* Translated by J. Zinkin. New York: International Universities Press. (Translation of *Dementia Praecox, oder Gruppe der Schizophrenien* (1911). Leipzig: Deuticke.)

Bleuler, M. (1963) 'Conceptions of schizophrenia within the last fifty years and today.' *Proceedings of the Royal Society of Medicine 56*, 945–52.

Bleuler, M. (1978a) *The Schizophrenic Disorders: Long-Term Patient and Family Studies.* New Haven, CT: Yale University Press. (First published in German in 1972.)

Bleuler, M. (1978b) 'The long-term course of schizophrenic psychoses.' In L.C. Wynne, R.I. Cromwell and S. Matthysse (eds) *The Nature of Schizophrenia.* New York: Wiley.

Bleuler, M. (ed) (1979) *Beiträge zur Schizophrenielehre der Zürcher Psychiatrischen Universitätsklinik Burghölzli (1902–1971).* Darmstadt: Wissenschaftliche Buchgesellschaft.

Bleuler, M. (1982) 'Manfred Bleuler'. In M. Shepherd (ed) *Psychiatrists on Psychiatry.* Cambridge: Cambridge University Press.

Bynum, W.F. (1983) 'Psychiatry in its historical context.' In M. Shepherd and O.L. Zangwill (eds) *Handbook of Psychiatry,* Vol.1. Cambridge: Cambridge University Press.

Dörner, K. (1969) *Tödliches Mitleid.* Gütersloh: Verlag Jakkob von Hoddis.

Griesinger (1861) *Die Pathologie und Therapie der psychischen Krankheiten* 2nd edition. Stuttgart: Krabbe.

Hare, E. (1979) Review of *The Schizophrenic Disorders: Long-Term Patient and Family Studies* by Manfred Bleuler. *British Journal of Psychiatry 135*, 474–80.

Hecker, E. (1871) 'Die Hebrephrenie.' *Virchows Arch. pathol. Anat. 52*, 394–429.

Kahlbaum, K.L. (1874) *Die Katatonie oder das Spannungsirresein.* Berlin: Hirschwald.

Kleist, K. (1908) *Untersuchungen zur Kenntnis der psychomotorischen Bewegungsstörungen bei Geisteskranken.* Leipzig: Voegel.

Kraepelin, E. (1899) *Psychiatrie* 6th edition. Leipzig: Barth. (First edition 1887.)

Lifton, R. (1986) *The Nazi Doctors.* London: Macmillan.

Meynert, T. (1884) *Psychiatrie: Lehrbuch der Erkrankungen des Vorderhirnes, begründet auf dessen Bau, Leistung und Ernährung.* Vienna: Braumuller.

Morel, B.A. (1852) *Études cliniques: traité théorique et pratique des maladies mentales.* Paris: Masson.

Morel, B.A. (1860) *Traité des maladies mentales.* Paris: Masson.

Rihner, F. (ed) (1982) *Prof. Dr. Manfred Bleuler: zum 80. Geburtstag.* Zürich: W. Woodtli.

Scharfetter, C. (1983b) 'Schizophrenia.' In M. Shepherd and O.L. Zangwill (eds) *Handbook of Psychiatry,* Vol.1. Cambridge: Cambridge University Press.

Stierlin, H. (1967) 'Bleuler's concept of schizophrenia: a confusing heritage.' *American Journal of Psychiatry 123*, 996–1001.

Wernicke, C. (1881–83) *Lehrbuch der Gehirnkrankeheiten.* Berlin: Fischer.

Winnicott, D.W. (1971) *Playing and Reality.* London: Tavistock.Scharfetter, C. (1983a) 'Psychosis.' In M. Shepherd and O.L. Zangwill (eds) *Handbook of Psychiatry,* Vol.1. Cambridge: Cambridge University Press.

CHAPTER 3

The Ubiquity of Psychotic Anxieties

Robert M. Young

When I began composing this chapter, I could not decide whether the point I am trying to make is banal and obvious or really rather important. Perhaps it's both at once. As Wilhelm Reich said, it is essential to subject things to the searching scrutiny of naive questions. My point is that the Freudian definition of the unconscious and, *a fortiori*, the Kleinian one, says in a quite flat-footed way that fundamentally irrational processes are going on all the time in our inner worlds. The difference between the Freudian and the Kleinian versions of this point is that on the Kleinian account these processes are in a complex interplay with other, less irrational ones, from moment to moment, and the way Kleinians write about them and make interpretations of them makes them seem more extreme – in a word, crazier, playing a larger and more manifest part in everyday behaviour. Kleinians, of course, believe that one can work with these processes and that interpretations should be made at the deepest level one can reach. Whatever one may want to say about the difference of tone or degree or technique between Freudian and Kleinian accounts, it is not startling news that crazy things go on in the unconscious. It is worth recalling that on both accounts, by far the larger part of what goes on in the mind is unconscious, where the rules of Aristotelian logic do not apply. All of this could be said to be banal and well-known.

Why, then, might my point be rather important? There are a number of interrelated reasons. Why are psychotherapists and psychoanalysts on the whole wary of and out of touch with psychosis, and why are most psychiatrists equally (perhaps more) out of touch with psychodynamic formulations of psychotic phenomena? There seems to be a barrier or, at least, imperfect communication. Therapists and analysts do not commonly treat psychotics. All but a tiny minority of psychiatrists would not dream of using 'the talking cure' as the treatment of choice with such patients. Indeed, I am told that in America, an analyst was recently successfully sued for doing so and that the ensuing debate is ongoing in the American psychiatric journals. There are notable exceptions, to some of whom I shall return: Wilfred Bion, Hanna Segal, Herbert Rosenfeld Donald Meltzer, Murray Jackson, Joseph Berke, Haya Oakley, Michael Conran, Michael Sinason and a few others in this country, and, most notably, Harold Searles in America. But it is not common and is usually seen as research with limited therapeutic goals. Searles, work with a number of patients over decades is the object of bemusement and ridicule in some circles, although I am bound to say that the more I do psychotherapy with psychotics, the more I admire him and envy his ability to find and convey the meaning and sense in what psychotics say (Young 1992a).

Then there is the burgeoning literature on so-called 'borderline states' and 'pathological organisations', categories which are problematic and whose legitimacy are the subject of intense debate in some quarters, at the same time as the literature about them is rich and fascinating for what it suggests about the inner world and the refractory structures in individuals (Rey 1994; Rosenfeld 1987; Searles 1986; Silver and Rosenbleuth 1992; Spillius 1988, Vol. 1, Part 4; Steiner 1993).

This leads on to the question of nosology, a topic which has a narrow and a wide focus. The narrow focus is the gulf that exists between psychoanalysts and psychotherapists on the one hand and psychiatrists on the other with respect to the relevance of psychiatric classification of mental disorders. This gulf may be described quite simply. Psychotherapists do not think much in terms of disease entities or syndromes. Of course they do in a loose way, but their overwhelming emphasis is on unconscious dynamics. Orthodox psychiatrists tend to think in terms of categories, while therapists tend to think in terms of levels and movements back and forth between positions or emotional states.

We find a big difference of emphasis with respect to the extent to which psychotherapists and psychiatrists use classifications of the sort found in the American Psychiatric Association's *Diagnostic and Statistical Manual* (APA 1987), which has just passed from its third edition, revised *(DSM-III-R)*, to its fourth. We also find that the distinctions between normal and neurotic and psychotic are not much used, at least in Kleinian circles. I hasten to add that the distinctions are around and relevant, and that I carry around in my head terms which I attach to my patients in some reflective moments and in supervision, for example, 'paranoid', 'borderline', 'pathological organisation', 'depressed', 'schizoid', 'hysterical', and so on. But these are rarely in my mind during sessions.

The wider focus of the topic of nosology is the problematic role of classifications in medicine and science in general. Classifications are put forward as facts of nature, analogous, in the first instance, to disease categories in medicine, which, in turn, claim some affinity to natural classifications of species in biology and particles, elements and compounds in physics. This is a central feature of the scientific enterprise: the search for a definitive specification of natural kinds. The trouble with the attempt to find a natural classification in psychopathology is that the project of achieving such classifications opens up a very large can of worms about human nature, nature and the theory of knowledge: epistemology.

By this I mean that the attempt to classify mental phenomena has no language of its own. It is a consequence of Cartesian mind–body dualism that bodies are described in terms of primary qualities – extension and figure, treated geometrically and mathematically – while mind is negatively defined as that which does not pertain to body (Young 1989, 1994, Chapter 1). The languages employed by scientists, including medics and therapists (regarded as rather pale shadows of 'proper' scientists), are generated *by analogy* from more scientifically respectable disciplines. For example, the 'association of ideas' was itself dreamed up as an analogy to the ways physical particles were thought to interact in the seventeenth and eighteenth centuries – a sort of billiard-ball impact physics (Young 1970, pp.94–100).

The very notion of *psycho*pathology was an attempt, begun in the mid-nineteenth century, to found the theory of mental disturbance on the disease model – hence 'mental disease'. A description of the features of such disorders was made analogous to the exciting new findings of the study of the pathology of organs and cells – hence the use of terms such as 'syndrome' and 'morbid anatomy'. The term 'psychopathology' entered English in 1847 as a transliteration of the title of a book by Baron von Feuchstersleben, and there were titles around mid-century, such as *Elements of the Pathology of the Human Mind* (Mayo 1838), *Chapters on Mental Physiology* (Holland 1852) and Henry Maudsley's *Physiology and Pathology of Mind* (1867). Books with psychopathology in their titles continue to appear (Berrios 1991; Summers 1994), and I currently lecture on the subject in several psychotherapy trainings.

The history of ideas in psychopathology is the history of the extended use of a somatic analogy which, it was thought by Freud's teachers, would soon be securely founded on the actual findings of cerebral pathology (Amacher 1965). Indeed, it is worth recalling that it was in this field that he chose to work (Bernfield 1944, 1949, 1951; Kris 1950). It was the subject of his first book, *On Aphasia* (Freud 1891; Riese 1958; Stengel 1954). He turned to treating neurotics because he could not afford to continue working as an academic researcher (Gay 1988, pp.22–37; Young 1986). Throughout his writings we find analogies and metaphors drawn from physics, anatomy, physiology and pathology. Anatomical and reflex models were pervasive in *The Interpretation of Dreams* (Freud 1900), and at the end of his life he was still thinking this way in the *New Introductory Lectures*, one of which was entitled 'The Dissection of the Psychical Personality' (Freud 1933, Chapter 31)

Not only is it the case that psychopathological nosology is based on an extended and increasingly dubious analogy to the natural and biomedical sciences, but these efforts at placing the vicissitudes of human suffering on the bedrock of putatively natural classifications also turn out, according to recent research in the history, philosophy and social studies of science, to be eminently *historical*. Disease categories in psychiatry are also historical and change over time as a result of wider forces in the history of ideas and the history of culture. If that was not obvious before systematic nosological work was attempted, it should be transparent from the fact that, as I have indicated, the official *Diagnostic and Statistical Manual* has gone through four revisions in its short history since it first appeared in 1952 (APA 1987 pp.xviii–xix). You could say that they are moving progressively towards a refined truth, but the changes are not of that kind. It is more like the history of encyclopaedias, which may have been conceived in the belief that knowledge accumulates in a linear way. In fact, however, its categories, frameworks and terms of reference have also changed in successive editions. I have the eighth edition of the *Encyclopaedia Britannica*, dated 1860. It includes a long article entitled 'Deluge', which goes into lots of complicated matters about the Biblical flood and its relationship with then-prevailing theories in geology. The next edition, which appeared less than two decades later, has no such entry but does have a new one called 'Evolution'. The eighth edition was completed before Darwin's epoch-making *On the Origin of Species* appeared: the ninth reflected a fundamental change in the framework of ideas about the earth, life and humankind. As a result, the categories, the chapter headings of knowledge, had to be re-thought. There are interrelated changes throughout the edition, including the disappearance of a preliminary volume of essays called 'Dissertations and Discussions', which sought to encompass all of knowledge.

You might think I am leading up to a sharp distinction between human knowledge and natural knowledge, but I submit that the example I have just given points the other way and shows that the historicity of categories also applies to natural knowledge. As I have tried to show in my films and other writings, ideas of nature have a history (Young 1973, 1985, Chapter 6; Young and Gold 1982; Young and Postle 1981). One inspiration for this approach is Georg Lukács, who argued, the idea of nature in any period is 'the theoretical reflection and projection of' the social milieu of the times (Lukács 1923, p.38). 'Nature is a societal category. That is to say, whatever is held to be natural at any given stage of social development, however this nature is related to man and whatever form his involvement with it takes, i. e. nature's form, its content, its range and its objectivity are all socially conditioned' (p.234).

What is true of nature in general also applies to the framing of natural kinds or classifications. So the attempt to found the understanding of human distress on an analogy to somatic pathology – which is, in turn, reducible to physiology, biochemistry, chemistry and physics – fails to take note that the bedrock is itself changing as a function of broader movements in the culture. This is less obvious in the physico-chemical sciences, but it is still the case. It is obviously so in medicine, as a brilliant and pioneering series of essays by Karl Figlio has shown, with respect to the rise and fall of certain eminently somatic diseases: chlorosis and miner's nystagmus (Figlio 1978, 1979, 1985). Figlio has moved on, inspired by Harold Searles' profound book, *The Nonhuman Environment: In Normal Development and in Schizophrenia* (1960), to explore how we experience and deploy the external world in our unconscious projective processes (Figlio 1990). Searles shows how the external world is taken up and made use of for projective purposes; Figlio integrates this with his own work on the historicity of disease categories and, more generally, of our ideas about nature and the environment.

Note carefully that I am not saying that there was no such thing as chlorosis or miner's nystagmus, or that there is no nature out there, independent of the psychological uses we make of it. The medical textbooks and hospital records prove that there were such diseases and that their natures changed over time until they eventually disappeared from the textbooks. These syndromes were discovered and treated as natural kinds. One had as its pathognomonic symptom a kind of anaemia, the other a disorder of eye movements. They waxed and waned in the medical literature as the constellation of social forces which evoked them changed over decades. The same is true of the nosological categories in *DSM*; an example is 'ego-syntonic homosexuality'. It has simply ceased to be a disease; it became one in the 1950s and ceased to be one in the 1970s, although if you have the 'non-ego syntonic' variety you are still – according to the current classification – sick. I learned this system of ideas – what anthropologists call a belief system – as a psychiatric aide in Arizona (where promiscuity and priapism were still considered grave illnesses, resulting in long-term incarceration in a state mental hospital) and got to be a dab hand at making diagnoses. I later learned to do assessment interviews in a psychotherapy department and to make dynamic formulations which met the prevailing standards. Even diagnostic categories which have been challenged can elicit high degrees of reliability that meet scientific standards of intersubjective validation, as Alex Tarnopolsky (1992) has shown with respect to borderline disorders. What is true of particular somatic and psychological diseases is also true of our broader and deeper conceptions of nature and human nature.

You could be forgiven for thinking that I am spending a long time in the foothills of my argument. My reply would be that I am at the summit of it in a number of respects. Even so, if I may vary the metaphor, I am poised for re-entry to the part of my text which concentrates on the modifier 'psychotic'. My vehicle for re-entry is Peter Barham's breathtakingly wise book, *Schizophrenia and Human Value* (1984), in which he argues that we must move off the nosological relegation of schizophrenics to demented chronicity and learn to think of them as living lives, of which it can be said, 'thereby hangs a tale', that is, a narrative which has meaning and value and merits our attentiveness, whether or not the cause of schizophrenia turns out to be largely biochemical. (I have never understood why people think that biological causation diminishes the meaningfulness of what psychotic people say and do.) Barham has gone on to say that because they tell a recognisably meaningful story – 'mented', as it were, rather than 'de-mented' – the lives of these people merit provision appropriate to fellow human beings, who, like people in wheelchairs, are in need of certain kinds of spaces which facilitate their doing whatever they can, rather than the stark alternatives of hospitals or park benches and cardboard cities (Barham 1984).

Barham argues his thesis on general humanitarian grounds but also draws on writings by Alisdair MacIntyre and Richard Rorty which are critical of the hegemonic claims of scientific rationality and seek to promote narrative, story-telling, evaluative and humanocentric ways of speaking about things, especially human things, by which I mean *not* treating the relations between people as if they were relations between things (reification). This goes against the grain of the history of scientism, whereby scientific rationality and materialist explanations were offered as the models for all of knowledge – a movement which peaked in the 1950s and has recently been under attack in general philosophy and in the philosophy of both the natural and the so-called human sciences (Rorty 1982, Chapter 12).

It is at this point that two strands of my argument meet. The first strand, drawn from my critique of psychiatric classifications based on analogies from somatic medicine, is a widespread and growing turning-away from reductionist explanations based on the increasingly historicised bedrock of natural science. The second, and closely allied, strand is a philosophical critique of rationalist views of human nature in psychology and social studies – moving away from enlightenment and positivist models and towards a more tolerant and inclusive view of the role of primitive processes in our lives. These strands meet at the point where human phenomena are increasingly described in terms which are recognisably human, rather than – as was the case at the high tide of scientism – in terms which reduce the human to the parameters of scientific rationality and human nature to a split between the rational and the Other, whereof one cannot speak.

I hope I have said enough to make it plausible and worthwhile to embark on the project of addressing my title and pointing out the ubiquity of psychotic anxieties. I have set the stage in the way I have in order to make clear that what I shall now say about Freudian and Kleinian ideas is not just a re-hash but a *repositioning* of these ideas in the context of a broader movement in philosophy and the study of humanity, society and the world. It puts primitive processes in the context of a broader cultural movement which is challenging forms of discourse drawn directly or by analogy from natural science.

That movement is not entirely new. It has a distinguished history. What *is* new is that the claim that primitive and irrational processes are central to human nature, and it should not provoke a scandalised response. There is a good analogy to related developments in epistemology. The word 'ideology' and the adjective 'ideological' have had pejorative meanings since Napoleon trashed the movement which went by that name in the early nineteenth century: *les Idéologues* (Rosen 1946; Young 1971, 1973, 1977). But ideology only held its terrors in virtue of being in paired opposition to 'science', rather as 'fact' and 'value' are paired. But if the strong claims hitherto made for science are seen to melt away, then ideology – the colouring of accounts of things by the values of interest groups – becomes the norm, not the deviation (Haraway 1989, 1990; Young 1992b). If the science/ideology and the fact/value distinctions are undermined, because science is ideological and facts are value-laden, then the closely related split between psychotic and non-psychotic (or normal) should also be reconceptualised. The rational and putatively objective cannot be sharply distinguished from the irrational and subjective.

The distinguished history to which I refer is easily recalled. Plato banished the poets and songsters from his rationalist republic. The role of the senses and accidental connections was, in very different ways, one of sullying knowledge in the purest of both the rationalist and empiricist traditions. But David Hume, the deepest of the empiricists, made passion central to human nature and knowing. Illumination from witches and hermetical and magical processes remained strong themes in Renaissance thought, but also in the eminently respectable writings of Paracelsus, van Helmont and other figures in alchemy and early chemistry and, most notably, in Newton's world view (Webster 1982). The point of this is that the official line – that meaning and purpose and the so-called 'final causes' of the Aristotelian tradition were banned from scientific explanation – leaves out the hugely important fact that they remained active in the deepest assumptions of the greatest scientists, such as Newton and Darwin (Rattansi 1973; Young 1985, 1989, 1992c.)

If we look at the history of painting for evidence of the profound truths which have been believed to inhere in the irrational, one need only mention Bosch, Breughel, Goya, van Gogh, Surrealism and Dada for a continuous tradition of illumination sought from primitive, irrational and disturbing images. Think of Magritte and Man Ray and the films of Buñuel. Similar stories can be told about literature, culminating in the significance attached in recent times to automatic writing and stream of consciousness.

The history of psychiatry tells the same story, as Foucault (1967) has shown in *Madness and Civilisation*, and as was made part of a movement, in aspects of the so-called anti-psychiatry movement which was (in part wrongly) associated with the work of Laing, Cooper and Esterson (Cooper 1972; Laing 1960; Laing and Esterson 1970; Boyers and Orill 1972; Ingleby 1981). There is a common theme here: that we must pay attention to what is usually called psychotic. It has a meaning. This is sensitively demonstrated in Laing's writings and exemplified in detail by Barham's analyses of discussions among chronically schizophrenic patients (Barham 1984, Chapters 4 and 5). It could be said that most of the four volumes by Harold Searles demonstrate the meaningfulness of psychotic utterances (Searles 1960, 1965, 1979, 1986), while his gladiatorial dialogue with Langs defends his special competence in this utterly demanding work (Langs and Searles 1980, especially Chapter 4 and Appendix).

Let's take stock. I have granted that there are banal and potentially illuminating versions of my thesis that psychotic processes are everywhere. I have reminded you of certain differences of preoccupation and approach between psychiatrists and those who think psychoanalytically. I have contrasted psychiatric classification of mental disease syndromes with psychotherapeutic dynamics. I have made a critique of the claims of classification to be based on an unproblematic idea of the natural, since the natural (including disease categories and the concept of nature itself) is itself historical – part of the history of culture. Finally, I have begun an attempt to bring the primitive and irrational – the psychotic – to the centre of our humanity. In doing so I have been implicitly undermining orthodox, ego psychology models, along with orthodox psychiatric ones.

I turn now to psychotic anxieties *per se*. Lest it be thought that the strands of my argument are not being interwoven into a recognisable pattern, let me say what I want you to discern in the final product. It is that human distress, if we are to treat it as human, must be interpreted as intelligible and part of our sense of what it means to be human – all the way to its deepest roots as well as its broadest determinations. A whole set of interpreters has helped us to place ideas – including scientific, medical, psychiatric and psychological ideas – inside the broader history of culture. They have not been as assiduous in doing this with primitive forces in human nature, although, God knows, we have plenty of evidence at the moment for the baleful effects of such forces. These, too, must be treated as part of the mainstream of human nature in the individual and in groups, institutions, cultures and communities. The fact that it is hard to find a language adequate for characterising and interpreting pre-linguistic and sub-linguistic feelings only makes the problem more difficult and challenging. It does not excuse abrogating the constitutive role of intense irrational motives in how we think, feel and behave. To say with the philosopher that 'nothing human is foreign to me' is to open the door of theory and practice to the ubiquity of psychotic anxieties and to begin to break down the barriers of mutual incomprehension and subcultural separation between psychotherapy and psychiatry. I see these as institutionalised forms of the splitting-off of deep and irrational feelings from the received account of how we think. If science is to be reintegrated with meaning, purpose, goals and values – including ideology and politics – then psychotherapy, psychoanalysis and psychiatry must, as part of the overall project, be reintegrated with the deepest sources of the evaluative dimension. This has implications for both the psychiatric and the psychotherapeutic communities and for training as well as practice.

I begin with some classic texts; this from Freud's 'Formulation on the Two Principles of Mental Functioning' (1911):

'With the introduction of the reality principle one species of thought-activity was split off; it was kept free from reality-testing and remained subordinated to the pleasure principle alone. This activity is *phantasying*, which begins already in children's play, and later, continued as *day-dreaming*, abandons dependence on real objects' (p.222).

'The strangest characteristic of unconscious (repressed) processes...is due to their entire disregard of reality testing; they equate reality of thought with external actuality, and wishes with their fulfilment – with the event – just as happens automatically under the dominance of the ancient pleasure principle' (p.225).

Freud says here that the persistence of the irrational is fundamental to human nature and remains so as we develop.

This is from Joan Riviere's classic Kleinian essay 'On the Genesis of Psychical Conflict in Early Infancy' (1952b):

'I wish especially to point out...that from the very beginning of life, on Freud's own hypothesis, the psyche responds to the reality of its experiences by interpreting them – or rather, *mis*interpreting them – in a subjective manner that increases its pleasure and preserves it from pain. This act of *subjective interpretation of experience*, which it carries out by means of the processes of introjection and projection, is called by Freud hallucination; and it forms the foundation of what we mean by *phantasy-life*. The phantasy-life of the individual is thus the form in which his real internal and external sensations and perceptions are interpreted and represented to himself in his mind under the influence of the pleasure-pain principle. (It seems to me that one has only to consider for a moment to see that, in spite of all the advances man has made in adaptation of a kind to external reality, this primitive and elementary function of his psyche – to misinterpret his perceptions for his own satisfaction – still retains the upper hands in the minds of the great majority of even civilized adults.)' (p.41)

In claiming that experience is characteristically misinterpreted at source and that hallucination is at the foundation of experience, Riviere is saying that there is no neutral observation language in everyday life. You don't start with pure sense data which then get subjectively distorted. The very act of *having* experience is coloured by irrational processes. The same claim about there being no neutral observation language is made of science in recent work in the philosophy of science.

I want to turn now to the history of ideas about psychotic processes in Klein, Bion and Meltzer. Klein described schizoid mechanisms as occurring 'in the baby's development in the first year of life characteristically...the infant suffered from states of mind that were in all their essentials equivalent to the adult psychoses, taken as regressive states in Freud's sense' (Meltzer 1978, Part 3, p.22).

Klein says in the third paragraph of her most famous paper, 'Notes on Some Schizoid Mechanisms' (1946), 'In early infancy anxieties characteristic of psychosis arise which drive the ego to develop specific defence-mechanisms. In this period the fixation-points for all psychotic disorders are to be found. This has led some people to believe that I regard all infants as psychotic; but I have already dealt sufficiently with this misunderstanding on other occasions' (Klein 1975, Vol.3, p.1). Meltzer comments: 'Although she denied that this was tantamount to saying that babies are psychotic, it is difficult to see how this implication could be escaped' (Meltzer 1978, Part 3, p.22).

Kleinian thinking evolved in three stages. As in the above quotation, Klein saw schizoid mechanisms and the paranoid-schizoid position as fixation points, respectively, for schizophrenia and manic-depressive psychosis. Then the paranoid-schizoid (ps) and depressive (d) positions became developmental stages. Her terminology included 'psychotic phases', 'psychotic positions' and then 'positions' (Klein 1975, Vol.1, pp.275 (footnote)–276 (footnote), 279). Next, in the work of Bion and other post-Kleinians, these became economic principles and part of the moment-to-moment vicissitudes of everyday life. The notations 'ps' and 'd' were connected with a double-headed arrow – 'ps↔d' – to indicate how easily, frequently and normally our inner states oscillate from the one to the other and back again (Meltzer 1978, Part 3, p.22).

In Bion's writings on schizophrenia an ambiguity remained as to whether or not the psychotic part of the personality is ubiquitous or only present in schizophrenics (Bion 1967, especially Chapter 5), but Meltzer concludes his exposition of Bion's schizophrenia papers by referring to the existence of these phenomena in patients of every degree of disturbance, even 'healthy' candidates in training to be therapists (Meltzer 1978, p.28). Going further, he and colleagues have drawn on the inner world of autistic patients to illuminate the norm (Meltzer *et al.* 1975); Frances Tustin (1986) has essayed on autistic phenomena in neurotic patients, while Sydney Klein (1980) has described 'autistic cysts' in neurotic patients. In his most recent writings on *The Claustrum* (1992), Meltzer has elegantly shown that desperate defences against schizophrenic breakdown account for much of the psychology and behaviour of competitive and dramatically successful executives and leaders. Those who live in the claustrum – the lower colon of the mental digestive tract, just inside the anus – have inner worlds dominated by virulent projective identification and fear of expulsion, which would have the consequence of schizophrenic breakdown.

Klein's views on these matters are based on Freud and Abraham's notions of oral libido and fantasies of cannibalism (Gedo 1986, p.94). She begins her essay, 'A Contribution to the Psychogenesis of Manic-Depressive States' (1935), with claims about the extreme feelings of all babies: 'My earlier writings contain the account of a phase of sadism at its height, through which children pass during the first year of life. In the very first months of the baby's existence it has sadistic impulses directed, not only against its mother's breast, but also against the inside of her body: scooping it out, devouring the contents, destroying it by every means which sadism can suggest' (Klein 1975, Vol.1, p.262). Once again, the projective and introjective mechanisms of the first months and year give rise to anxiety situations and defences against them, 'the content of which is comparable to that of the psychoses in adults'.

Orality is everywhere, for example, in the 'gnawing of conscience' (p.268). Riviere says that 'such helplessness against destructive forces within constitutes the greatest psychical danger-situation known to the human organism; and that this helplessness is the deepest source of anxiety in human beings' (Riviere 1952b, p.43). It is the ultimate source of all neurosis. At this early stage of development, sadism is at its height and is followed by the discovery that loved objects are in a state of disintegration, in bits or in dissolution, leading to despair, remorse and anxiety, which underlie numerous anxiety situations. Klein concludes, 'Anxiety situations of this kind I have found to be at the bottom not only of depression, but of all inhibitions of work' (Klein 1975, Vol.1, p.270).

It should be recalled that these are pre-linguistic experiences developmentally, and sub-linguistic in adults. They are hard to characterise and hard to think about. It is a characteristic of the world view of Kleinians that the primitive is never transcended and that all experiences continue to be mediated through the mother's body. Similarly, there is a persistence of primitive phantasies of body parts and bodily functions, especially biting, eating, tearing, spitting out, urine and urinating, faeces and defecating, mucus, genitals. One of the reasons we don't like to think about these matters is that it is very hard to characterise them, and they are so yukky.

Why is all this such an innovation? Riviere points out that anxiety was of great significance to Freud, but that much of his rhetoric was scientific, especially physiological. He did not concern himself with the psychological content of phantasies. Indeed, he and many of his so-called 'Freudian' followers have tended to use scientist analogies instead of conveying human distress in evocative language. By contrast, 'Anxiety, with the defences against it, has from the beginning been Mrs Klein's approach to psycho-analytical problems. It was from this angle that she discovered the existence and importance of aggressive elements in children's emotional life…and [it] enabled her to bring much of the known phenomena of mental disorders into line with the basic principles of analysis' (Riviere 1952a, pp.8–9).

This contrast between Freud and Klein takes us back to one of the major themes of my argument – the need to break away from describing the inner world in terms drawn from a metapsychology based on analogies from physics, chemistry and biology. I am advocating, instead, the bold use of terms adopted from the language of everyday life – including, and especially, primitive emotional life – and the employment of any way of representing primitive processes that comes to hand which keeps contact with real feelings. This involves a move from the didactic and objectivist language of natural science, and the epistemologies which kow-tow, to it, towards evocative and phenomenological ways of attempting to convey the inner meaning of experience. Mental space need not be reduced to the realm of extended substances; it can be filled and populated by whatever kind of account helps us to keep feeling alive. Rather than defer to the impoverished vocabularies implied by the canons of Cartesian dualism, our criterion should be whether or not a given account resonates with the dialectic of experience.

Kleinians have consistently written in a language which eschews physicalist scientism, although Klein retained a notion of instinct, even though this was largely redundant as a result of her object relations perspective. They went on to propose elements of a general psychology, including the claim that there is 'an unconscious phantasy behind every thought and every act' (Riviere 1952a, p.16). That is, the mental expression of primitive processes '*is* unconscious phantasy' (ibid.). It is not only a background hum, as it were. Susan Isaacs claims that 'Reality thinking cannot operate without concurrent and supporting unconscious phantasies' (Isaacs 1952, p.109). And again: 'phantasies are the primary content of unconscious mental processes' (pp.82, 112). 'There is no impulse, no instinctual urge or response which is not experienced as unconscious phantasy' (p.83). 'Phantasies have both psychic and bodily effects, e. g., in conversion symptoms, bodily qualities, character and personality, neurotic symptoms, inhibitions and sublimations' (p.112). They even determine the minutiae of body language (p.100). The role of unconscious phantasy extends from the first to the most abstract thought. The infant's first thought of the existence of the external world comes from sadistic attacks on the mother's body (Klein 1975, Vol.1, p.276; Vol.3, p.5). 'Phantasies – becoming more elaborate and referring to a wider variety of objects and situations – continue throughout development and accompany all activities; they never stop playing a great part in mental life. The influence of unconscious phantasy on art, on scientific work, and on the activities of everyday life cannot be overrated' (Klein 1975, Vol.3, p.251; cf. p.262).

These anxieties are not only ubiquitous: they interact in complicated ways. As Riviere (1952) points out,

'It is impossible to do any justice here to the complexity and variety of the anxiety-situations and the defences against them dominating the psyche during these early years. The factors involved are so numerous and the combinations and interchanges so variable. The internal objects are employed against external, and external against internal, both for satisfaction and for security; desire is employed against hate and destructiveness; omnipotence against impotence, and even impotence (dependence) against destructive omnipotence; phantasy against reality and reality against phantasy. Moreover, hate and destruction are employed as measures to avert the dangers of desire and even of love. Gradually a progressive development takes place…by means of the interplay of these and other factors, and of them with external influences, out of which the child's ego, his object-relations, his sexual development, his super-ego, his character and capacities are formed.' (pp.59–60)

It was on the foundation of these ideas about individual psychology that the classical work on groups and institutions of Bion, Elliott Jaques and Isabel Menzies Lyth was built. Bion argued that group phenomena required a deeper explanation than the Freudian one employing the family and id, ego and superego. He did not repudiate these but delved deeper into the realm of psychotic anxieties, which he believed operated in all groups. The forms of distress that converted sensible 'work groups' into mad ones dominated by what he called 'basic assumptions', 'correspond so closely with extremely primitive part objects that sooner or later psychotic anxiety, appertaining to these primitive relationships, is released'. The defensive measures to which the groups resort are the same as those which individual babies employ in the face of their earliest anxieties (Bion 1955, p.456). Bion suggests that these primitive anxieties 'contain the ultimate sources of all group behaviour' (p.476).

Jaques begins his essay, 'Social Systems as a Defence against Persecutory and Depressive Anxiety' (1955) by reiterating that 'social phenomena show a striking correspondence with psychotic processes in individuals', that 'institutions are used by their individual members to reinforce individual mechanisms of defence against anxiety', and 'that the mechanisms of projective and introjective identification operate in linking individual and social behaviour'. He argues the thesis that 'the primary cohesive elements binding individuals into institutionalised human association is that of defence against psychotic anxiety' (Jaques 1955, pp.478–9). He points out that the projective and introjective processes he is investigating are basic to even the most complex social processes and directs us to Paula Heimann's claim that they are at the bottom of all our dealings with one another (p.481, 481 (footnote)).

His conclusion is cautionary and points out the conservative – even reactionary – consequences of our psychotic anxieties and our group and institutional defences against them. He suggests that as a result of these reflections on human nature:

'it may become more clear why social change is so difficult to achieve, and why many social problems are so intractable. From the point of view here elaborated, changes in social relationships and procedures call for a restructuring of relationships at the phantasy level, with a consequent demand upon individuals to accept and tolerate changes in their existing patterns of defences against psychotic anxiety. Effective social change is likely to require analysis of the common anxieties and unconscious collusions underlying the social defences determining phantasy social relationships.' (p.498)

I turn finally to the investigator who, in my opinion, has made the most of this perspective, Isabel Menzies Lyth, who built her research on the shoulders of Bion and Jaques. She has investigated a number of fraught settings, extending from the fire brigade to the British Psycho-Analytical Society, but the piece of research which has deservedly made her world-famous is described in a report entitled 'The Functioning of Social Systems as a Defence against Anxiety' (1959). It is a particularly poignant document, which addresses the question why people of good will and idealistic motives do not do what they intend, that is, why nurses find themselves, to an astonishing degree, not caring for patients and leaving the nursing service in droves. It would be repetitious to review the mechanisms she describes. They are the ones discussed above. What is so distressing is that they operate overwhelmingly in a setting, the hospital, which has as its very reason for existence the provision of sensitivity and care. Yet that setting is full of threats to life itself and arouses the psychotic anxieties I have outlined. She says, 'The objective situation confronting the nurse bears a striking resemblance to the phantasy situations that exist in every individual in the deepest and most primitive levels of the mind. The intensity and complexity of the nurse's anxieties are to be attributed primarily to the peculiar capacity of the objective features of her work situation to stimulate afresh those early situations and their accompanying emotions' (Menzies Lyth 1959, pp.46–7).

The result is the evolution of socially structured defence mechanisms which take the form of routines and division of tasks which effectively preclude the nurse relating as a whole person to the patient as a whole person. 'The implicit aim of such devices, which operate both structurally and culturally, may be described as a kind of depersonalisation or elimination of individual distinctiveness in both nurse and patient. For example, nurses often talk about patients not by name, but by bed numbers or by their diseases or a diseased organ: "the liver in bed 10" or "the pneumonia in bed 15". Nurses deprecate this practice, but it persists' (pp.51–2). She lists and discusses the reifying devices which reduce everyone involved to part-objects, including insight into why the nurse wakes you up to give you a sleeping pill (p.69). There is a whole system of overlapping ways of evading the full force of the anxieties associated with death, the ones which lie at the heart of the mechanisms which Klein described (pp.63–64; cf. Riviere 1952, p.43).

Menzies Lyth also draws a cautionary conclusion: 'In general, it may be postulated that resistance to social change is likely to be greatest in institutions whose social defence systems are dominated by primitive psychic defence mechanisms, those which have been collectively described by Melanie Klein as the paranoid-schizoid defences' (Menzies Lyth 1959, p.79). In recent reflections on her work and that of her colleagues, she has reiterated just how refractory to change institutions are (Menzies Lyth 1959, pp.1–42 and personal communications).

That completes my exposition of the Kleinian and post-Kleinian literature. I find it sobering and profoundly challenging to any hope for a better world. I do not think it can be squared with at least two other traditions. The first is the orthodox and neo-Freudian one where the ego's mechanisms of defence manage to keep irrational forces at bay or to neutralise or tame them before they enter consciousness. Nor do I find it compatible with the convenient distinction between people who are either normal (or normally miserable and neurotic) and others who are in a different state called psychotic, with allowances for periods in the repair shop called 'breakdowns'. I am not saying that there are not psychotic people or people who have breakdowns. I am saying that those people are not as strange to the rest of us as the nosologists would have you believe. My point is that we are not strangers to psychotic processes in our everyday lives, families, groups, institutions and societies. They are about all the time – not just in the wars and conflicts we see all around us, particularly at the moment. I refer also to what all too often happens in psychotherapeutic and psychoanalytic training organisations: scapegoating, outgrouping, paranoid atmospheres, splits. What is surprising at first glance is that this sort of behaviour occurs at all in and between psychotherapeutic, psychoanalytic and group relations institutions – the cradles of the very psychodynamic enlightenment which I have been trying to illuminate. But, on reflection, that's not really surprising, either. It is true in the churches, academic institutions and charities, the schools, asylums and major corporations, monasteries and nunneries, orphanages and sports teams, political parties and communes. I am not listing institutions for completeness' sake. I have in mind quite specific incidents and histories. Psychotic processes are not evident or dominant all the time, but they are present and having effects all the time in all institutions. We are all partly psychotic all of the time and all of us display psychotic parts of our personalities part of the time. Bion insists that the move into basic assumption functioning is involuntary, automatic and inevitable (Bion 1955, p.458).

Having objects into which to project is the *sine qua non* of mental well-being. But we do so in a vulnerable space, on one side of which is nameless dread and a black hole and on the other the intense projections of outgrouping, racism and virulent nationalism. All of us become humans by learning to project and members of groups by being socialised into their projective identifications, some good, some very nasty (Young 1994, Chapters 6 and 7). The same is true of professions, even and especially helping professions like nursing, medicine, psychiatry, psychotherapy and psychoanalysis.

I recall that eminent neo-Freudian, Joseph Sandler, describing psychotherapy as a process of making friends with the unacceptable parts of ourselves. Just as Bion said we had to delve deeper than Freud to get at the ultimate sources of all group behaviour, I think we have to grant that the ubiquity of psychotic anxieties means that we are up against much more in ourselves that we are inclined to believe. So there are even more unacceptable parts to be befriended or neutralised or repressed by the thin veneer of civilisation. To deny their ubiquity or to overestimate the strength of that veneer strikes me as ostrich-like and to tempt us to hide our eyes from the lessons of the nursery, the family, society and international relations. I think this blinkered attitude helps to explain why psychiatrists and psychotherapists try to restrict the range of their obligations, the people with whom they work and the issues upon which they reflect.

We split off these feelings and try to confine them to 'psychotics'. I suggest that much official psychopathology and classification serve defensive purposes and protect us from our own and others' psychotic anxieties. These are forms of control which – like the banishment of purposes and goals in scientific explanation – sequester existential risk and politics and drive underground the legitimate angst of suffering people. The official healers in society do their jobs humanely but get turned into minders. While I was still writing this paper I saw a film about the huge oil spill of the Exxon Valdez in Alaska, in which phalanxes of reasonably conscientious officials never got into a hands-on tactile relationship with the millions of gallons of sludge or the fatal coating their ways of working and their blinkered notion of energy had allowed to stifle life. It struck me as a metaphor for the urgency of the reconceptualisation I am proposing.

I think Freud pointed the way in the concluding passage in his presciently realistic though pessimistic essay, *Civilization and Its Discontents* (1930). He wrote that the history of civilisation is 'the struggle between Eros and Death, between the instinct of life and the instinct of destruction, as it works itself out in the human species. This struggle is what all life essentially consists of... And it is this battle of the giants that our nurse-maids try to appease with their lullaby about Heaven' (Freud 1930, p.122).

REFERENCES

Amacher, P. (1965) 'Freud's neurological education and its influence on psychoanalytic theory.' *Psychological Issues 4*, 4, Monograph 16.

APA (American Psychiatric Association) (1987) *Diagnostic and Statistical Manual of Mental Disorders.* Third edition, revised. *DSM-III-R.* Washington, DC: American Psychiatric Association.

Barham, P. (1984) *Schizophrenia and Human Value.* Oxford: Blackwell. (Republished Free Association Books, London, 1993.)

Barham, P. (1992) *Closing the Asylum: The Mental Patient in Modern Society.* Harmondsworth: Penguin.

Bernfield, S. (1944) 'Freud's earliest theories and the school of Helmholtz.' *Psychoanalytic Quarterly 13*, 341–62.

Bernfield, S. (1949) 'Freud's scientific beginnings.' *American Imago 6*, 3–36.

Bernfield, S. (1951) 'Sigmund Freud, M.D., 1881–1885.' *International Journal of Psycho-analysis 32*, 204–17.

Berrios, G. E. (1991) 'British psychopathology since the early 20th century.' In G.E. Berrios and H. Freeman (eds) *150 Years of British Psychiatry 1841–1991*. London: Gaskell.

Bion, W.R. (1955) 'Group dynamics: a re-view.' In M. Klein *et al.* (eds) (1955).

Bion, W.R. (1961) *Experiences in Groups and Other Papers*. London: Tavistock.

Bion, W.R. (1967) *Second Thoughts: Selected Papers on Psycho-Analysis*. London: Heinemann. (Republished Maresfield, London, 1984.)

Boyers, R. and Orrill, R., (eds) (1972) *Laing and Anti-Psychiatry*. Harmondsworth: Penguin.

Cooper, D. (1972) *The Death of the Family*. Harmondsworth: Penguin.

Feuchstersleben, E.F. von (1847) *The Principles of Medical Psychology*. London: Sydenham Society.

Figlio, K. (1978) 'Chlorosis and chronic disease in nineteenth-century Britain: the social constitution of somatic illness in a capitalist society.' *International Journal of Health Services 8*, 589–617.

Figlio, K. (1979) 'Sinister medicine: a critique of left approaches to medicine.' *Radical Science Journal 9*, 14–68.

Figlio, K. (1985) 'Medical diagnosis, class dynamics, social stability.' In L. Levidow and R.M. Young (eds) *Science, Technology and the Labour Process: Marxist Studies*, Vol. 2. London: Free Association Books.

Figlio, K. (1990), 'The environment: topographies of the internal and external worlds.' Talk delivered to the Centre for Psycho-analytic Studies, University of Kent.

Foucault, M. (1967) *Madness and Civilisation: A History of Insanity in the Age of Reason*. London: Tavistock.

Freud, S. (1953–73) *The Standard Edition of the Complete Psychological Works of Sigmund Freud*. 24 Vols. London: Hogarth. (S.E.)

Freud, S. (1891) *On Aphasia: A Clinical Study*. New York: International Universities Press, 1953.

Freud, S. (1900) *The Interpretation of Dreams*. Standard Edition, Vol.4–5.

Freud, S. (1911) *Formulation on the Two Principles of Mental Functioning*. Standard Edition, Vol. 12, 218–26.

Freud, S. (1930) *Civilization and Its Discontents*. Standard Edition, Vol.21, 59–145.

Freud, S. (1933) *New Introductory Lectures on Psycho-Analysis*. Standard Edition, Vol.22, 3–182.

Gay, P. (1988) *Freud: A Life for our Time*. London: Dent.

Gedo, J. E. (1986) *Conceptual Issues in Psychoanalysis: Essays in History and Method*. New York: Analytic Press.

Haraway, D. (1989) *Primate Visions: Gender, Race, and Nature in the World of Modern Science*. London: Routledge.

Haraway, D. 1990) *Simians, Cyborgs and Women: The Reinvention of Nature*. London: Free Association Books.

Holland, Sir H. (1852) *Chapters on Mental Physiology*. London: Longman, Brown, Green and Longmans.

Ingleby, D. (ed) (1981) *Critical Psychiatry: The Politics of Mental Health*. Harmondsworth: Penguin.

Isaacs, S. (1952) 'The nature and function of phantasy.' In M. Klein *et al*. (1952).

Jaques, E. (1955) 'Social systems as defence against persecutory and depressive anxiety.' In Klein *et al*. (eds) *op.cit.*

Klein, M. (1975) *The Writings of Melanie Klein*, 4 vols. London: Hogarth.

Klein, M. (1935) 'A contribution to the psychogenesis of manic-depressive states.' In M. Klein (1975), Vol. 1, 262–89.

Klein, M. (1946) 'Notes on some schizoid mechanisms.' In M. Klein (1975), Vol. 3, 1–24.

Klein, M., Heimann, P., Isaacs, S. and Riviere, V. (1952) *Developments in Psycho-Analysis*. London: Hogarth. (Republished Karnac, London, 1989.)

Klein, M., Heimann, P. and Money-Kyrle, R.E. (eds) (1955) *New Directions in Psycho-Analysis: The Significance of Infant Conflict in the Patterns of Adult Behaviour*. London: Tavistock. (Republished Maresfield, London, 1977.)

Klein, S. (1980) 'Autistic phenomena in neurotic patients.' *International Journal of Psycho-analysis 61*, 395–402.

Kris, E. (1950) 'The significance of Freud's earliest discoveries.' *International Journal of Psycho-analysis 31*, 108–16.

Laing, R.D. (1960) *The Divided Self: An Existential Study in Sanity and Madness*. London: Tavistock. (Republished Penguin, Harmondsworth, 1965.)

Laing, R.D. and Esterson, A. (1970) *Sanity, Madness and the Family: Families of Schizophrenics*. Harmondsworth: Penguin.

Langs, R. and Searles, H.F. (1980) *Intrapsychic and Interpersonal Dimensions of Treatment: A Clinical Dialogue*. London/New York: Aronson.

Lukács, G. (1923) *History and Class Consciousness: Studies in Marxist Dialectics*. London: Merlin, 1971.

Maudsley, H. (1867) *The Physiology and Pathology of Mind*. London: Macmillan.

MacIntyre, A. (1977) 'Epistemological crises, dramatic narrative and the philosophy of science.' *The Monist 60*, 453–72.

MacIntyre, A. (1981) *After Virtue*. London: Duckworth.

Mayo, T. (1838) *Elements of the Pathology of the Human Mind*. London: Murray.

Meltzer, D. (1978) *The Kleinian Development*. London: Clunie.

Meltzer, D. (1992) *The Claustrum: An Investigation of Claustrophobic Phenomena*. London: Clunie.

Meltzer, D., Brennan, J., Hoxter, S., Woddell, D. and Wittenberg, I. (1975) *Explorations in Autism: A Psycho-Analytic Study*. London: Clunie.

Menzies, Lyth, I. (1959) 'The functioning of social systems as a defence against anxiety.' *Human Relations 13*, 95–121. (Reprinted in *Containing Anxieties in Institutions: Selected Essays*. Free Association Books, 1988.)

Rattansi, P. M. (1973) 'Some evaluations of reason in sixteenth- and seventeenth-century natural philosophy.' In M. Teich and R. M. Young (eds) *Changing Perspectives in the History of Science*. London: Heinemann.

Rey, H. (1994) *Universals of Psychoanalysis in the Treatment of Psychotic and Borderline States*. London: Free Association Books.

Riese, W. (1958) 'Freudian concepts of brain function and brain disease.' *Journal of Nervous and Mental Diseases 127*, 287–307.

Riviere, J. (1952a) 'General Introduction.' In Klein *et al.* (1952).

Riviere, J. (1952b) 'On the genesis of psychical conflict in early infancy.' In Klein *et al.* (1952).

Rorty, R. (1980) *Philosophy and the Mirror of Nature.* Oxford: Blackwell.

Rorty, R. (1982) *Consequences of Pragmatism (Essays: 1972–80).* Minneapolis: University of Minnesota Press.

Rorty, R. (1989) *Contingency, Irony, and Solidarity.* Cambridge: Cambridge University Press.

Rosen, G, (1946) 'The philosophy of ideology and the emergence of modern medicine in France.' *Bulletin of the History of Medicine 20*, 328–39.

Rosenfeld, H. (1965) *Psychotic States: A Psychoanalytic Approach.* London: Hogarth. (Republished Maresfield, London 1982.)

Rosenfeld, H. (1987) *Impasse and Interpretation: Therapeutic and Anti-Therapeutic Factors in Psychoanalytic Treatment of Psychotic, Borderline, and Neurotic Patients.* London: Routledge.

Searles, H.F. (1960) *The Nonhuman Environment: In Normal Development and in Schizophrenia.* Madison, CT: International Universities Press.

Searles, H.F. (1965) *Collected Papers on Schizophrenia and Related Subjects.* London: Hogarth. (Republished Karnac, London 1986.)

Searles, H.F. (1979) *Countertransference and Related Subjects.* Madison, CT: International Universities Press.

Searles, H.F. (1986) *My Work with Borderline Patients.* London: Aronson.

Segal, H. (1981) *The Work of Hanna Segal: A Kleinian Approach to Clinical Practice.* London: Aronson. (Republished Free Association Books/Maresfield London, 1986).

Silver, D. and Rosenbleuth, M. (eds) (1992) *Handbook of Borderline Disorders.* Madison, CT: International Universities Press.

Spillius, E.B. (1988) *Melanie Klein Today.* 2 vols. London: Routledge.

Steiner, J. (1993) *Psychic Retreats: Pathological Organizations in Psychotic, Neurotic and Borderline Patients.* London: Routledge.

Stengel. E.A. (1954) 'A re-evaluation of Freud's book *On Aphasia*: its significance for psychoanalysis.' *International Journal of Psycho-analysis 35*, 85–89.

Summers, F. (1994) *Object Relations Theories and Psychopathology: A Comprehensive Text.* London: Analytic Press.

Tarnopolsky, A. (1992) 'The validity of the borderline personality disorder.' In Silver and Rosenbleuth (eds) *op.cit.*

Tustin, F. (1986) *Autistic Barriers in Neurotic Patients.* London: Karnac.

Webster, C. (1982) *From Paracelsus to Newton: Magic and the Making of Modern Science.* Cambridge: Cambridge University Press.

Young, R.M. (1970) *Mind, Brain and Adaptation in the Nineteenth Century: Cerebral Localisation and Its Biological Context from Gall to Ferrier.* Oxford: Clarendon Press. (Republished Oxford University Press, 1990.)

Young, R.M. (1971) 'Evolutionary biology and ideology: then and now.' *Science Studies 1*, 177–206.

Young, R.M. (1973) 'The human limits of nature.' In J. Benthall (ed) *The Limits of Human Nature.* London: Allen Lane.

Young, R.M. (1977) 'Science *is* social relations.' *Radical Science Journal 5,* 65–131.

Young, R.M. (1985) *Darwin's Metaphor: Nature's Place in Victorian Culture.* Cambridge: Cambridge University Press.

Young, R.M. (1986) 'Freud: scientist and/or humanist.' *Free Associations 6,* 7–35.

Young, R.M. (1989) 'Persons, organisms…and primary qualities.' In J. Moore (ed) *History, Humanity and Evolution: Essays for John C. Greene.* Cambridge: Cambridge University Press.

Young, R.M. (1990) 'The mind–body problem.' In R.C. Olby, G.N. Cantor, J.R.R. Christie and M.J.S. Hodge (eds) *Companion to the History of Modern Science.* London: Routledge.

Young, R.M. (1992a) 'The vicissitudes of transference and countertransference: the work of Harold Searles.' *Journal of the Arbours Association 9,* 24–58.

Young, R.M. (1992b) 'Science, ideology and Donna Haraway.' *Science as Culture 15, 3,* 7–46.

Young, R.M. (1992c) 'Darwin's metaphor and the philosophy of science.' *Science as Culture 3,* 16, 375–403.

Young, R.M. (1994) *Mental Space.* London: Process Press.

Young, R.M. and Postle, D. (1981) 'Behaving ourselves.' Television film in the series *Crucible: Science in Society.* Channel Four.

Young, R.M. and Gold, M. (1982) 'A history of nature.' Television film in the series *Crucible: Science in Society.* Channel Four.

CHAPTER 4

Schizophrenia
A Constructive Analogy or a Convenient Construct?

Richard Marshall

I find little value in the concept of what is termed 'schizophrenia' itself; indeed, I regard it primarily as a social construction which indicates more about a variety of social and professional structures than it does about individuals who are unfortunate enough to be so designated. The questions which I find most interesting and relevant concern the processes which maintain the concept, and promote it as being based upon scientific knowledge. Such considerations are, I feel, more than quaint philosophical deliberations which have little relevance to the real world of psychological distress. It is my view that the concept of schizophrenia, the accompanying implicit notion of an illness, and belief in physiological and genetic underpinnings, have served many purposes, the most significant being to provide a model for viewing a whole range of conducts in biological terms.

The implications are that all other areas of psychological distress and what might be called 'unwanted conducts' could eventually be subsumed under reductionistic and biologically-determined explanations. Meanwhile, psychological and sociological considerations will gradually be pushed to a periphery of quaint notions left over from the 1960s which, whilst noteworthy, will be seen to have little to do with the real business of scientific understanding. In this process psychotherapeutic thinking, socio-economic relevances, and attempts to find meanings in context, would come to be regarded as anti-scientific and unworthy of more than passing consideration. For those reasons alone, then, I regard it as obligatory that we pay serious attention to the concept of schizophrenia and its promotion as a biological entity.

The chief driving force behind the ideas in this paper have their origins in seeing at first hand the damaging effects of psychiatric hospitals systems on those labelled 'schizophrenic', and in working closely with such individuals. I had rather presumptuously supposed that some of my concerns were a result of recent perceptions, and I was a little surprised to find many of them articulated by Stanton Peele (1981), an American psychologist known for his overviews, in a paper written over a decade ago. He warned that a growing consensus was emerging that the best hope for understanding and dealing with psychological problems lies with work being done in genetics, biology, and the neurosciences. The public is kept abreast of progress in this field in article after article in semi-popular scientific publications and the more serious periodicals and news-papers. Psychologists, themselves, appear to be so eager to accept neurological and biochemical explanations for behaviour that psychology is in danger of losing its status as an independent body of knowledge. I have asked final year undergraduates in psychology the causes of schizophrenia, and palled when told in all confidence that it was a virus.

Peele points out that this reductionistic trend of thought, as well as having major scientific implications, affects popular attitudes towards self-regulation in key areas of human functioning. Reductionism is not a theory, since it does not present a testable hypothesis. It is more of a philosophy or a faith in the ultimate nature of things. The eventual goal of this faith is to find neurobiological correlates for individual actions, perceptions, feelings, thoughts and memories – as well as for entire behaviour syndromes such as addiction and schizophrenia.

I am particularly aware that there is nothing new in what I am saying, and that it has been far more precisely articulated by others. I do think, however, that such views are being heard less frequently in recent years as the various relevant disciplines become more preoccupied with professional issues, and have tended to concentrate on non-psychotic forms of distress. Mainstream psychiatry, par-ticularly in Britain, has established such a rigorous party line that anything questioning the dominant beliefs is likely to be rejected for publication, and denigrated in shrill fashion when appearing in presses outside its control.

A theme of this paper, then, is that the dominant concept of schizophrenia, as a phenomenon to be understood in terms of biological determinism, is what Peele would describe as a 'faith in the ultimate nature of things'. I will attempt to justify this, and then outline the possible consequences of such faith, as well as consider how such faiths have come into being.

Perhaps we should begin at the most fundamental level. Theodore Sarbin (1991), for long a writer in these matters, has pointed out that because the word 'schizophrenia' belongs to a grammatical class (noun), there is a readiness to regard its referent as 'a thing' (the reification process). He aptly quotes from John Stuart Mill well over a century ago:

'The tendency has always been strong to believe that whatsoever received a name must be an entity or being, having an independent existence of its own. And if no entity answering to the name could be found, men did not for that reason suppose that none existed, but imagined that it was something particularly abstruse and mysterious.'

It is interesting that, around the same time, or a little later, Lewis Carroll seems to have been attempting to put such thoughts into Alice's reformulating words:

> "'What's the use of their having names", the Gnat said, "if they won't answer to them?" "No use to *them*", said Alice, "but it's useful to the people that name them, I suppose. If not, why do things have names at all?"'
> (Carroll)

Rather closer to the present, the late and much-missed Don Bannister (1968) argued that 'schizophrenia', as a concept, as a semantic Titanic, doomed before it sails; a concept so diffuse as to be unusable in a scientific context. So, any effort to criticise or clarify the concept of 'schizophrenia' must begin from the position that 'schizophrenia' is a hypothesis. In spite of the huge literature directed towards establishing empirical validity it remains a hypothetical construct. It would seem wise to state, at this point, that I am in no way diminishing the reality of the distress involved in what is termed 'schizophrenia', both for the individuals and for those around them.

THE CLAIM TO A SCIENTIFIC BASIS

It is sometimes difficult to avoid the impression that the notion of 'science' is abused. On the one hand are those who actually work in a meaningful, constructive, empathic and intuitive way with those termed 'schizophrenic'. Understandably, they regard the so-called scientific literature as being as far removed from this reality as some distant planet. On the other hand are those whose notions of science are more akin to what has been termed 'scientism'. As Notcutt (1953) put it:

> 'Scientism is to science as the Pharisee is to the man of God. In the psychology of scientism there is everything to impress the onlooker – enormous libraries, and a systematic search of the journals, expensive instruments of exquisite precision and shining brass, multi-dimensional geometrics and differential equations... all the equipment is there to make the psychologist feel that he is being really scientific – everything except ideas and results.'

If we accept that science is derived from the root 'to know' then science is about not only what we know, but how we come to know what we know. In this context, then, Kuhn's classifications of how much we seem to know what we are talking about in science are particularly relevant. Here science is not defined in terms of its numerical analysis, techniques, or specialised vocabulary. At the upper range of the level of certainty we have laws and theories; at the lower end, paradigms or models, and lastly metaphors or analogies. Paradigms or models are ideas which seem to explain a group of facts pretty precisely. At the lowest level, metaphors or analogies are ideas which *look as though* they might fit a group of facts, where there is no clear evidence that they do. From a point of view of problem-solving, metaphors and analogies have their uses – they help to turn images into thoughts. But, in Kuhnian terms, they are at the lowest rung of the ladder of certainty of what we are talking about.

The 'illness' notion on which schizophrenia is based is at the level of metaphor or analogy. It is simply a result of an analogy with organic illness. It is metaphorical thinking – it is *as if* what is termed schizophrenia *is* illness, a result of organic defect. What appears to have occurred, however, is that the 'as if', the defining quality of a metaphor, has taken its leave. More important, the awareness that it began as an analogy has concurrently been lost. So-called 'theories' of biological causation have become uncritically accepted. From a true scientific viewpoint, then, an illegitimate and unwarranted assumption has been made. We have moved from the realms of science and into the reaches of belief.

Returning to the reductionistic notions of thinking – it is not difficult to find reasons for their appeal. It lies in their concreteness and conciseness. As Peele (1981) points out

> 'it organises behaviour into exact, discrete categories. By drawing physical connections between behaviour and the nervous system, it offers compact causal explanations. Finally, and most important to its appeal, reductionistic thought holds out the promise of clear-cut remedies to problems that otherwise seem painfully beyond solution.'

The mechanistic, reductionistic worldview is not the only metaphysical framework. The other might be described as contextualism (Sarbin 1991). Unlike mechanistic constructions in which the human being is a passive object reacting to happenings within the body, the contextualist perspective directs the scientist to perceive human beings as agents, actors, performers. Within such a framework, asserts Sarbin, the clinician would begin his study by posing questions such as 'what is the person trying to do or say?', 'what goals is he or she trying to reach?', 'what story is he or she trying to tell?'. Here the aim is to make sense of the world as it is experienced by human beings. Any psychological analysis or treatment which fails to incorporate individual personality and subjective needs or situational and cultural variables, is bound to be incomplete (Sarbin 1991).

In a critical overview of what is termed schizophrenia it is usual to review the literature on 'reliability' and 'validity'. In other words, how much consistency is there in what diagnosers witness, and how does this relate to some consensus notion of what is deemed to be schizophrenia? There is only space here to mention that there is a range of studies which illustrate lack of interjudge agreement so far as schizophrenia or its subcategories are concerned. And to mention that there are studies which indicate low interjudge agreement for alleged attributes of the class of schizophrenics. There are also studies which indicate high overlap of the characteristics of the schizophrenic category with other categories. It would also be necessary to discuss studies of unequal incidence rates indicating diagnostic confusion, and studies which show how judge characteristics manifest themselves. This would, in itself, take up a great deal of time, but would lead to serious reservations about the reliability and validity of the concept of schizophrenia itself.

In a paper advocating the need for twin and adoption studies, Kringlen (1993), himself a psychiatrist, cautions against the optimism generated by genetic linkage studies:

> 'our classification of mental disorders is without strong scientific evidence, although it is more or less agreed upon by the psychiatric establishment. Thus the whole problem of phenotype is debatable. Without an improved phenotype, linkage studies are not likely to succeed...classification problems, combined with ignorance about mode of genetic transmission, suggest that linkage studies in the field of psychiatry will continue to be a dubious enterprise for some time.'

It is worth spending a little time on a review of the literature by Sarbin and Mancuso (1980). They examined nearly 400 papers on schizophrenia over a 20 year period, published in the *Journal of Abnormal Psychology*, and later went on to review a further 10 years' worth of publication. They found that underlying the typical research hypothesis was the Kraepelin premise that those called schizophrenics are basically flawed organisms. About 80 per cent of the reports showed that 'schizophrenics' performed poorly on a variety of psychological tests, in comparison to controls. But the differences were very small. In fact most 'schizophrenics' could not be differentiated from normal controls in a wide variety of experimental tasks. In the two studies in which they performed better, this was interpreted as being a result of their taking the instructions too literally – and is not literalness a sign of thought-disorder?

Sarbin (1990) points out that the small differences in performance between controls and those designated schizophrenic tend to earn the 'schizophrenia hypothesis' a modicum of credibility. But even these small differences dissolve into meaninglessness when we consider the number of hidden variables which could account for observed differences; for example, neuroleptic mediation, socio-economic status, education, effects of patienthood, and so on.

Sarbin and Mancuso (1980) concluded that 30 years of psychological research produced no marker that would establish the validity of a schizophrenic disorder. They add that biochemical, neurological, and anatomical studies also indicate that studies using somatic variables follow the same pattern as for psychological studies.

Yet, in spite of all these limitations, it is not only presented to lay and professional people that schizophrenia is some proven entity, but that furthermore it is an entity with proven origins, and that these origins are biological. A rare caution is provided by Bruce Charlton (1990), a psychiatrist turned anatomist:

'It is useful to reflect on the implicit rationale or philosophy underlying much biological psychiatry research: the idea that psychiatric illness is caused by alterations in neurotransmitter function. This view is so firmly embedded in most research programmes that it seldom surfaces to consciousness, and we forget that there is no direct evidence to link any specific psychiatric diagnosis with a neurotransmitter change.'

One of the major ramifications of the concept of 'illness' is that potential meaningfulness of conduct and thought is denigrated to the level of random aberrations of disordered molecules. As Karon and VandenBos in *The Psychotherapy of Schizophrenia* (1981) point out, genetic and physiological theories are usually generated by investigators who have never talked or listened to any schizophrenic individual for any length of time. It often appears that the most cogent, scientifically-based, arguments against the concept of schizophrenia come from those with a rich grounding in clinical work. Names such as Szasz, Sarbin, Bannister and Laing come to mind. Sarbin (1990) describes his early clinical experiences and traces how these led him to see that the reported imaginings and expressed beliefs were so specific to the individual's life story that it was difficult to accept the explanation that some brain anomaly could account for the hetereogeneity. Only by redefining conduct as 'symptoms' of a still-to-be discovered disease entity could we obliterate the specificity, the individuality, and the problem-solving features of each person's conduct. Furthermore, the illness analogy renders irrelevant the search for intentions behind perplexing interpersonal acts. It makes irrelevant the search for meanings of beliefs and imaginings of persons engaged in solving – often with limited skills – existential and identity problems. Perhaps it is as U'Ren (1992) would have it – psychiatry will continue to generate new diagnoses from old experiences because an increasingly harsh market demands it.

A recently-published WHO report (Jablensky *et al.* 1992) on a ten-country study of schizophrenia is likely to be greeted with great acclaim. The authors make considerable play of their finding that 'schizophrenia is ubiquitous'. It is hardly surprising that people trained in the ways of redefining conduct as 'symptoms' will all find some people to call schizophrenic. Yet in the greatest leap of faith I have come across in this field this simple finding is very seriously presented as evidence that schizophrenia must be genetic in origin. In contrast to this almost religious belief a rare perspective is provided by Kringlen (1993), a long-respected researcher in the genetics of psychological disorders:

'It would also benefit psychiatry if psychiatric research workers were more interested in being scientists than ideologists. The study of schizophrenia illustrates how ideas within psychiatry have been influenced by the *Zeitgeist...* during the last 10–20 years we have witnessed a biological wave in psychiatry, partly based upon the biological revolution, and partly based on the spirit of the times.'

Unusual for a writer in a psychiatric journal Kringlen considers such developments in a wider context:

'Political manoeuvres have been rife, this time fought by biologically-oriented psychiatrists, backed by the pharmaceutical industry, who attempt to show that almost every social phenomenon is genetically determined. The Americans are again leading the way with such slogans as "the decade of the brain".'

Kringlen begins to address issues that verge on the sociology of scientific knowledge as he asserts that

'one encounters today well-known scientists who cite only findings that support their own view. This selectivity has even crept into textbooks of psychiatry. Such dishonesty is sad and will hurt psychiatry in the long run, because progress must be based on facts and rationality.'

One of the many dangers of the mechanistic, objective, positivist, reductionist, notions is that they are often confused with science itself. That then often leads us to question the validity and meaningfulness of our own and others' experiences. It becomes axiomatic that the only worthwhile 'research' consists of assembling large cohorts of people designated as schizophrenics, without any reference to individuality. Discussion of individuals is considered anecdotal, and therefore as irrelevant to the real business of science. Yet it is only here that individual meaning is to be located, and Karon and VandenBos (1981) properly emphasise the importance of regarding the content of so-called hallucinations and delusions as having deep personal meaning and relevance.

There have been attempts to move away from what Don Bannister (1968) described as 'the notions of science which came with our first chemistry set'. Kellian theory does attempt to make a science of the individual possible, but such approaches, lacking the macho accoutrements of 'real science' are considered third-rate to the studies which dazzle with numerical analysis, large samples, control groups, and biochemical analysis. Yet as Richards (1992) points out, anyone familiar with current philosophy of science must acknowledge that there is no consensus at all on what 'being scientific' uniquely consists in. In the 1950s and 1960s the strategy was to look for 'markers' of schizophrenia in blood and urine samples. A series of observations led to the identification of the 'mauve' spot in the chromatographs of the urine of hospitalized patients. Great excitement ensued. This biochemical notion of schizophrenia lost ground when the marker, the mauve spot, was found to be a metabolite of the very medication designed to control patient behaviour.

So much for notions of science. At least some learning took place, and when the next hypothesis, waiting in the wings, appeared, investigators were very careful to control for drug effects. I remember the great excitement at the prospect of a breakthrough when the 'Pink Spot' was discovered. 3,4 DMPE was found, in places as far afield as Japan and Scotland, in the urine of schizophrenics, but hardly in the urine of the vast control groups.

There was no particular point at which an adjudicator wrapped up the issue.

The belief slowly died away. Sarbin (1991) estimates that biochemical theories have a half-life of five years. One careful researcher, declining the belief that science is about big numbers and technology, perused the literature carefully and came up with some meaningful hypotheses. Using three student volunteers, whose diet was carefully controlled, he found that he could produce the 'Pink Spot' at will. It was a metabolite of tea. Common, ordinary, tea. Perhaps those who had been so careful in their experimental design had never experienced life on the back wards of mental hospitals in the early 1960s. If they had, they would have known that coffee was a very scarce commodity. They may well have known that medical student controls prefer coffee.

It is highly significant that this period of excitement is never referred to in contemporary literature or textbooks. Trainee psychiatrists and researchers in the field are, by and large, unaware of this story and many others like it. There is a kind of professional amnesia. There are many lessons in this cautionary tale, not least of which is the seeming paradox that a belief in the pursuit of biochemical or biological investigation gained, rather than lost, ground. In addition, the very concept of schizophrenia as a reification was reinforced rather than weakened.

It is difficult to comprehend such seeming paradoxes without recourse to the sociology and psychology of scientific knowledge. We might begin by looking at an article entitled 'The end of ideology in behaviour modification'. Perry London (1972) concluded that 'it never was theory, anyhow, but ideology for professional purposes, and mostly metaphor for clinical purposes'. Ideology carries the meaning that knowledge is situationally-determined: in other words, the worldview and the social status of the scientist influence the content of knowledge. Sarbin (1991) points out that an examination of ideological premises illuminate how an entrenched professional organisation can become so bound to a situation that members cannot recognise facts which would dissolve its power. An ideology has a sacred quality. A challenge to a claim based upon ideological premises usually invokes passionate rather than reasoned responses. Note the heated responses to the writings of Laing and Szasz and other critics of the official schizophrenia doctrine.

I would like to offer a synopsis of my own and others' work examining the crucial evidence of genetic studies. I chose to examine the field of schizophrenia genetics for several reasons, the chief being that what is termed 'evidence' has become a cornerstone of the belief in biological aetiology, and has furthered the reification process (Marshall 1990). By this, I mean that the widely-believed assumption is that if there is a genetic entity there must be a schizophrenia entity.

As I mentioned earlier, the thinking becomes so sloppy that we find a WHO report (Jablensky *et al.* 1992) which then moves on to make this a reciprocal matter: 'If it's schizophrenic it must be genetic'. At such points I begin to have a better appreciation of Lewis Carroll. Sometimes the researchers unwittingly provide the 'Alice Effect'. Kety (1974), probably the leading authority on, and supporter of, the genetics and pathophysiology of schizophrenia wrote: 'If schizophrenia is a myth, it is a myth with a strong genetic component'.

During the 1970s and 1980s the claims for an overwhelmingly important genetic basis were increasingly promoted by some of the leading authorities in the field, and gradually their claims have seeped into the knowledge-base as accepted wisdom. By 1977 Gottesman and Shields were asserting that: 'Environmental factors contribute only 20 per cent of the variance to the combined liability to developing schizophrenia'. They were quite explicit about the significance of this:

'It implies a biochemical and/or biophysical cause of the malfunctioning of the brain that leads to schizophrenia.'

It is clear, then, that the genetic evidence is crucial. Yet several careful examinations of the genetic evidence have shown that the methodologies, statistical manipulations, and inferences fall far short of what is required in matters of such personal, social, and scientific importance. Perhaps the best illustration of this is to be found in Kallmann's (1946) massive twin study. His concordance rates of 86 per cent for identical twins for schizophrenia, and only 15 per cent for fraternal twins, have dominated textbook accounts for about half a century. Careful perusal leads to the conclusion that such work was of little or no value. Statistical distortions, biased methodology, and deeply held eugenic beliefs, appear to have profoundly influenced his research. As Ben-Yehuda (1986) points out, scientists have profound interests in the success of their ideas and disinterestedness does not appear to be a realistic norm.

The following excerpt is not an isolated statement in Kallmann's writings:

'Despite various advances in recent years, psychiatric research is still battling on many fronts...for general recognition of genetic concepts and for practical realisation of biological principles. The key position of this battle seems to be held by the disease group of schizophrenia, which continues to crowd mental hospitals all over the world, and affords an unceasing source of maladjusted cranks, asocial eccentrics, and the lowest type of criminal offenders.' (1938, p.xii)

More modern claims for genetic underpinnings are derived from other twin studies and adoption studies. Again, these are duly reported in the literature and textbooks as providing definitive evidence, but several careful reviews have evaluated the evidence and found it wanting. The Danish Adoption Studies, for example, are reviewed by Rose, Kamin and Lewontin (1984) in *Not in Our Genes* and they conclude that the weaknesses of the studies are so obvious that it is difficult to understand how distinguished scientists could have regarded them as eliminating all the artefacts which beset family and twin studies of nature and nurture. Sarbin and Mancuso's (1980) analysis describe the studies as being of small value. Lidz and Blatt (1983) conclude that the evidence indicates that careful examination would suggest that genetic influences may play only a limited role in the aetiology of schizophrenia. A team of French researchers (Cassou *et al.* 1980), took ten authoritative reviews in the field, all of which were unanimous in stating that the importance of genetic factors had been convincingly demonstrated. The team found that the original evidence just did not warrant the conclusions. They concluded that 'after a meticulous and exhaustive re-evaluation, we therefore conclude that there is *no* evidence for a genetic effect in the schizophrenic process'.

Perhaps more important, they went on to assert that the process through which a consensus is reached on matters of great social importance is, itself, seriously problematic. They add: 'The very existence of such contradiction shows the potential danger of relying on expert opinion on matters of social importance'.

It is difficult to avoid the impression that science, ideology, and belief have become intertwined. If, in a field as subjective and fluid as this, even the 'harder' evidence is distorted in a particular direction, it seems relevant to examine this process. We attempted to trace this distortion process in the way in which the *crucial* twin concordance figures are analysed (Marshall and Pettitt 1985). Our analysis illustrated the process by which seemingly objective, detached, scientific method can be distorted in 'reports of reports' to lend strong support to genetic and biological beliefs. We looked at one particular study (Kringlen 1967) whose results indicated a modest genetic component. When reanalysed, using what we considered to be illegitimate statistical manipulations, the results were, in the words of the writers, 'within shouting distance of Kallmann's'. Pettitt and I concluded that the recommended techniques for analysing such data were unscientific, and appeared to be a further attempt to drive the hereditability factor to a level which allows for no other understanding of the disorder called schizophrenia.

Yet it is interesting to note how these new and illegitimate methods of calculation have passed into conventional wisdom. Kendler (1983, 1987), another leading US authority, provides data from other studies and subjects it to the new calculations, but the reader is not aware that he/she is being presented with *corrected* data. Kendler's conclusion is that

'there is substantial agreement across the major twin studies of schizophrenia that the hereditability of schizophrenia is between .6 and .9. Twin studies consistently suggest that genetic factors play a major role in the familial transmission of schizophrenia.'

The role of ideology is apparent in more ways than statistical manipulations. Even if we were to accept what I term gross exaggerations of evidence, at face value, there is, it seems to me, a basic error of logic, so characteristic of ideological influence. Accepting the figures, for a moment, does not show that 'schizophrenia is inherited', or that there is some known mechanism or 'known gene' for schizophrenia. Karon and VandenBos (1981) suggest that it would indicate that there might be some unknown inherited factor or factors that tend to increase the frequency of schizophrenia. If we assume that what is termed schizophrenia consists of extreme methods of adaptation, part of the potentialities of all human beings, our inferences would be very different. In this context anything which makes life adjustment more difficult is going to increase the rate of schizophrenia. Hollingshead and Redlich's (1958) study, for example, showed that schizophrenia is 12 times as frequent in the lowest socioeconomic groups as in the highest. Cassell (1976) has shown that all disorders, physical and mental, accompany the experience of a wide range of distressing conditions, from poverty, social estrangement and unemployment to feelings of powerlessness, low self-esteem, and social marginality and loneliness.

To accept the more modest contribution of genetics is to accept that non-genetic factors are important. Remedies now become psychosocial, economic and political, and concepts such as 'illness' and 'schizophrenia' would come to be regarded as convenient social constructs, which serve a range of purposes. Such purposes include professional imperialism, biologically-oriented research funding, and pharmaceutical interests, political philosophy and expediency, explanations for therapeutic failure, and, as I will later suggest, the application of genetic/biological principles to a wide range of human functioning.

This kind of analysis takes us directly into the realms of the sociology of scientific knowledge. Gould (1981), in his book *The Mismeasure of Man* has shown how scientific claims about the nature of intelligence owe much to the beliefs and attitudes of dominant groups in wider society. Bernal (1965), a distinguished chemist and historian of science, goes somewhat further, in an elegant sentence:

'Often enough the ideas which statesmen and divines think that they have taken from the latest phase of scientific thought are just the ideas of their class and time reflected in the minds of scientists subjected to the same social influences.'

In fact, when we consider the genetic approach in such a context, a historical analysis becomes more meaningful. We might begin with Victorian psychiatry, and the dominant notions in that society of hereditary degeneration upon which psychiatry based its social and scientific vision. We now find an excellent illustration of Bernal's notion of the interaction between science and dominant influences in society. The genetic-disease model fitted neatly into dominant thinking in Western societies in the nineteenth century. Predominant myths of the Victorian period were the inheritance of delicate, weak, or raw nerves, and the myth of the 'degenerate'. 'Degeneracy' was considered to be passed from one tainted generation to the next, with each generation becoming progressively worse: the alcoholic father was likely to have a prostitute daughter, or a criminal, even idiot, son. Such hereditarian beliefs allowed the possible negative impact of social and economic forces upon individuals to be neglected. The source of social dysfunction was located squarely within the individual's genes. George Albee (1982) explains the strong appeal of genetic determinism in terms of the powerful influence of Calvinism with its notions of predestination and dualism, and especially the concept of unchangeable man.

Genetic explanations provide a ready, apersonal, ahistorical, asocial focus. They appear to bear the hallmark of scientific respectability. The medicalisation of a range of conducts in the late nineteenth century, when the medical profession was becoming established, led to what Foucault has termed 'the strict, militant, dogmatic medicalisation of society'. Virginia Berridge (1987), in her book *Opium and the People* notes that this found its expression in the late nineteenth century in the establishment of 'diseases' affecting a whole spectrum of conditions. Homosexuality, insanity, addiction, even poverty and crime were classified in a biologically-determined way. Berridge illustrates the ways in which the concept of addiction become reifed in late nineteenth century, an analysis which could equally apply to other fields. She wrote:

'The scientific nature of medical concepts was somehow underlined by increasing specialisation and the emergence of different schools of thought. The controversies between advocates of different theories of addiction and its treatment were intense and acrimonious...but they nevertheless demonstrated a form of professional self-affirmation.'

This seeming expertise, in turn, served to provide support for the reification process.

Psychology, too, has reflected its social context. It is, says Alan Buss (1979), tied to the infrastructure of a society or socially-defined groups. There is, therefore, an intimate relationship between statements of value and statements of fact. So the particular researcher, and his or her theories, are tied to particular values, beliefs, and ideologies.

Stephen Gould (1981), speaking of science more generally, aimed to demonstrate that it is a socially-embedded activity which must be understood as a social phenomena, at times serving as a mirror to social movements. No doubt the authors of *Not in our Genes* (Rose *et al.* 1984) would concur with this. They note that the rise in biological determinism during the 1980s reflects the rise of New Right governments which find their social nostrums so neatly mirrored in nature: 'if inequalities are biologically determined, they are therefore inevitable and immutable'.

Sarason (1981) has pointed out that western psychology has been, by and large, an asocial, individual psychology, and built into it, part of its world view, is the polarity: man and society. This can make it easy to focus on one and ignore the other; it could ignore not only the study of the social order, but social history as well. Although psychology located the origins of schizophrenia conduct at a less reductionistic level than psychiatry, it nevertheless has tacitly accepted the illness model by making 'schizophrenia' the object of its studies. In this way psychology lent its scientific credibility to the diagnostic process, the concept, and this model. It thereby assisted in the reification process which left the illness model unquestioned.

Perhaps such discussions tend to leave us feeling rather anchorless, with a feeling that all is relative, rather like floating in space, where 'up' and 'down' become arbitrary directions. I tend to find Gould's (1981) comments constructive: he does not claim that a factual reality does not exist, but that the roads to it are lined with preconceived ideas and attitudes which exert considerable influence. I would hope that this kind of analysis might assist the process of discriminating between reported observations and the inferences derived.

IMPLICATIONS

Tucked away in the literature is a report by Karon (1989), who reviewed the studies in the field of treatment of schizophrenia. His overall conclusions made clear that, in the long run, psychosocial treatments – in which the patient participates as an agent – have better outcomes than medication.

Yet there is little doubt in the minds of many, professional, lay, and policy-makers alike, that Kallmann's battle for schizophrenia is won. That was, you may remember, the 'key position of the campaign', a campaign to capture the conceptualisation of all disordered behaviour, and to cast it into a biological mould. There are numerous signs that this process is already showing results, and it is not impossible to envisage a future in which all unwanted conduct or distress might be reconstrued as being a result of constitutional factors. An example of such beliefs is to be found in the article by Marks et al. (1986). They concluded that there was evidence for genetic effects on normal fear and anxiety, on anxiety disorders as a whole, and on panic and obsessive–compulsive disorders, agora-phobia, and even on blood-injury phobias. Taking this one step beyond the speculative Crowe et al. (1987) concluded that any candidate genes mapped to chromosome 16q22 would be the logical candidates for study in panic disorders and agoraphobia.

Lewontin (1992) has pointed out that the genomes projects are, in fact, administrative and financial organisations rather than research projects in the usual sense. He noted that they had been created over the previous years in response to an active lobbying effort, by scientists, aimed at capturing very large amounts of public funds and directing the flow of those funds into an immense co-operative research program. Lewontin adds that the rage for genes reminds us of Tulipomania and the South Sea Bubble in McKay's *Great Popular Delusions of the Madness of Crowds*.

Using the most prestigious general American scientific journal, *Science*, as an example Lewontin points out that it is an energetic publicist for large DNA sequencing projects, and carries major adverts from biotechnology equipment manufacturers. The editor has visions of genes for alcoholism, unemployment, domestic and social violence, and drug addition: 'What we had previously imagined to be messy moral, political, economic issues', writes Lewontin,

'turn out, after all, to be simply a matter of an occasional nucleotide substitution. While the notion that the war on drugs will be won by genetic engineering belongs to Cloud Cuckoo Land, it is a manifestation of a serious ideology that is continuous with the eugenics of an earlier time.'

One of the few writers to express concern and caution about this trend, Pat Spallone (1992), says

'Genes become the cause of an ever-expanding list of human conditions. Genetic technology becomes the solution. Genetic intervention becomes prevention.'

She warns about the 'stupendously expensive' gene-mapping projects – for example, the genome project aims to explore the links between genetics and all human behaviour – not just those associated with illness. The recent WHO study focuses in its conclusion on 'linkage studies and genome mapping techniques, which are preparing the ground for a 'molecular' epidemiology of schizophrenia'. More ominously the WHO is creating an international, clinical and epidemiological database on schizophrenia and *related disorders* worldwide.

This so-called 'decade of the brain' may well become a struggle for definition of human problems and their causes. Personal knowing and understanding of the issues is important, but it would seem that a more organised challenge to scientism and the overstated case of biological determinism will be required if some form of brake is to be applied to the runaway notion of man's problems in living as arising simply from his biology.

REFERENCES

Albee, G.W. (1982) 'The politics of nature and nurture.' *American Journal of Community Psychology 10*, 4–36.

Bannister, D. (1968) 'The logical requirements of research into schizophrenia.' *British Journal of Psychiatry 114*, 181–188.

Bentall, R.P., Jackson, H.F. and Pilgrim, D. (1988a) 'Abandoning the concept of "schizophrenia": Some implications of validity arguments for psychological research into psychotic phenomena.' *British Journal of Clinical Psychology 27*, 303–324.

Bentall, R.P., Jackson, H.F., and Pilgrim, D. (1988b) 'The concept of schizophrenia is dead: long live the concept of schizophrenia.' *British Journal of Clinical Psychology 27*, 329–331.

Ben-Yehuda, N. (1986) 'Deviance in Science.' *British Journal of Criminology 26*, 1, 1–27.

Bernal, J.D. (1965) *Science in History*, 3rd edition. London: Watts.

Berridge, V. (1987) *Opium and the People: Opiate Use in Nineteenth Century England*. London: Yale University Press.

Buss, A.R. (1979) 'The emerging field of the sociology of psychological knowledge.' In A.R. Buss (ed) *Psychology in Social Context*. New York: Irvington.

Cassell, J. (1976) 'The contribution of social environment to host resistance.' *American Journal of Epidemiology 104*, 107–123.

Cassou, B., Schiff, M. and Stewart, J. (1980) 'Génétique et schizophrénie: ré-évaluation d'un consensus.' *Psychiatrie de L'Enfant*, 87–201. (Schiff, M., Cassou, B., Stewart, J. (1980) Genetics and schizophrenia: The Reconsideration of a Consensus. Unpublished English translation.)

Charlton, B.G. (1990) 'A critique of biological psychiatry.' *Psychological Medicine 20*, 3–6.

Crowe, R.R., Noyes, R., Wilson, A.F., Elston, R.C. and Ward, L.J. (1987) 'A linkage study of Panic Disorders.' *Arch. Gen. Psychiatry 44*, 933–937.

Gottesman, I.I. and Shields, J. (1977) 'Contributions of twin studies to perspectives on schizophrenia.' In B.A. Maher (ed) *Contributions to the Psychopathology of Schizophrenia*. London: Academic Press.

Gould, S.J. (1981) *The Mismeasure of Man*. New York: Norton.

Hollingshead, A.B. and Redlich, F. (1958) *Social Class and Mental Illness*. New York: John Wiley and Sons.

Jablensky, A., Sartorius, N., Ernberg, G., Anker, M., Korten, A., Cooper, J.E., Day, R. and Bertelsen, A. (1992) 'Schizophrenia: manifestations, incidence and course in different cultures. A World Health Organization ten-country study.' *Psychological Medicine: Monograph Supplement 20*.

Kallmann, F.J. (1938) *The Genetics of Schizophrenia*, New York: J.J. Augustin.

Kallmann, F.J. (1946) 'The genetic theory of schizophrenia.' *American Journal of Psychiatry 103*, 309–322.

Karon, B.P. (1989) 'Psychotherapy versus medication for schizophrenia: empirical considerations.' In S. Fisher and R.P. Greenberg (eds) *The Limits of Biological Treatment for Psychological Stress*. Hillsdale, NJ: Lawrence Erlbaum Associates.

Karon, B.P. and VandenBos, G.R. (1981) *The Psychotherapy of Schizophrenia: The Treatment of Choice*. New York: Jason Aronson.

Kendler, K.S. (1983) 'Overview: a current perspective on twin studies of schizophrenia.' *American Journal of Psychiatry 140*, 1413–1425.

Kendler, K.S. (1987) 'The genetics of schizophrenia: a current perspective.' In H. Meltzer (ed) *Psychopharmacology: The Third Generation of Progress*. New York: Raven.

Kety, S. (1974) *American Journal of Psychiatry 131*, 957–962.

Kringlen, E. (1967) *Heredity and Environment in the Functional Psychoses*. London: Heinemann.

Kringlen, E. (1993) 'Genes and environment in mental illness: perspectives and ideas for the future.' *Acta Psychiatrica Scandinavica: Suppl. 370,* 79–84.

Lewontin, R.C. (1992) 'The dream of the human genome.' *The New York Review,* May 28th, 31–40.

Lidz, T. and Blatt, S. (1983) 'Critique of the Danish-American studies of the biological and adoptive relatives who become schizophrenic.' *American Journal of Psychiatry 140,* 426–431.

London, P. (1972) 'The end of ideology in behavior modification.' *American Psychologist 27,* 10, 913–920.

Marks, I.M. *et al.* (1986) 'Genetics of fear and anxiety disorders.' *British Journal of Psychiatry 149,* 406–418.

Marshall, J.R. (1990) 'The genetics of schizophrenia: axiom or hypothesis?' In R. Bentall (ed) *Reconstructing Schizophrenia.* London: Routledge.

Marshall, J.R. and Pettitt, A.N. (1985) 'Discordant concordant rates.' *Bulletin of The British Psychological Society 38,* 6–9.

Notcutt, B. (1953) *The Psychology of Personality.* London: Methuen.

Peele, S. (1981) 'Reductionism in the psychology of the eighties: can biochemistry eliminate addiction, mental illness and pain?' *American Psychologist 36,* 8, 807–818.

Richards, G. (1992) 'Reflexivity problems in psychology: Too embarrassing even to talk about.' *Newsletter of the History and Philosophy of Psychology Section of the B.P.S. 15,* 7–22.

Rose, S., Kamin, L. and Lewontin, R.C. (1984) *Not in Our Genes.* London: Penguin.

Sarason, S. (1981) *Psychology Misdirected.* London: Collier Macmillan.

Sarbin, T.R. (1990) 'The social construction of schizophrenia.' Unpublished paper presented at the conference *What is Schizophrenia?* Clark University, Worcester, MA, June 9–10, 1990.

Sarbin, T.R. (1991)'The social construction of schizophrenia.' In W. Flack, D. Miller and M. Wiener (eds) *What is Schizophrenia?* New York: Springer-Verlag.

Sarbin, T.R. and Mancuso, J.C. (1980) *Schizophrenia: Medical Diagnosis or Moral Verdict.* New York: Pergamon.

Spallone, P. (1992) *Generation Games: Genetic Engineering and the Future for Our Lives.* London: The Women's Press.

U-Ren, R. (1992) 'Psychiatric diagnosis and the market.' *Perspectives in Biology and Medicine 35,* 4, 612–616.

CHAPTER 5

Knowledge and its Pretenders
Bion's Contribution to Knowledge and Thought

D.L. Bell

Bion frequently used the term 'selected fact', which he borrowed from the mathematician Poincare. This refers to an observation or an idea which organises hitherto disparate elements of data into a coherent structure in which they are linked together. There are, potentially, a number of selected facts for any particular set of data, each of which will create a different vertex or point of view.

The history of psychoanalysis can be examined from any number of such points of view where the phenomena are structured around a particular selected fact. For example, one can demonstrate a movement from a primary concern with the mind's relation to the demands of external reality, to a primary concern with internal reality; or a movement from instinct theory where illness is caused by the frustration of instinctual drive (Freud's first theory of dammed up libido), to a theory primarily concerned with moral conflict where illness is caused by excess of hate over love (later Freud and much of Klein's work (where this perspective is considerably enriched by the concept of internal objects which can be damaged or repaired)); to a theory primarily concerned with the development of self-knowledge where illness is based on the mind's incapacity to know itself, replacing knowledge with its various pretenders (Bion, Money-Kyrle, Steiner). This development, however, is not linear. In Freud's work, for example, one can see elements of all three perspectives, although he lacked the adequate theoretical framework to contain all of them.

His aphorism 'where id was there ego shall be', his invitation to the patient to free-associate, his description of the 'momentous' changes brought about at the inception of the reality principle where 'what was represented in the mind was no longer what was agreeable but what was real, even if this happened to be disagreeable' (Freud 1911) – in other words to distinguish what is good from what is true – all bear testimony to his conviction that self-knowledge is central to psychic health and development.

The history of psychoanalysis demonstrates a constant movement between theory and practice – new observations demanded new theories which in turn brought new observations. Klein's play technique enriched the concept of transference and permitted the observation of more primitive mental states laying the ground for her analysands – Segal, Rosenfeld and Bion – to analyse the first psychotic patients using psychoanalytic technique. Work with these patients, whose difficulties centre on the process of thinking and the acquisition of knowledge, has immeasurably enriched psychoanalysis. Armed with his own development of Klein's theory and his refinement of technique resulting from his work with these patients, Bion returned to Freud and developed a metapsychology that gives an almost explosive new content to notions such as 'consciousness', 'thinking', 'knowledge', the relation of inner to outer, the nature of the psychoanalytic object, and thus to the task of the psychoanalytic session.

One of Bion's great achievements is to bring the process of the acquisition of knowledge to the centre of psychoanalytic scrutiny, to distinguish real knowledge, in the sense of coming to know oneself through experience (K) from its various substitutes. This problematic concept is the centre of his focus from his work on groups onwards. His philosophical base was idealist philosophy and his method is best described as phenomenological in that his principal aim is accurately to describe and discriminate different experiences, to provide models that both considerably widen the field of observation and also give coherence to the apparently incoherent. He was fond of metaphors from the physical sciences and his approach may be likened to a chemist who analyses complex compounds into their constituent elements. The use of the phenomenological method results in the focus being on mental states, experience, rather than on individual patients.

The analysis of experience – for example distinguishing truth from lies, not-knowing from ignorance, knowledge from omniscience, knowledge gained through experience from knowledge as an accumulation of facts – constitutes for Bion the basis of the therapeutic work. For Bion, truth is to the mind what food is to the body – lack of the capacity for truth about oneself leads to a type of mental rickets.

He quotes Dr Johnson: 'Whether to see life as it is, will offer us much consolation, I know not; but the consolation which is gained from truth, if any there be, is solid and durable; that which may be derived from errour must be, like its original, fallacious and fugitive' which compares easily with Freud's aphoristic statement of the aim of psychoanalysis 'to convert hysterical misery into ordinary unhappiness'.

I would like briefly to illustrate how Bion's approach illuminates a very ordinary clinical situation.

Mr A is informed that his analyst is taking an unexpected break. He senses the analyst's wish for him to discuss how this affects him, his beliefs/fantasies and so forth concerning the purposes of the break. He, however, resorts to attempting to discover the actual reason which, given that he moves in some circles in common with his analyst, he has some chance of realising. On what seems to be very insufficient evidence, he claims to know … and that is the end of the matter.

So, rather than avail himself of the opportunity of finding out something new about himself and thus gaining knowledge – which for various reasons he is unable to do – he acquires facts whose truth is less important than his feeling that he possesses them. He trades knowledge for omniscience.

And now a clinical situation that isn't so ordinary. Miss B comes to her session in a state of wild panic and announces that her cousin died yesterday and on her way into the session she saw X (a friend who is an analyst and the object of unbearable envy). This material might offer a number of possible interpretations. However, the pressing difficulty seemed to be that she had been violently intruded upon by events which she lacked the capacity to think about, and she conveyed to me a feeling that her mind was about to explode. On this being suggested to her she went on to say she left home without her identity card and went home to get it in case she died on the bus and no one knew who she was.

The above serves as an introduction and the rest of my chapter falls into two sections: first, returning to my title, I will give examples of how knowledge is replaced by its various pretenders (different types of omniscience), giving examples from individual, group and the larger institution. In the final part of the chapter I will describe Bion's model of the preconditions for the acquisition of knowledge and give illustrations of the quality of experience when these preconditions do not pertain.

KNOWLEDGE SUBSTITUTED BY RELIGION/CULT

The first example comes from a group I participated in some years ago.

One of the group members had developed the habit of always speaking after I spoke – explaining to the other group members what I meant, to their apparent satisfaction. In one session I had suggested that the group members feared encountering certain types of emotional states. My interpreter then duly informed the group that what I meant was that they would not get better until they expressed certain feelings such as anger, sadness and so forth. There followed various desultory attempts to be angry or sad and then the group members looked towards me appealingly. There ensued a conversation on religion.

I suggested that the group members' behaviour suggested that they were subscribers to a religion in which they had to express their feeling in order to obtain the cure for their difficulties.

There followed an explosive situation in which it seemed that the group might come to a precipitate end and I felt under enormous pressure to retract what I had said.

Anyone who has read Bion's first major work *Experiences in Groups* (1962a) will find this material familiar. A religious cult has developed in which one member has taken on the role of deciphering my comments in the same way that a disciple may interpret the oracle. Interpretations aimed at understanding current anxieties have been transformed into oracular instructions – activities to carry out in order to be granted cures. My interpretation threatened the premises on which the cult was based and were greeted with the same attitude as that which might be directed towards an heretic at a religious meeting.

Bion distinguished two levels of group functioning which he termed 'the work group' and the 'basic assumption group'. A group of people who meet, say, to discuss scientific problems (the work group) may find that their functioning is constantly disrupted by powerful and primitive states of mind, for example, extreme dependence on one member who becomes the fount of all knowledge (the dependency group). The two other basic assumption groups 'pairing' and 'fight–flight' I leave for our present purposes. The principal task of a therapeutic group is to examine the basic assumptions as they develop – in other words, to develop knowledge through experience of the transference situations as they emerge.

In the example given, this process of acquisition of knowledge has been transformed into the ritual of 'expressing emotions' which provides the comfort derived from a religious cult which protects against that doubt which is a precondition for the process of 'coming to know' – lack of doubt is the hallmark of omniscience.

Mr A, a patient in analysis, told me after some years that each time I spoke to him he silently altered the interpretation, saying to himself 'what he really means is … '. For example, when I commented on the meaning of his lateness (he was late for every session) this was re-interpreted as my telling him that he ought to come on time, with the implication that coming on time, not self-knowledge, would result in release from his chronic depression. That aspect of him which tells him 'what I really mean' represents the same phenomenon in my patient as was localised in the disciple in the group.

The following example is from a 'firm' meeting at the Cassel hospital – namely, a meeting of all the patients on a unit at the Cassel, myself and the nursing staff. One of the patients has recently had an 'assessment meeting' (this is a meeting of staff occurring after the patient has been in hospital for about six weeks in which we attempt to reach a formulation of the patient's central difficulties and suggest tasks that the patient may take on while in the hospital that might be useful for his development. This meeting is followed by a brief meeting with the patient to discuss this with him).

Miss Jones reported that following her assessment meeting she had been given one or two things to think about. She gave the impression that she was sure that a lot more went on in the meeting from which she had been excluded. She smiled mischievously when saying this. Mrs Smith said, slightly excitedly, that following her assessment meeting she'd been given four things to focus on. Mr Brown said angrily that he'd only had one.

The group has thus transformed this apparently straightforward process of 'feedback' (the work group) into something awesome and magical. It is as if the nurse had been sent up the mount to commune with the gods. The number of 'commandments' she returns with is some measure of how much the individual patient is valued by the gods. The 'feedback' from the assessment has turned into messages from the oracle or tyrannical commands from an all-knowing god 'Do this and you will be cured – don't and you will be punished'. The patient's mischievous smiling suggests that the feelings of exclusion are suffused with excited thoughts concerning the forbidden secrets of the parental bedroom.

These examples serve to illustrate the transformation of thoughtful ideas – into rituals and cults.

The history of psychoanalysis is replete with examples of attempts to degrade and institutionalise psychoanalytic ideas into techniques and procedures, or to deify psychoanalysts into gods to be worshipped; both these activities serve to evade confrontation with the unknown. In some psychiatric hospitals the fruitful idea that it might be helpful if an individual becomes able to experience emotions previously avoided degenerates into cults similar to that in the group described above. All patients and staff are encouraged to express their feelings, or at least to appear as if they are, regardless of cost in an atmosphere of 'dictatorial morality'. Main (1990) described this process as a movement from possessing an idea to becoming possessed by it. In the case of 'the staff group' it is often the sequestration and institutionalisation of a radical idea into a position where it can do no harm. It also represents an allegiance to a different perspective concerning the nature of mental illness from that dominant in the culture, but a lack of the necessary resources to do anything with this point of view.

I also think that this transformation of analysis into cult is an issue in all analyses – a vertex from which the transference can be usefully examined. Some patients attend their sessions, for example, religiously – believing that doing so and following the rituals of the analytic session is in itself a protection against illness.

TRANSFORMATION OF KNOWLEDGE INTO AN ACCUMULATION OF FACTS

Here I am referring to a process where the accumulation of facts is idealised at the expense of the process of coming to know. The facts may be of various types (e.g. facts about psychoanalytic theories, or the theories of one analyst, facts about oneself, facts about the world).

Bion (1977, p.16) describes a patient who made a number of statements which, taken as they stand, might lead to a potentially interesting discussion. However, the analyst is gripped by a sensation that could only be described as 'so what'. The communications are experienced by the analyst as dead facts, empty of resonance or meaning. Such situations, if not primarily due to difficulties in the analyst's capacity to receive, are indications of severe disturbance, often of a paranoid nature.

Staff intensively involved with very disturbed patients very often experience a dread of not-knowing. An understandable wish to encourage a free flow of information as and when necessary can turn into a demand for endless meetings where information is 'fed-back' from other meetings. The feed-back activity swells until it occupies and takes over a space which might have been filled by thought. This activity, common in psychiatric hospitals, and often called 'handover', easily degenerates into lists of facts. Such a process, frequent in institutions, serves to rid the mind of responsibility and, in my experience, often serves a tyrannical organisation which demands to know all the facts, and threatens terrible persecution for any lapse (such as being held responsible for a suicide).

A psychotic patient was internally dominated by such an organisation. He attended his sessions, religiously, attempting to tell me all the facts that had occurred since his last session. He called this process 'filling me in'. He would say 'Tuesday I went to visit John that was good, Wednesday I helped in the hostel and then had lunch which was followed by feeling slightly angry with Mary who had promised to help ... that wasn't good...' etc. These statements had no emotional link between them and were felt by me to be inanimate, stripped of meaning. The patient was dominated by a tyrannical organisation sometimes felt to be in him, sometimes in me and sometimes in neither, which demanded that he fill me in with all this data. If he became unwell he was internally told this was his punishment for neglecting to tell me something.

One can see how knowledge, in the sense of apprehending the unknown, bearing doubt, is not possible in such situations. These situations are not confined to psychotic patients – a patient of Strachey's told his analyst after some years that he experienced the invitation to free-associate as ('You free-associate or I'll kick you out of analysis').

In other situations the wish for knowledge about the self is replaced by a wish to accumulate knowledge about the analyst. This can be a reasonable and worthwhile activity. Certainly in any analysis the analysand will spend time and trouble exploring the innards of his analyst – exploring the contours, strengths and weaknesses of the 'container' – in this sense it might represent acquiring some very important knowledge. Sometimes, however, the patient accumulates facts about his analyst to avoid knowledge of himself. I gave an example of this at the beginning of the paper (the patient who acquired facts about my coming break). When this situation dominates, all interpretations are understood not as invitations to the patient to examine certain areas of experience but as revelations of the analyst's state of mind. Ms C, for example, habitually spent weekends relating aspects of her analysis to her boyfriend – together they would criticise the interpretations, enacting an oedipal situation in which the analyst has projected into him the feelings of exclusion. However, when I commented on this my comment was understood as asking to be informed in detail of their conversation. Bion describes this situation as follows:

> 'the patient grasps the gist of what I say. The totality of the statement, including the implication that I am the analyst, is evacuated (the mechanism represented by the theory of projective identification). He identifies himself with the analyst and by virtue of his intuition is able to "see" the meaning of my interpretation. The meaning that he thus "sees" is that I am annoyed, jealous, envious at my exclusion from participation in or understanding of his sexual life.'

It is striking how in such cases the patient is able to have considerably more certainty than his analyst as to the sources of his analyst's interpretations.

KNOWLEDGE REPLACED BY THE 'DICTATORIAL ASSERTION OF MORALITY'

Psychoanalysis is, of course, not amoral – in the sense that the search for personal truths is a moral exercise. There are certain universal truths which have to be faced – such as the reality of the passage of time, differentiation between the sexes and generations, the reality of death. It is important to distinguish this sense of truth from Truth with a capital 'T' – ultimate truths and assertions of moral superiority. Bion described an activity he termed '-K' – in which the process of coming to know is reversed. Experiences are stripped, denuded of their meaning, leaving 'residues' which acquire a moral tinge which is derived from a 'superego' (a very primitive omnipotent structure completely distinct from Freud's use of the term). Such a superego asserts the moral superiority of un-learning, misunderstanding, hates development. (It is seen at its most extreme in certain types of schizophrenia where a vacuous stupidity is idealised and knowledge mocked.)

It is possible to examine the above accounts of religious cult and the colonisation of that space for thought by the process of the accumulation of facts from the perspective of this archaic morality.

For example, handing on of information may primarily serve not the possibility of thought and understanding but the attempt to avoid blame (this has to
be distinguished from taking responsibility).

In a staff meeting following a patient's suicide there was an attempt to discuss
what might be learnt from it. This search for understanding quickly degenerated
into accusation and blame. In the staff meeting the previous week, considerable
time had been spent discussing the strain the nurses were under resulting from
their re-grading. It was soon asserted that this had been used to avoid discussion
of the patient, with the implication that had we done so the suicide might have
been averted. In the next staff meeting I found myself wanting to discuss any of
my patients who were potentially suicidal. Gradually the word 'potentially'
expanded its reference – I then thought that maybe the ones I thought weren't
potential suicides could be just the ones who might do it – as sometimes it is
those patients for whom one is least concerned who harm themselves – I soon
found myself wanting to talk about all my patients. I hope you can see that this
activity has little to do with realistic attempts to improve the care of the patients
(work group), but more an attempt to evade being held responsible for a suicide
(basic assumption group).

When the quest for knowledge is replaced by the morality derived from the
psychotic superego, issues of blame and accusation soon surface. This 'super ego'
is interested in the cause of behaviour not for the process of furthering understanding but only in order to ascribe blame. All of us are prey to this process in
certain circumstances – for example, it is not easy to have a 'scientific discussion'
of child abuse without it degenerating into this type of primitive morality.

It is worth recalling here Freud's statement concerning the momentous step
taken at the institution of the reality principle where what is good can be
distinguished from what is true. Where there is no proper psychic equipment to
distinguish between true and false it is replaced 'by the dictatorial assertion that
one is right and the other wrong'. The primitive morality described here asserts
that what is good is true and what is true is good. It is in this sense uni-dimen-
sional.

There are patients whose whole psychic life is dominated by this type of
morality. The aim of analysis for such patients is discovery of the Truth. Rosenfeld
(1971) describes a psychotic patient who seemed to be co-operating in his
analysis. The patient brought material about his difficulties and engaged intensely
in unearthing aspects of himself to bring to analysis. Rosenfeld subsequently
realised that there was indeed a powerful alliance in this analysis but not one that
could be described as therapeutic. From the patient's point of view he was allied
with the analyst in the energetic conduct of a criminal investigation, whose aim
was to bring all aspects of his ill self to the courtroom of the session where he
could be punished through humiliation. (This is reminiscent of Bion's (1957)
perspective of the myth of Oedipus where the cause of the disaster is Oedipus's

arrogant insistence on Truth at any cost regardless of warnings and regardless of suffering.)

These issues, in a more subtle way, intrude into any analysis. Indeed, there is often a powerful pressure on the analyst to take this sort of moral stance.

In the above I have attempted to illustrate different types of phenomena that although apparently manifestations of knowledge are, in fact, attempts to evade it.

I will now turn to examine those processes which Bion suggests underlie the capacity to acquire knowledge.

I would like to emphasise that what follows should not necessarily be taken as an empirical description of what goes on between babies and mothers – although it may well be. Bion's approach is, as stated above, phenomenological and, thus, his primary aim is to widen the field of observation and to bring clarity to hitherto inexplicable phenomena; it is by these criteria that we must judge its worth.

Bion suggested that the capacity to gain knowledge about the self was based on the development of an 'apparatus' (or function) that transforms raw sense impressions into experiences which can be known and felt. This apparatus or function develops through the interaction between the infant and mother. The infant, assailed by raw impression such as the fear of dying, at first an unthinkable thought, projects this experience into the mother who, through her 'reverie', transforms the raw experience in such a way that it becomes thinkable. The mother's psyche provides a container for the experience – is affected by it, transforms it and returns it. Through repeated interactions, the infant not only receives the experience but also acquires the function (which he termed alpha function) to enable the infant to think for himself – namely to experience his experiences and through thinking about them come to know himself and consequently the world. For Bion it is not thinking which produces thoughts but unthought thoughts which require an apparatus for thinking them. Freud distinguished between primary and secondary processes. Dreaming, an activity of the primary process, Freud tended to equate with psychosis. However, for Bion the distinction is between the unthought thoughts – raw experience which he termed 'beta elements' – and the process of their transformation into felt experiences which can be linked together in a meaningful way.

The failure of this function leads to psychotic problems. Dreaming, a product of alpha function, is, for Bion, an achievement of the non-psychotic personality. Dream activity, as with Freud and Klein, is a continuous activity which we are only aware of at certain times. It is an activity which, along with fantasising and myth-making, gives meaning to experience and so is essential for psychic health. The psychotic personality neither dreams nor is fully awake but, as he poetically puts it, 'moves not in a world of dreams, but in a world of objects which are ordinarily the furniture of dreams' (1967a, p.51).

At the beginning of life the absent object is not experienced but is replaced by an hallucination. When this fails the infant does not experience an absence, but the presence of something bad. The no-breast becomes a thing in itself which persecutes, and therefore suffers the fate of all such objects – namely projection (here Bion follows Klein very closely). The development of the capacity for alpha function means that the absent object can be thought about – the 'no-breast becomes a thought' (1967b, p.112).

Due to circumstances of constitution and environment this process can fail – and the result is primitive catastrophe. The projected fear of death is not detoxified but instead is returned denuded of its life-giving aspects (fear of death implies the existence of the will to live) and returns as a primitive horror he termed 'nameless dread'. Bion describes the world of the psychotic using imagery that is both poetic and evocative. A personality built around such foundations cannot learn. The result may be actual psychosis or a compromise where any contact with life and knowledge is dreaded. The patient lives in the chilling world of '-K'. He is internally tyrannised by rigid objects that do not contain experience but denude it and render it useless for psychic work.

The relation to animate human life, including his own, is of a type that would be more appropriate to inanimate objects. It is a mechanical, Kafka-esque world depicted in horror movies of robots and automatons. There is no sense of a mental space for experience. Intense emotion may be felt as the sudden draining away of what life there is as it is violently projected into a space which is felt to be infinite. These patients often talk of black holes.

To fend off this sort of catastrophe – the contact with life – the patient has to manufacture a personality which evades such contact whilst giving an appearance of it.

As to the preconditions for such a state, they would include the lack of an experience of containment through the limitations of the container or through constitutional factors. Bion imagines the situation in which the infant approaches the breast in its function of love and understanding but when this is available attacks it so that all that is left is the material comfort. This results in a situation in which there is endless greed for material comfort combined with a lack of any experience of satisfaction. This bears certain resemblance to the state in which there is an endless hunger for facts and not experience.

Bion brought great clarity to the problem of the distinction between the neuroses and the psychoses by distinguishing not between psychotic and neurotic patients but between neurotic and psychotic personalities. The psychotic person-ality differs from the non-psychotic personality, not through the negation of reality, but through the destruction of that apparatus (or function) that is concerned with the awareness of internal and external reality.

'... the end result is that all thoughts are treated as if they were indistinguishable from bad internal objects; the appropriate machinery is felt not to be an apparatus for thinking, but an apparatus for ridding the mind of bad internal objects.' (Bion 1962b, p.112)

A patient living in such a world (i.e. when the psychotic personality dominates mental functioning) lives in a world which is both omnipotent and concrete. As a result of the violent projective processes, the patient is constantly menaced by the hostile objects which have been evacuated. It is also a world which is one-dimensional: the categories 'good–bad', 'true–false', 'inside–outside' collapse into one dimension where what is true is good is inside; what is bad is false is outside.

John is a very disturbed seven-year-old child who is constantly menaced by 'germs'. His analysis is dominated by the existence of the negation sign. He repeats over and over again 'I'm a person, you are a thing'. As contact with a living mind is felt to be so catastrophic he has constantly to render me inanimate. All interpretations are negated and treated as bad objects which he evacuates, utilising obsessional rituals aimed at removing these bad objects, for example, by repeating the words until they become incoherent and then literally taking them out of his mouth with his hands or, in the 'language of the oldest instinct', spitting them out. From her point of view my interpretations are my attempts to rid my mind of these bad objects and force them into him. Much of his motor activity, similarly, appears to be an attempt to rid his mind of bad objects. Thinking depends on differentiating – beginnings, ends, boundaries between spaces. John negates all such differentiation in a state of great excitement. In three years John still claims not to know what time his sessions begin or end.

John spends almost all his time desperately defending herself against an imminent catastrophe, which Bion termed catastrophic change. This results when the internal container is overwhelmed by sensation – the result is that it is felt to disintegrate – possibly it is this sort of process which underlies the feeling of breaking down, falling to pieces.

Mr Z is a 17-year-old adolescent whose mother suffered from severe mental illness and was institutionalised intermittently throughout his childhood. He relates his life as a series of meaningless biographical facts. In his behaviour he creates the appearance of an automaton. Bion said of such patients '... they feel pain but will not suffer it and so cannot be said to discover it ... the patient who will not suffer pain fails to "suffer" pleasure'.

In one session he was telling me of a friend he met who praised him as being unusually in touch with his feelings. He continued to talk about this incident in a mechanical way not conveying to me any feeling. Whilst he was talking I noticed his hand jerking as if there were something on it he wished to flick off.

This brought to my mind the possibility that his words were vehicles not for communication of experience but for evacuating it ('Talking ... must be considered as two different activities – one as a mode of communicating thoughts and the other one as the employment of the musculature to disencumber the personality of thoughts' (Bion 1977, p.83)).

I asked him if he believed the friend's assessment to be correct or whether he believed he'd evoked a false assessment as maybe he does in the session where his primary concern is to be rid of emotion. He was silent and then complained of discomfort.

He arrived for his session the following day in a state of panic, fearing imminent breakdown.

As he was less disturbed than John, Mr Z had allowed some contact between himself and me which had maybe led to the possibility of a new thought. As he lacked the equipment to manage this thought it was felt as a bad object that had lodged itself inside him and which threatened to overwhelm even the limited capacity for containment available to him.

CONCLUSION

In this chapter I have attempted first to introduce some of Bion's central ideas, along with giving some flavour of his mode of thinking, which I have characterised as essentially phenomenological. I have attempted to show how, using his method, we can differentiate different categories of experience – focusing particularly on the function he called 'K' – the process of coming to know oneself through experience.

He held the view that there is an epistemophilic instinct (ie., a basic drive towards knowledge which is not reducible to other instincts). The acquisition of knowledge brings the rewards of feelings of confidence gained from ever-widening experience. I have tried to describe different types of phenomena which although they may superficially give the appearance of knowledge are, in reality, strategies for evading it. These strategies stem from the functioning of a particular type of omniscience which functions like an institution found in the mind of individual patients, in groups and also in higher levels of social organisation.

In the latter part of the chapter I have outlined Bion's model of the development of the capacity to learn from experience which is, of course, closely related to his model of the analytic task.

I have, finally, brought some clinical material to illustrate the type of difficulty that is being avoided when omniscience replaces knowledge.

Bion's ideas have such extreme novelty that there has been some difficulty in their containment within the psychoanalytic community of thought and it is no coincidence that he was preoccupied with the question of how a group can contain a new idea. His theory outlines some of the requirements – the container of the new idea has to accept it without being overwhelmed by it and yet not compress its meaning, nor deform it by turning it into cult. Another way of putting this would be to say that it is sufficiently pliable to accept the new idea without suffocating it and sufficiently durable to not be disrupted by it.

I will close with a short poem by Brecht which, to my mind, describes a dream in which a powerful internal storm destroys the rigidity in the personality but is also met by a resilient but pliable container.

Iron

In a dream last night
I saw a great storm
It seized the scaffolding,
it tore down the iron cross clasps
What was made of wood stayed and swayed. (Brecht)

'And refashioning the fashioned lest it stiffen into iron is a work of endless vital activity.' (Heine)

REFERENCES

Bion, W.R. (1957) 'On arrogance.' In W.R. Bion (1967) *Second Thoughts*. London: Maresfield.

Bion, W.R. (1962a) *Experiences in Groups*. London: Tavistock.

Bion, W.R. (1962b) 'A theory of thinking.' In W.R. Bion (1967) *Second Thoughts*. London: Maresfield.

Bion, W.R. (1967a) 'Differentiation of the psychotic and non-psychotic personalities.' In W.R. Bion *Second Thoughts*. London: Maresfield.

Bion, W.R. (1967b) 'A theory of thinking.' In W.R. Bion *Second Thoughts*. London: Maresfield.

Bion, W.R. (1977) 'Learning from experience.' In W.R. Bion (1977) *Seven Servants*. New York: Jason Aronson.

Freud, S. (1911) 'Formulation on the two principles of mental functioning.' *Standard Edition*, Vol.12, 218–26. London: Hogarth.

Main, T. (1990) 'Knowledge, learning and freedom from thought.' *Psychoanalytic Psychotherapy*, 5, 1, 59–78. (Paper originally given at the Third Annual Congress of the Australian and New Zealand College of Psychiatrists in 1966.)

Rosenfeld, H. (1971) 'A clinical approach to the psychoanalytic theory of the life and death instinct: an investigation into the aggressive aspects of narcissism.' *International Journal of Psycho-analysis 52*, 169–178. Reprinted in E. Spillius (ed) (1988) *Melanie Klein Today* Vol. 1. London: Routledge.

CHAPTER 6

Murderousness in Relationship to Psychotic Breakdown (Madness)

Arthur Hyatt Williams

Gradually I have come to think of the state of murderousness as one which has been derived from a failure to work through the emotional disturbance engendered by a constellation of experiences, thoughts, feelings and phantasy constructs to do with death. This constellation may have originated in a number of different ways, such as loss through death or continued absence of a loved person, physical illness of a life-threatening kind, a life-threatening accident to the self, to one's loved or hated persons or seeing such an accident in relationship to persons unknown. In addition, there is the witnessing of cruelty being inflicted upon other people or the experience of it being inflicted upon the self. These last two instances are more traumatic when the individual is unable to retaliate, to escape and is more or less pinned down in the situation. Each of these life-threatening or psychically shocking experiences may be emotionally metabolised under satisfactory circumstances so that there is a relative or complete recovery, thus leaving little or no residue of 'problems to do with death' inside the individual. Of course, it is recognised that there is a problem to do with death in everyone, but problems concerning the inevitability of death for each individual may be relatively uncomplicated by unmetabolised experiences to do with death or may be interwoven with what I have labelled the 'Death Constellation'. Problems to do with personal death one would expect to increase with advancing years but this is not always or even usually so. The dangerousness of introjected experiences to do with death seems to be greater when the tide of life is running strongly. It is when young people, particularly young males, are confronted with such experiences that massive projection of them commonly occurs and results in homicide or, if there is a massive introjection, suicide. Sometimes, unmetabolised experiences to do with death are split off and encapsulated within the psyche. In this situation they tick over rather in the same way as an abnormal cerebral rhythm goes on quietly until some internal or external factors trigger it off into an epileptic fit. The 'Death Constellation' (a dangerous enclave to do with death) may give occasional evidence of its presence, or it may be so well encapsulated that no evidence of its existence is given until some further experience, stemming either from the intra-psychic world or from the external world, detonates it into sudden catastrophic activity. Usually, internal events and external ones act synergically. Sometimes the factors to do with death are present in such a way that they constitute an *alter ego*, or secondary manifestation of the self, like a Mr Hyde to a Dr Jekyll.

A number of people seen in prison, some in ordinary everyday life, and some seen as patients with emotional disorder have been aware of murderous phantasies and/or impulses. Impulses are much nearer to action than are phantasies. In several of these people, the primary complaint was that they had impulses to kill other people. Sometimes the choice is of a particular kind of person, such as all white people or all coloured men, or all prostitutes or all homosexuals. Sometimes the object of murderous impulses consists of the person who is, so to speak, 'in the way'. This may be the 'other woman', the 'other man', the hated sibling, the evil-eyed mother, or the tyrannical father. In some people who have such phantasies, there is guilt and remorse about having them at all (this is what one would expect). What happens is that many people, perhaps most, are able to bear the kind of guilt and remorse just described in such a way and for long enough for intra-psychic atonement to take place. It is to be noted that this atonement is for the crime of murder which has not been committed in external reality but which has been committed in the inner world of the mind in phantasy. This situation – which is the favourable one – does not always happen, because the pain of mourning over the murder not committed in external reality cannot be tolerated, and therefore the whole situation is denied, projected elsewhere, or defended against in one way or another, so that no ongoing intra-psychic work takes place. This intra-psychic work is at the depressive position or at the threshold to the depressive position. When there is a shift from a state of mind which approaches the depressive position to one nearer to the paranoid/schizoid position, so that the individual becomes dominated by paranoid anxiety, the outlook is very much worse. The situation whereby the pain of mourning over a crime committed only in the inner world was in a position in which intra-psychic work followed by emotional development could proceed, is itself designated as a *persecution*. Of the various ways in which this persecutory state can be dealt with, the one which leads on directly to the deed or murder is when the object of mourning or reproach, i.e. the object wished dead, is attacked for causing the psychic pain. A simple and common – albeit milder – example of this is when a mother whose child has crossed the road and narrowly missed being killed beats the child once the latter is safely in her hands again. If one can visualise a situation in which there is an escalation of destructive activity, it is easy to follow the steps leading to the murderous deed itself.

At any point in this spiral of destructive activity there can be a halting of the sequence of events or a deflection of it into some state in which, although there is no real working-through (as there might have been if the pain of the self-blaming state could have been borne) secondary measures – the task of which is to avoid the actual deed of murder – are able to become effective. Among these measures is the kind of psychotic breakdown which renders such consecutive and purposeful action as is necessary for the accomplishment of the deed of murder impossible to attain. Thus the mental illness is used unconsciously for moral and in some cases even altruistic purposes, its function being to immobilise the individual and to prevent him or her from committing homicide.

There occurs the opposite use of mental breakdown into psychosis. After study in depth of some murderers and their deeds, it becomes evident that the mental breakdown and the abandonment of effective reality-testing allows the individual to do that which when sane he or she could not have done. It is said that in Scotland, homicide takes place only when the murderer is drunk or at least has consumed a lot of alcoholic drink. What has to be found out from the personal history of each of these homicidal individuals, however, is what the alcohol was intended to do: whether it was to prevent the murderous impulse from being acted out, or whether it was temporarily to put out of action the forces set against the enaction of such a deed of homicide.

Consciously contained murderousness may be held in check and action avoided in a number of different ways. Sometimes the renunciation of murderous impulses is associated with a depressive illness. In other cases the murderous phantasies may themselves be eroticised and woven into a masturbation ritual. This provides a pleasure component and itself helps to perpetuate the *status quo*. By means of the secretly practised ritual of masturbation, contained within the murderous constellation, the acting out of the deed of murder is avoided, but the state of murderousness is perpetuated. In other words, the Death Constellation is held in a precarious state of equilibrium. This is all very well unless or until a further shift towards the paranoid/schizoid end of the spectrum takes place for whatever reason. Then the old pattern which had become relatively stable – perhaps enduring over long periods of time with little change – is found to function effectively no longer. The ensuing state, which is rather similar to the pharmacotoxic crisis described by Rado in 1932, constitutes a catastrophic change. The restoration of some kind of intra-psychic and external reality in the form of a psychotic breakdown is necessary, or there may be a 'mad' enaction of the whole phantasy constellation in a frantic attempt to make the old masturbatory set-up function again in both a relieving and even pleasurable way. The acting out may take place in a third way: namely by removing the self from what is regarded as the scene of the crime. Physically this may consist of a fugue while psychically there are at least six ways in which it may occur: suicide; amnesia; resort to alcohol in what usually amounts to a dipsomanic episode; the taking of drugs either to diminish psychic pain or to cause an elation in which a grandiose, not-caring state of mind becomes predominant; religious conversion; and the seeking of therapeutic help.

Of those few murderous people who committed the crime after they had been leucotomised, the trouble seems to have been that their internal or intra-psychic control system was disrupted sufficiently to allow the murder constellation, which had previously been held in check, to erupt into a catastrophic enaction. No study, as far as I know, has been made of the murders these people did commit, but I would venture to guess that they consisted of the acting out in detail of phantasy constellations which had long smouldered in a precariously maintained intra-psychic limbo. Madness can consist of the extrusion of a constellation of mad impulses and fantasies into a victim. This kind of madness has to be distinguished from madness due to a breakdown of psychic integration caused in the frantic attempts – or in spite of the frantic attempts – to contain and keep mad, murderous fantasies under control. Killing the enemy was not considered to be mad both in ancient and in more recent times. If we think of Ajax who killed the animals belonging to his own side that were being reserved for their food, because he was allegedly suffering from the delusion that they were Trojan soldiers, one might suspect that, motivated by sibling rivalry because of some dissatisfaction with his own position in the pecking order of the Greek top-brass, there had been a muddling of the splitting and polarisation which would have enabled him to recognise the enemy and not find such an enemy within the Greek encampment. Somewhat later in the *Oresteia*, Athene's orders to the Greeks were that they were to refrain from killing within the family but to reserve killing for the enemy in war involving risk to the State: the State had to be protected. She, Athene, exhorted her people not to become like 'some mad mate-murdering bird', killing inappropriately. Such killing was therefore even then considered to be a manifestation of madness.

Bion refers to the confusion between internal object images and their external realisations. He wrote of the mad way in which a certain young man, wishing to make an adult sexual relationship with a young woman with whom he regarded himself to have fallen in love, evacuated (projected) the internal intra-psychic images of his anti-sex parents who would not allow him such a relationship. He evacuated this disturbing intra-psychic constellation into his external parents after a very minor refusal and killed them both, disposing of their bodies down a cliff and into the sea. He then went off in his father's car to find the girl with a feeling of emancipation and of the sudden acquisition of adult status. This, of course, was quite mad, and it was not many days before sanity returned and with it the appropriate feelings of horror at what he had done and guilt and remorse about the irreversibility of his mad actions. The girl, who seemed to be very fond of him, accompanied him to the police station in order for him to be able to give himself up. He is alleged to have stated that he was willing to die for what he had done.

The *crime passionnel* is not based upon an overwhelming first-time situation but upon a catastrophic repetition of a previously experienced one. In the old situation there had been the same intra-psychic patterning and possibly, as in the oedipal situation itself, the same internal/external object relationships. In the *crime passionnel*, however, the power balance is very different. In the childhood instance where father could not be prevented from having sexual relationships with mother, there were three important factors: the subject – the child – was small, weak and dependent upon his parents; father and mother probably loved each other and in any case had more than a casual relationship with each other; and despite hatred, the child also loved both parents although maybe in widely different ways. The problem in childhood, therefore, was how to sustain ambivalent feelings against the father for having taken mother sexually and/or against the mother for her lack of fidelity to the child, the subject. The subsequent intra-psychic attack on the part of the child may be directed against the parents' sexuality, and by a small transformation may then be directed against the sexual parents. By introjection the attack becomes directed against the sexuality of the internal parents who are, of course, important parts of the child. This unresolved equation or constellation may remain in a state in which it gives little or no trouble until the tide of adolescent sexuality is running high. Then, if the situation becomes unbearable, and if the intra-psychic patterning is matched by something taking place in the external world, sometimes there is a massive projection of the internal anti-sex parental images. This projection may take place into the external parents as in the case just described, and the whole fatal episode may be triggered off by some trivial refusal which may have more symbolic than concrete significance. In the case mentioned by Bion (1967, Chapter 7, p.81), the little boy self of the young man, antipathetic towards the sexuality of his parents, therefore ascribed to them the attitude of being against his sexuality. When in a state of mind dominated by persecutory anxiety, actions are in accordance with the Talion principle. The young man concerned killed his parents in the mad belief that by obliterating them his sexuality would be able to develop. He had suffered from learning difficulties and was educationally, although not intellectually, retarded. Another way of describing his state of mind is that he was troubled by the part of himself which did not allow mating, whether it be of a male or female human being or of ideas and thoughts which fitted together. As he found that he needed the vehicle of an internal father (penis) to approach – i.e. make the journey to – the girl (mother), he asked his father for the car (the car which belonged to his father) to go and make contact with the girl who was some hundreds of miles away. Father's refusal was abrupt and mother supported it. At that moment the catastrophe fulminated so that symbol slipped into symbolic equation, as described by Segal (Segal 1981, see also Bion 1962), and the dreadful crime followed automatically. The breaking down of the capacity to symbolise, so that what is usually expressed symbolically is concretely acted out, is an essential feature of murderous deeds. The breakdown of the capacity to symbolise characterises psychotic patients. Apart from the impulsive murders which some schizophrenics do commit, the psychotic state is characterised by splitting and fragmentation of such a kind and to such a degree that planning and carrying out in action intra-psychically nurtured phantasies are precluded by the fragmentation. Sometimes the schizophrenic makes a false confession. If one can delineate an individual who contains, has to bear, tolerate and work through a constellation to do with death, pressing to be expressed in the form of murderous actions, the safe metamorphosis is by way of an increasing capacity to symbolise, not a tendency to resort to concretisation. When there is a sound capacity to symbolise, murderous phantasies are able to be tolerated until intra-psychic healing proceeds and emotional growth mitigates them. Thus, what ensues is an enactment with all its associated horror and disastrous consequences. Owning all the various parts of the self and reaching a relatively satisfactory state of poise and balance are features of sanity. They are characteristics of maturity and integration. In such a psychic state there is no real risk of there being a resort to murder, and any residual murderousness within the self is distributed in a safe way and not detached from its intra-psychic moorings in such a manner that it may 'take on a life of its own'. When murderousness does take on a life of its own, what happens next is that there is an attempt to make a take-over bid by the murderous part of what one would usually regard as the more sane part of the self.

Murderousness militating towards acting out, that is towards the deed of homicide, characterises the failure to integrate and to come to terms with an important part of personal psychic content. In its turn this leads to difficulties in relating to a coming-to-terms with important features of situations in external reality. Many more people have the burden of the death constellation than the comparatively small numbers who kill, either themselves or anyone else. What, therefore, are the processes involved in the minds of those who do develop psychotic breakdown or those who avoid such a breakdown by resorting to murder? Those who break down in the process of containing the death constellation, and who, by reason of their psychotic breakdown, do not kill, unconsciously use the defence of a psychosis against the acting out of murderous impulses. Sometimes this defence is not successful, and there may then follow a particularly mad, impulsive murder. At the opposite end of the scale are those who murder in order to remain sane, and again it must be stressed that this is an unconscious process. What usually happens is that during a phase of great anxiety and tension, the anxiety being of the persecutory kind of course, there is a murderous acting out, and this seems to clear the air for the murderer (at least for a while). But the murder is accomplished by designating the victim as inferior, sub-human, a 'cabbage' as Brady said during his trial, or as wholly bad and deserving death as a Hell's Angel said of his sexy life-loving young male victim. In this latter case it is quite clear that the murderer projected into the victim a very death-seeking, psychically sick part of himself and killed it in the victim. It must be stressed, however, that it was the victim and not he who died. Another young man who killed a very old lady projected the death-seeking part of himself into the old woman and killed her instead of himself, making yet another suicidal attempt. What had facilitated this massive projection into her was her own statement to her killer that she would be glad when her life was over, as she wished most sincerely to join her beloved and much-lamented late husband. This form of killing – choosing a victim into whom to project – can be accomplished only by the loss of those parts of the self which are jettisoned into the victim. Again, I must stress that these processes are unconscious. At successive interviews it may appear that there were real grievances which the killer had against the victim, and some of these may sound quite reasonable and convincing. At greater depth, however, they are able to be seen as the excuses for an action or actions which can be regarded as a kind of parasitism. These actions constitute the ultimate in the 'I'm all right, Jack' formula. I have seen this attitude shared between a small group of friends, all of whom had committed their separate murders, and the sharing of their experiences did seem to mitigate the guilt feelings which had been reactivated when all of them had been granted parole, thus being set free from the prison walls to enjoy the green world of life and sexuality. After a murderous action, the projected parts of the murderer may not remain in the victim for long and a rapid return into the murderer sometimes results in the suicidal attempt or actual self-killing of the latter. When a murderer is 'on the run' from the police authorities, it is not only from them that he is a fugitive, but perhaps more importantly he is fleeing from and making every effort to avoid the return of parts of himself which he has murdered in someone else. Even when he has been caught and perhaps admitted the killing, been convicted and sentenced, he is likely to attempt to show himself in a better light than the reality would allow. Most murderers try to show themselves to themselves as well as to the authorities in a wishfully self-excusing way: for example, one man and his mind converted a ten-centimetre wound in the chest of his young victim into a ten-millimetre wound. When the reality was pointed out to him he was horrified, and time after time reverted to his rather plaintive question 'How did that little cut kill her?' Another man, who shot a young person with a shotgun, multiplied the distance between himself and the victim, until he made the latter into some kind of distant target which he mistook for an animal. In fact the shooting had been at point-blank range.

What I am attempting to make clear is that murder committed as a defence against madness is associated with the projection of unbearable parts of the psyche of the murderer into a victim. The victim is not an arbitrarily chosen person, though the choice is unconscious, and there may not be any recognition of who it is for whom the victim stands in place. Although in a formal sense the murderer may appear to be sane, the mechanism by which he gets rid of unbearable parts of himself is psychotic and the catastrophic deed itself may keep those parts of the murderer at bay for only a short time. The deed itself is mad and is associated with a breakdown in the capacity to symbolise, so that it does take the form of – and in fact is – a symbolic equation. Not all murders are of this kind, but certainly those perpetrated upon an unknown victim tend to be of this kind.

Let us ask ourselves what kind of person commits murder. At the risk of being criticised for teleological arguments, it is a person who has within himself or herself a constellation of memories, impulses, fears and experiences to do with death which cannot be, or at least have not been, psychically digested and metabolised, so that the life-threatening enclave which I have loosely termed the 'death constellation' is in a safe state within the psyche. In this safe state it is either safely attached or dispersed within the psyche so that it does not stultify emotional growth and development on the one hand, and does not threaten a collapse into symbolic equation on the other hand. Symbolic equation would mean action leading to the death of the self or that of some victim unconsciously chosen for specific reasons. Clinically, it is found that murderers and potential murderers are paranoid. Paranoid attitudes are far more constant than overt aggressiveness. When one comes to give psychotherapy to people with this kind of psychic configuration, what is revealed is a failure in the primary negotiation of the depressive position and subsequent failures to do so in all the crises of life when such negotiation would have been desirable and necessary. In some murderers, the failure to negotiate the depressive position seems to have been due not to absence of compassion on the part of the potential murderer, but to a failure of reparation, and a ricochet back from the approaches to the depressive position to a paranoid/schizoid state of mind (Williams 1960). Among the causes of failure at the threshold of the depressive position is a lack of a containing person in the life of the potential murderer. This lack of a containing person may well have occurred in the very early life of the individual suffering from difficulties to do with the metabolisation and detoxification of the death constellation. Help during and after a bereavement is one such situation, particularly if one parent dies and the surviving parent is so disturbed and distressed that he or she cannot give the necessary, and perhaps not even the usual, containment to the child. The child or young person splits off, by-passes or represses the threatening situation, which therefore does not get worked through. Twenty years ago, the separation from the absence of containing parents or parental figures during times of anxiety about death was of great importance in the prisoner-patients whom I saw. The constellation which had been laid down

30–35 years ago was derived from wartime evacuation, when children were separated from parents in an atmosphere of threat to life in the form of enemy bombing. The foster parents, those people who stood *in loco parentis* to the children, may or may not have been kind, but the salient fact was that the known parent was not there and was phantasised as being in the thick of the bombing, or alternatively as having a happy life all the time. That in the child's mind, absence is equated with death, was emphasised many years ago by Freud and his co-workers. The formula is something like the following: absence of the needed parent – needed in order to contain anxieties about death – plus the presence of the hated substitute parent, who made demands of 'dos' and 'don'ts' without the child being able to use him or her as a container for anxiety, is the first sequence. The present bad parent takes over all the hostility from the absent good parent who is subsequently felt to be bad. Meanwhile, no real containment of anxiety to do with death is possible.

The disburdening of the homicidal individual of elements of the death constellation into somebody else is a pathological parallel to the normal disburdening of the self which the infant does in relationship to the caring parent. In line with Bion's views (1967, pp.80–82), in the initial interchanges between murderer and victim there is usually some testing out of the capacity of the victim to contain and to detoxicate death constellation communications. There may be something like revenge in a further failure of a transaction (of projected identification) which has failed before.

Now it may well be asked what evidence there is for what I have put forward here. In several instances, I have been put into the position of the receiver of projective identification specifically in the form of psychic content to do with death. These communications were made by murderous patients, and when eventually I was able to sort out the nature of the anxiety with which I had been filled, I was able to make some statement to show that at least I could tolerate the communication, and that time had to be allowed before we could reach a more precise understanding of what had been communicated. After this countercommunication had been made in all these cases, the tension, which had reached a high peak of intensity, rapidly subsided. In taking detailed histories of potentially murderous or actual victims, it became clear that the dialogue between potential murderer and victim-designate consisted of communications of the kind which I have just described in the murderous patients' interaction with me. In some cases, with a fatal ending, it was clear that the victim, in panic, increased the anxieties of his assailant in one way or another, so that the interaction escalated into the murderous deed itself. In other cases, the victim-designate was able to contain, to tolerate and to communicate with the would-be assailant without hatred or panic. In these cases there was a de-escalation, just as there had been in my interviews with murderous persons, and the outcome was favourable in that no murder took place. One attractive girl, chosen by a murderous young man for rape and murder, smiled so pleasantly at her assailant that the whole escalation went into reverse, and the would-be murderer was caught by the police through allowing this potential victim to go free and unharmed.

I have mentioned the mechanism of projective identification discovered and named by Melanie Klein (1946). It is a primitive method of communication common to everyone, particularly in early life, but used excessively in psychotic patients and murderous individuals. It appears that projective identification is a link between the psychotic and the murderer. The other link is between the psychotic murderer and the person who kills in self-defence: let us take, for example, the citizen soldier when confronted by the enemy in time of war. The soldier becomes murderous because he has been sanctioned by an authority to kill an enemy who on his part has also been sanctioned to kill. It becomes a competitive transaction in which, at worst, one ends up dead and one alive and, at best, as in a game of chess where there is one who has total power over the other, slaughter is not necessitated, although there is always a risk of it happening. Anyone with a troublesome intra-psychic death constellation may find relief in the sanctioned life-and-death contest. But this is not mad in the way which I have described in those who have to kill in an attempt to preserve their sanity, or in those who go mad in order to prevent themselves from killing. It is clear that much more research in this area is needed.

REFERENCES

Bion, W.R. (1962) *Learning from Experience*. London: Heinemann.

Bion, W.R. (1967) *Second Thoughts*. London: Heinemann.

Klein, M. (1946) 'Notes on some schizoid mechanisms.' *International Journal of Psycho-analysis 27*, 99–110.

Segal, H. (1981) *The Work of Hanna Segal*. New York: Aronson.

Williams, A.H. (1960) 'A psycho-analytic approach to the treament of the murderer.' *International Journal of Psycho-analysis 41*, 532–539.

CHAPTER 7

Psychosis
The Sacrifice that Fails?

E.M. Armstrong-Perlman

Psychosis can be provoked by a sacrifice that fails. The subject has made heroic efforts to gain the recognition of an 'idealised' other. He or she fails to win the desired response: 'This is my beloved son or daughter, in whom I am well pleased'. When the failure of the response cannot be denied at the conscious level, the subject is exposed to the futility of his efforts. With the loss of the hope of acceptance and recognition by a good object, his desolate cry may become 'My God, My God, why have you forsaken me?' The idealised other is experienced as indifferent or hostile. The hope of being accepted by a 'good' object is lost; the chasm of psychosis beckons. If the loss and the disappointment cannot be contained, the 'ego' is at risk of being overwhelmed by unbearable affects that jeopardise its very survival.

My thesis builds on Fairbairn's account (1951) of the development of psychopathology. The Fairbairnian infant needs the responsive embodied warmth of the mother. If the relationship is too frustrating, his need and frustration are exacerbated. She develops a duality of aspects. The infant experiences the mother as excessively exciting and rejective; this gives rise to ambivalence. Given his unconditional need, he cannot reject her, yet she seems to be rejecting him. At this stage, his only hope is to convert the real object into a good one.

To cope with this intolerable experience, he internalises the relationship where at least it is under his control. For Fairbairn (1951, p.178), 'the internalisation of the unsatisfying object was regarded as a defensive technique designed to control the traumatic element in a situation involving the cathexis of an object which was unsatisfying.' But internalisation just transfers the problem to his inner world. The solution is the splitting of the internalised object. The child splits off the overexciting and over-frustrating elements of the internal object leaving the nucleus of the original object desexualised and idealised, shorn of its 'bad' features. This now acceptable object provides the nucleus of the superego but in its role of the 'ego-ideal'.

The child internalises bad objects to make the objects in his environment good, but 'outer security is purchased at the price of internal security, since it leaves the ego at the mercy of inner persecutors (Fairbairn 1951, p.164). This splitting of the emergent pristine self of the child preserves the conditions of safety but at the cost of repressed relationships with bad objects. However, internalisation and splitting do not after all eliminate the bad aspects of the real object that provoked and will later evoke the dilemma. They just transfer them to an internal theatre. If they continue to be intolerable, the child begins to identify with the internalised bad object. The process might be sketched out at a subjective level: 'if you are bad I would reject you but I can't because I need you. If I am good how can you be bad to me if you are good? The reason you are bad to me is because I must be bad.'

Let us take the Fairbairnian account a bit further. Taking on board the burden of the badness defends the other but does not solve the problem of the need for acceptance: 'To get what I need I have to become good in your eyes, so I have to do things which would make me a hero in your eyes. I need to be acknowledged as the beloved son or daughter in whom you are well pleased. I take on your values as the conditions of my self-esteem. If this fails, the subsequent disappointment may lead to a threatening reintegration of persecutory figures, which is intolerable. I try even harder, modelling myself on that which I think will secure your acceptance. I put the "you" over the "I".' Submission becomes a 'good', a worthwhile sacrifice for approval. The values of the other are seen as good from the standpoint of the central ego and are put over the self, a superego ideal.

The attempts to win the approval and acceptance of the significant, idealised other involve self-abnegation. The self puts the presumed will of the idealised, necessary other above its own wishes and desires. Heteronymy prevails over autonomy. The unquestioning idealisation of the presumed behest of the other entails a negation of the self. The will of the other constitutes the moral world, the superego ideal. The disowned features of the relationship are repudiated and repressed. According to Fairbairn (1951), the superego originates as a means of defence against bad objects. The barrier of continuous repression has to be maintained as long as the relationship with the idealised object is necessary for the maintenance of the self.

If, however, the sacrifice fails, the pride of the hair-shirt of self-denial no longer promises the gratification of conditional acceptance. Submission is no longer a 'good' but rather the resented price paid for an illusory, unobtainable acknowledgement.

If the idealised object is treated as an external object, the individual runs the risk of being re-traumatised. If the object carrying the hope disappoints too severely, disillusion can prevail. His eyes are opened; his sacrifice has failed to win the required acceptance; he has to face a God that fails. His efforts were futile; all his attempts have failed to win the acknowledgement of the other who carries the projection of the ego-ideal. The object of hoped-for acceptance becomes rejective and frustrating, blind to his basic need for acceptance and recognition. The rejective hatred can overwhelm the good. The ego-ideal can dissolve into a malign unacceptable terrifying persecutor, surely the core of the malign superego. The idealised object is no longer acceptable to the central ego.

The indifference or hostility of the external other who is the unwitting recipient of the idealised relationship may be real or projected. The essential feature is the lack of awareness and acknowledgement on the part of the significant other of his subjective and symbolic importance to the subject. This blindness of the significant other is a blow that threatens the virtual annihilation of the subject. The failure of acknowledgement is construed as indifference or hostility. This leads to a catastrophic hopelessness and risks the reactivation of early trauma when the subject did not have the resources either emotional or cognitive to work through the disappointment. At that time, faith in the loving concern and therefore the reliability and trustworthiness of the significant necessary other was eroded. There was a psychic catastrophe but a catastrophe that was dealt with by repression, splitting and acceptance of the badness. The fragile faith in the hoped-for responsiveness of the other was based on denial of the relational failure when the only hope of converting the bad object into a good one was by internalisation and splitting the object, and in consequence the self.

But now, faced with the loss of his good object, with no object either internal or external to turn to, he may be exposed to the full blast of intolerable persecutory anxiety. The intolerable anguish of abandonment, of the outer darkness 'where there is wailing and gnashing of teeth' becomes a psychic reality. He enters the intolerable anguish of the 'black hole' of seeing nothingness in the nonresponsive gaze of the other. Given the despairing, desperate need of the subject for solace and acceptance, this primitive agony may lead to the disintegration of the self.

Because of the break down of his defense system, he cannot maintain the splitting that served to preserve his conditions of safety. For Fairbairn (1943),

'the return of bad objects implies a failure of the defence of repression; but it equally implies a failure of the moral defence and a collapse of the authority of the super-ego.' (p.81)

The central ego can be overwhelmed by the reactivation of repressed relationships with bad objects. It can disintegrate with the failure of hope for recognition and acceptance by the idealised other. This heralds the return of relationships with bad objects from the unconscious. The benign, just Godhead can be polluted by the return of the demonic, the Virgin Mary adulterated by an unrepentant Mary

Magdalene. He is left with the full force of infantile ambivalence and with the full force of infantile need.

With some psychotic patients I have worked with, there has been a failure of a Herculean attempt to restore either the parental marriage or to obtain the approval of a parent or a parentified figure. This may operate at a severe cost to the self in terms of the individual's own maturational development. Even sexuality may be sacrificed to maintain the relationship with the object.

An example was a 20-year-old man, who, on an unskilled salary, had paid for his mother to return to her idealised ex-husband, also his idealised father, in their country of origin. The attempt was a miserable and acrimonious failure. After the failure, but prior to his breakdown, he had tried to live by himself. This attempt at independence failed. He became unemployed for the first time and retreated to the maternal household, leading a non-communicative existence, holed up in his bedroom.

This behaviour caused concern. The visiting psychiatrist deemed him to be on the brink of a psychotic breakdown. He referred him for family therapy. I was part of the supervisory team observing the case by means of a two-way mirror.

This young man seemed unsuitable for individual psychotherapy. He passively came with his mother and youngest brother, but his passivity exuded an atmosphere of barely controlled violence and sexuality; a volcano about to erupt. Even as an ex-Mental Welfare Officer accustomed to emergency admissions and having worked in a psychiatric hospital run as a therapeutic community, the body signals and the fixed gaze made me fearful of possible violence.

There was a history of multiple separations. His father had returned to their country of origin after the birth of his second brother. Then aged two, he and his infant brother had been left with the maternal grandparents. His father had not maintained contact. He had intermittent periods with his mother which entailed multiple separations from the maternal grandparents. His brother, who was ruthless in his use of the family, had an established record of delinquency. He was not seen during the therapy as he was in custody on remand. He was the 'bad boy' who appeared to have taken a psychopathic solution pursuing his own ends, devoid of concern for others. An eight-year-old brother, the son of a different father who had died some years earlier in a motorcycle accident, was an anxious, fearful child already causing concern at school because of learning difficulties.

The patient appeared to have been the 'good boy' who had taken the role of looking after and trying to please his mother. He had no peer group and there was no evidence of closeness with either of his brothers. But his attempts to be 'good' did not succeed. He did not manage to repair the parental couple. He did not win either the recognition or the appreciation of his father or his mother for his efforts. Rather, he became implicated in her acrimony over the failure of this illusory attempt to re-establish a relationship with her first husband.

From a psychoanalytic point of view, it was clear that he had made a Herculean attempt, not just in phantasy but in reality, to restore the primal couple, an omnipotent attempt at a reparative restitution that failed disastrously. It could not be denied; he was exposed to his impotence to convert his parents into a united couple that would presumably care for him and reconstitute the family from which he had been ejected at the age of two. It is a feasible speculation that this was a new edition of the initial trauma of the breakup of his parents' marriage. This failure in real terms also failed to win any recognition of his sacrifice. It was a failure that his conscious self had to acknowledge. Like Coriolanus, he had failed to create a better world and he had no other world to turn to.[1]

It became clear during the progress of the therapy that the mother was inappropriately bonded to her son and was conveying messages of his significance to her as her companion, but an intermittent, inadequate companion. She humourously referred to the fact that in pubs, people sometimes mistook them for a couple and referred to their relationship as having been a form of Darby and Joan. He appeared to be an intermittent appendage to his mother's psychic equilibrium. She was equally necessary to him. In Fairbairn's (1941) terminology, he had encountered difficulties at the transitional stage of differentiation and separation from the object. His mother's intermittent acceptance had not been in terms of his needs.

There appeared to be no history of any attempts to establish any form of a sexual relationship. However, he did emanate that indefinable feel that he was a young man, not a boy, but a prematurely old, joyless, young man. He had sexual presence, an attribute that observers presumably picked up when they assumed he and his mother were a couple.

He was exposed to his mother's active denigration of him as well as her concern. This was painfully evident in their interaction in the therapy. She appeared to have little capacity for an empathic awareness of him as a separate person, although she could recognise similarities in their behaviour when they became manifest in the therapy. His mother reported that he had torn up the family photographs and flushed them down the lavatory just as she had done to the wedding photographs after the breakdown of the marriage. The attempt to reconstitute the family could be multi- determined, to please and satisfy his mother, to find a rescuing father and to recreate the conditions for his own growth. However it had failed. He destroyed the family photographs.

For Fairbairn, failure at later stages of development can regressively reactivate relationships with bad objects. This patient's attempt to find an idealised father and unite the primal couple had failed. His attempt then to leave home also failed. He failed to find a 'good' father who could function as a bridge to enable him

---

1   I am grateful to Sally Boatswain for elaborating this connection in a paper given to The Guild of Psychotherapists in February, 1989.

to differentiate and separate from his mother. He had no stable representation of a good father either internally or externally to help him with this task of individuation available to him. He had not established a close relationship with his stepfather and his relationship with his grandparents had been intermittent and marked by multiple early separations. But primarily, he had failed to win the response 'This is my beloved son, in whom I am well pleased' from either his father or his mother.

At the beginning of the therapy he was locked in a state of dependence with his mother, but a dependence that reeked of barely controlled sexuality and aggression. There was a risk of internal reality overwhelming external reality, a risk of a psychotic breakdown that might necessitate further fragmentation of the self in attempts to preserve the relationships with 'good' objects both external and internal, uncontaminated by intolerable features of sexuality and aggression. He had sacrificed much but to no avail.

In another case, an adolescent girl, not diagnosed as psychotic, had been admitted to an adult psychiatric ward, run on therapeutic community lines. She was beyond the scope of a children's home to contain. After quite a lengthy and tumultuous admission, she became very co-operative and helpful, a 'good girl'. Her behaviour was so improved that a plan was set in motion to transfer her to an adolescent hostel. We failed to allocate responsibility to a specific person to discuss this with her on an individual basis. At this point, she gave her meagre possessions to Oxfam, prior to a clear psychotic episode of short duration. This of course necessitated an extended stay on the ward.

We, the ward team, had failed to appreciate what the transfer to another setting had meant to this girl. She was the illegitimate child of an Irish Catholic mother and a black American service-man who had left in infancy. Her mother had looked after her intermittently. There had been long episodes of care in a convent.

As the only adolescent on the ward, she received a lot of affection as well as boundary-setting. The ward sister, an ample-breasted Irish woman with a lot of gruff warmth had also given her individual attention. Both the male charge nurses, also kindly to her, were black. We had not considered the symbolic meaning of this environment to this girl. Apart from what might have been seen as an ejection from a symbolic, but idealised family, we did not realise that the separation might rearouse a situation with too close mnemic links to the early trauma. She had become cooperative and very helpful with others but her reward was discharge. We were pushing her towards a transitional stage of quasi-independence but failed to empathically relate and communicate with her the meaning of this separation. We were not sensitive to the psychic significance of our actions to this emotionally deprived adolescent. We had become the loved object failing to respond.

Fairbairn (1943) emphasises the role of precipitating factors in reality,

> 'an unconscious situation involving internalised bad objects is liable to be activated by any situation in outer reality conforming to a pattern which renders it emotionally significant in the light of the unconscious situation.' (p.76)

The external situation is rendered traumatic by symbolic significance in terms of previous vulnerability and trauma. We had unwittingly created the situation in external reality that evoked and provoked her response. We were responsible for our blindess to our symbolic transferential import to this girl. We acknowledged our failure, and tried to make good by re- establishing the connection with her. The psychotic episode was transient and of less than a few days' duration.

This adolescent girl did not destroy loved photographs like the previous patient but gave her possessions to the poor. Both, however, were severing their connection with their history. One with an act of symbolic violent destruction, the other by giving away her meagre inheritance.

The individual at risk of a psychotic breakdown, may make a St Francis-like sacrifice of his past. He gives away or destroys his inheritance. But the psychotic, unlike St Francis, fails to find a the symbolic father who acknowledges him. Rather, like Christ on the cross, he is left with the despairing cry of, 'Eli, eli lama sabachthani – My God, my God, why have you forsaken me?' But there is no answer, there is nothing there. He is left desolate in the wilderness, an emotional 'dosser'.

He is exposed to the futility of his efforts. The futility is manifest at two related levels. In the outer world, his sacrificial attempts have failed to win acknowledgement, so it is difficult to maintain that the other is good. In the inner world, this challenges his acceptance of the badness to maintain the other as good. If he is not bad the other must be bad.

But the psychic cost is high (Fairbairn 1943):

> 'It is better to be a sinner in a world ruled by God than to live in a world ruled by the devil. A sinner in a world ruled by God may be bad: but there is always a sense of security to be derived from the fact that the world around is good – "God's in His heaven – All's right with the world!(170; and in any case there is always a hope of redemption. In a world ruled by the devil the individual may escape the badness of being a sinner; but he is bad because the world around him is bad. Further, he can have no sense of security and no hope of redemption. The only prospect is one of death and destruction.' (p.67)

The central ego, a fragile construct, based on identification with the idealised object has failed in its task of functional adaptation to secure the acceptance of the idealised other. It can dissolve with the drastic dissolution of its object. It can be overwhelmed by the reactivated relationships with bad objects. If this happens, there is a danger that inner reality is super- imposed upon outer reality (Fairbairn 1943):

> 'When such an escape of bad objects occurs, the patient finds himself confronted with terrifying situations which have hitherto been unconscious. External situations then acquire for him the significance of repressed relationships with bad objects.' (p.76)

The individual then despairs but is also desperate. He can experience himself as a rat in a trap – an internal 'psychic' situation now externalised, of impotent fight or flight, or in a more malignant form kill or be killed; a metaphorical situation which now becomes only too real.

With one suicidal young man, I could only empathise with his predicament, of how appalling it was, to be so absolutely dependent on such a monstrous person as he experienced me to be. Later he referred to the fact that his internal reality when reactivated in the transference was only too real.

Such an individual is in danger of experiencing the reactivation of the malign dyadic situation of infantile ambivalence, a situation of murderous intensity, an emotional Hungerford.[2] But he is no longer an infant, an uncontrolled impulsive act actually can kill. Aggressive impulses, if not constrained, can destroy his objects in external reality.

But in this state of primary identification, with the self not as yet differentiated, the mother constitutes the world. She is absolutely necessary; loss of her is equivalent to loss of the self. The tragedy of such individuals is that they have no other world to turn to. Desperate measures are necessary to preserve both the self and the other, both internal and external, from annihilation. Killing the object either internally or externally is akin to psychic suicide. Grief or mourning for the lost object is not a psychological option given the level of psychic dependance. The defensive processes adopted to defend and preserve the self in relation to its objects have broken down. The need of the other is merely intensified. The individual re-enters the danger zone of imperative, impotent infantile, ambivalent need. He or she can be overwhelmed by desperate longings for the body of the mother.

These longings may be highly eroticised. Conscious incestuous fantasies may break through the weakened repression barrier overwhelming the central ego. Fantasies may emerge of the alluring withholding, frustrating mother. The image of a loving mother who is an acceptable object to the child may be polluted or contaminated by images of the exciting frustrating mother. The idealised loving

---

2   In 1987, a man in Hungerford, who had lived innocuously with his mother went on a random killing spree. The first victim was a young mother picknicking with her children. The last victims were his own mother and himself.

mother, shorn of sexuality is in danger of becoming the alluring, hated, tantalising prostitute who through her very allure excites murderous rage.

Desperate, violent, intrusive sexual impulses to rape – or, if the splitting has broken down disastrously, to murder – may flood the overwhelmed central self. Access to the maternal body, which is intrusive, frustrated and hostile, becomes a driving force. The near-psychotic adult is, unlike the infant, capable of actual incest and rape. For the suicidal young man, no punishment was cruel enough to punish rapists. According to Fairbairn (1944):

> 'It is because the child does have the experience of a physical relationship with his mother's breast, while also experiencing a varying degree of frustration in this relationship, that his need for his mother persists so obstinately beneath the need for his father and all subsequent genital needs.' (p.122)

But frustration leads to heightened ambivalent excited need, intensified by the historic and the current lack of emotional connectedness. Words have failed. If too often frustrated, this intensified excitable, eroticised need for the body of the mother is increasingly imbued by aggression, fear and resentment. Fairbairn argues that as the child comes to appreciate genital difference in the course of his own development (1944):

> 'his physical needs tends to flow increasingly (albeit in varying degrees) through genital channels, his need for his mother comes to include a need for her vagina. At the same time, his need for his father comes to include a need for his father's penis. The strength of these physical needs for his parents' genitals varies, however, in inverse proportion to the satisfaction of his emotional needs. Thus, the more satisfactory his emotional relationships with his parents, the less urgent are his physical needs for their genitals.' (p.122)

But if the relationships with both parents are too frustrating, 'some measure of ambivalence necessarily develops in relation to his mother's vagina and his father's penis' (p.122). The woman's vagina for the sake of psychic economy can become the rejected object, an object of disgust, while the penis functions as a symbolic breast, the necessary object of succour. Working analytically with psychotic patients, I have found fantasies of anal intercourse with the father flooding consciousness while the body of the mother is repudiated. Disgust for the breast and the vagina flood consciousness. These fantasies cause torment when they emerge in consciousness.

To mitigate 'the danger of violent outbursts of precipitate action' (Fairbairn 1941, p.52), the individual has to withdraw; the emergent connections have to be attacked. The individual requires desperate measures to preserve his internal and external objects. To avert a psychic murder, which is equivalent to suicide, he needs to restructure his objects. To preserve his external objects, he has to repress yet again and obliterate the emerging transferential connections. The emerging image or idea has to be separated from the affect.

The only alternative to incest or murder and rape may be a further flight from internal and external objects. Linking has to be attacked. This averts a reintegration that would have a catastrophic effect on his external objects. He withdraws emotionally even further from reality. However, to avoid primitive agonies, new connections with disembodied, fragmented, internalised objects are necessary. He stubbornly clings to an internal world constituted by increasingly fragmented objects. This compensatory world defends and protects his internal and external objects.

The flight into madness is, however, a retreat from the anguish of the failed response. He has failed to find a better world. The flight protects both himself and his objects from his eroticised ambivalence. But the cost of the necessary preservation is the fragmentation of the self.

An elderly patient, seeking my acknowledgement, said he had sacrificed his sexual life to prevent murder. Given my experience in the transference of the desperation and terror underlying his too eroticised need and rage, I was able to acknowledge his sacrifice with genuine conviction. It was also apparent that the cost of preserving his objects had been the ultimate act of renunciation. He had lost more than his sexuality, he had lost his 'self'.

REFERENCES.

Fairbairn, W.R.D. (1941) 'A revised psychopathology of the psychoses and psychoneuroses.' In *Psychoanalytic Studies of the Personality*. London: Tavistock/Routledge and Kegan Paul (1952).

Fairbairn, W.R.D. (1943) 'The repression and the return of bad objects with special reference to the "War Neuroses ".' In *Psychoanalytic Studies of the Personality*. London: Tavistock/Routledge and Kegan Paul (1952).

Fairbairn, W.R.D. (1944) 'Endopsychic structure considered in terms of object relationships.' In *Psychoanalytic Studies of the Personality*. London: Tavistock/Routledge and Kegan Paul (1952).

Fairbairn, W.R.D. (1951) 'A synopsis of the development of the author's view regarding the structure of the personality.' In *Psychoanalytic Studies of the Personality*. London: Tavistock/Routledge and Kegan Paul (1952).

Part Two

Treatment

CHAPTER 8

Working with Psychotic Processes in Art Therapy

Katherine Killick

INTRODUCTION

In this chapter I will describe the practice of art therapy with patients in acute psychotic states as it evolved in my work at Hill End Hospital, St Albans over a period of ten years between 1979 and 1989, when I practised in, and eventually managed, the hospital's Art Therapy Department. I will share some understandings of working with psychotic processes in art therapy, which developed through this work, and which continue to evolve in my clinical practice. I will introduce this with a short description of the work of an art therapist.

Most art therapists, myself included, arrive in relationships with patients having graduated first from a training in Fine Art (which involves three to four years' experience of working with creative processes in the making of visual imagery) followed by postgraduate training in art therapy, which introduces concepts and experience to the trainee in order to enable her to develop relationships of a psychotherapeutic nature with patients. Within these an understanding of the experiences involved in creating art objects can inform a psychotherapeutic process.

The art therapy relationship includes experiences of working with art materials, creating visual images which then exist as concrete objects, and working with the objects created. My art therapy training tended to focus on the experiences between therapist and patient that are possible when the patient is able to symbolise experience, to differentiate the concrete and the symbolic, and to converse with the therapist in consensually validated symbolic language.

Many art therapists who are employed in adult psychiatric settings find themselves trying to work psychodynamically with patients experiencing severe disturbances, and this precludes such therapeutic conversations. As a newly qualified art therapist in 1979, I found myself working with patients in acute psychotic states at Hill End Hospital, a predominantly medical-model psychiatric hospital. Patients going through schizophrenic episodes were often referred for art therapy by their psychiatrists.

It seemed to me that these patients often engaged with the art therapy setting, and with myself, in ways which seemed to facilitate positive changes in their experiences of themselves and of the world of human relationships, although the nature of this engagement differed from that which I had been trained to understand. I became interested in understanding more about these patients, about the way they related to the setting, and about myself in relation to them as someone attempting to be of service to a therapeutic process (Killick 1987, 1991).

Over time, an approach evolved from this enquiry, which I now propose to describe. Many elements of the approach which evolved in my work have been maintained by those staff of the Art Therapy Department, Hill End Hospital, who are presently working with acute in-patients, and these have been described in *The Handbook of Art Therapy* (Case and Dalley 1992).

My current theoretical understanding of this subject is informed by ideas offered by psychoanalysis and analytical psychology. I will be making particular use of my understanding of Bion's ideas of 'catastrophe' (1962) and 'faith' (1970) and of Eigen's (1985) elaboration of these ideas in this chapter. I will also refer, directly and indirectly, to ideas offered in the work of Searles (1962), Winnicott (1965, 1974), and Segal (1991). Theoretical understanding, however, as these authors can remind us, has its limitations, and I am indebted to past and present patients and to my own analysis and supervision for helping me to remember this.

SCHIZOPHRENIC REGRESSION

Searles (1962) proposes that the schizophrenic patient's relationship with reality is 'desymbolised', and that accordingly the patient's experience of both the truly concrete and the truly symbolic is foreclosed. They are 'de-differentiated' in schizophrenic regression, as a result of attacks on those ego functions concerned with symbolisation. I will briefly explore this state of affairs, and go on to explore the idea that the art therapy relationship can offer opportunities for experiences which foster evolution of these symbolising ego functions.

I will start by borrowing a living metaphor for the psychic situation experienced by the patient in a state of schizophrenic regression, and thus also encountered by the therapist attempting to form a relationship with the patient. Mr A made an image (Figure 8.1), and spoke about it as follows:

Figure 8.1

'*Maybe it's a shell for some sort of creature. Something that needs protection from its enemies. Its enemies are trying to devour it all the time. Thousands of enemies, everywhere. Risks, dangers. If anything tries to come in this way, it can get out that way. I suppose life is very simple for it. Without the shell there would be nothing, a blob. Maybe it would melt into nothingness if it left the shell. Maybe it's worried about its relationships. Maybe it can survive some of the time without it, but not all the time. Maybe it's a decoy. The enemies could be surrounding it and watching it, thinking the blob is inside, when all the time the blob could be watching them from under a stone. It probably found some way of building the shell itself, but, by now, the blob is getting very lonely and confused ... It can't get close to other blobs because it may eat them by mistake in the gloom and darkness of the shell ... Is the blob very clever, or a fool? It receives what it needs to eat materially but not emotionally. It is very alone.*'

My understanding of the image, and of the meaning with which it was invested, only became possible after Mr A's capacity to differentiate the concrete from the symbolic, to make use of symbols, and to use symbolic language in conversation with me had developed within the relationship. The session in which this took place was approximately four years into his therapy. This metaphor evokes experience of the psychic situation we encountered in his earlier state of schizophrenic regression.

In this state, consciousness of feelings and sensations, memory, attention, judgement, and thought, all of which form links to inner and outer reality, is foreclosed. Links to reality, which are experienced by the 'blob', are experiences of what Bion (1963) describes as 'catastrophe'. In the absence of functions which can transform the experience of catastrophe into meaningful events, experienced as occurring within a frame of reference, these contacts with reality are felt to threaten the psyche with destruction.

These functions, which evolve in the early infant–mother relationship, are those which I understand Bion (1963) to mean by the word 'containing'. The early mother is a source of meaning, a matrix of living thought, feeling, and sensation, offering her baby a frame of reference for raw experience. The baby lives in a world of experience in which affects, images, sensations and perceptions are fused. The quality of this experience is described by Bion as 'catastrophic', in that it is pervaded by the fear of dying.

The mother's psyche is open to receive the signs of catastrophe which her baby emits and her reverie is an act of 'faith' (Bion 1970) which contains these unthinkable experiences and transforms them into meaningful events which can be received and assimilated by the baby. Faith, as I understand it, is a sense of continuity of being which is experienced in the realm of feeling. Eigen (1985, p.328) suggests in his discussion of Bion's work that it is a form of mindlessness which can meet the mindlessness of catastrophe and foster the birth of meaning.

Eigen says, 'Over and over the baby dies out and is reborn' (p.329) in this exchange between mother and baby. The baby receives and assimilates both the transformed experience and the function which transforms, developing faith, a sense of continuity of being which persists through catastrophe. The baby becomes increasingly able to think for himself, to experience experiences without the fear of dying, and to learn from experiences.

Experiences of loss contained in this way foster the evolution of the capacity to symbolise, in which two objects are brought together. The resemblance between the two is manifest while their differences remain unimpaired, forming a third object (Bion 1967). Faith, in the continuity of being which persists through catastrophe, allows those experiences of interplay between falling apart and coming together, tearing apart in order to build anew, which are essential to creative mental activity of all kinds. If experiences of containment are 'good enough', in the sense described by Winnicott (1965), it is possible to risk the encounter with the unknown involved in creative activity.

In the world of schizophrenic regression, the experience of a container is fragile or non-existent. Possibly via experience of an actual mother who was disturbed by the baby's signs of catastrophe, the baby learns that intense experiences destroy the container, and that raw experience returns in a magnified form, increasing his fear of dying. Contact with reality is a catastrophic experience which threatens destruction, and accordingly it is defended against.

In the absence of thinking, both the bad experiences which ensue from contact with reality, and those functions which foster contact with reality, are split by projective processes into minute fragments. These are projected into outer objects, which are felt to have the qualities of the parts of the psyche which are projected into them. Bion (1967) describes these as 'bizarre objects'.

The absent container is experienced as a present world of persecutory objects which terrorise the psyche and strip experience of meaning and feeling, arriving at a state of mindlessness and disconnection. Links to reality are foreclosed, differentiation negated, and thought employed as a defence against contact with reality by a primitive superego operating in the service of the pleasure principle.

The absence is filled by hallucinatory experience and omnipotent phantasies, a made-up reality, which is how we can understand Mr A's 'shell'. The experience of the unknown is eliminated, replaced by an empty knowing which serves to ward off persecution. Accordingly, the possibility of creativity, which requires sufficient faith to engage in an encounter with the unknown, is foreclosed.

Contact with reality, mediated, as it were, by the 'blob', is masked by the dominance of omnipotent phantasy intended to destroy awareness of reality, seeking a state which is neither alive nor dead. This phantasy is a fact to the patient, and my experience is that most images made, and words spoken, in the early stages of working with acute schizophrenic patients, are signs of, and indeed part of the fabric of, this 'shell'.

SIGNS OF MEANINGLESSNESS IN ART THERAPY

The patient's relation to reality is what Searles describes as 'desymbolised'. The links and linking functions which make symbolisation possible are attacked by splitting and projective processes, as are the functions of differentiation and articulation. The patient lives in a world of the 'bizarre objects' described by Bion, neither truly concrete nor truly symbolic. The images made in art therapy, if images are made at all, form part of the attack on reality.

Although the images produced in art therapy can appear rich in symbolic meaning to the therapist, I think they are often what Eigen (1985) describes as 'signs of meaninglessness' (p.325), the end products of a disintegrated capacity to think. As he says in his paper discussing the work of Bion,

'What passes for symbol may be an elemental sign of distress and horror. The psychotic patient signals rather than symbolises his ongoing sense of catastrophe. The materials he uses may resemble symbols but they are used to point to an unnameable psychic reality.' (p.323)

In order to convey something of the quality of this experience as it is encountered by the art therapist, I will share some material from an early session with a patient, to whom I will refer as Mr B. He showed me this image, (Figure 8.2) and this is some of what he said in relation to it:

Figure 8.2

'*That's a train which runs with a bomb on it from King's Cross to Manchester, and then to Liverpool, which is the future sort of train, and it's going to travel at 70 mph. It's going to be quite cheap, but I don't know how much it will cost because I haven't designed it. Maybe I should design it ... British Rail is run by the Germans. Maybe one day I'll drive the Penzance to Paddington train if Sir Peter Parker allows. Therefore this train should be utterly destroyed in the year 1999 ... Maybe to drive the Euston to Glasgow would be better because I've read more about it. That's King's Cross and that's Victoria ... and quite frankly if that's what King's Cross looks like I don't want to know it ... This Ramsgate to Victoria freak, it doesn't exist ... That train is the sort of train that goes from somewhere in Cornwall to somewhere in London. The head code is dubbed and that doesn't exist.*'

While recognising the meaningless state of affairs which this communicated, I needed to keep in mind that there was, as it were, a 'blob' somewhere, who put in fleeting appearances, and with whom I hoped to engage in a conversation. I am not sure how to think of the nature of the 'blob' but I find ideas of 'soul' and 'self' coming to mind, a core of personhood which persists, even if ego is laid to waste and the sense of personhood destroyed.

I would like to explore the idea that this defensive use of visual image-making can change over time into an area of evolving meaning and mindfulness within the therapeutic relationship. I will now discuss the value of the realm of experience offered by the concreteness of art-making processes available within the art therapy setting, which can form a transitional, or intermediary, area of thinking for the patient in relation to the living presence of a therapist. The pre-verbal thinking functions involved in the creative use of visual image-making can contain and transform the raw material of experience within the therapeutic relationship, paving the way of symbolisation, and the experience of relatedness to the therapist can foster the possibility of a symbolic relation to the images.

The potential for this intermediary role of image-making needs to be actively established in relationships with schizophrenic patients, for whom the faith which might enable an experience of the unknown to be lived through is missing. It is this containing experience, fostering the patient's sense of continuity of being which can survive and learn from the apparently catastrophic, that I think is significant in all psychotherapeutic approaches to psychotic processes. I will now introduce the form that this containing experience can take in the art therapy setting.

THE ART THERAPY SETTING

Within the approach which evolved in my work at Hill End, in-patients would usually attend the art therapy department for at least five two-hour sessions per week, many attending for ten sessions. Of these, one hour would be allocated to an individual interview with a therapist in an individual therapy room. The rest would be spent within the main room of the department, a large space with tables, chairs, art materials, facilities for tea and coffee making and for playing music, and access to grounds full of trees, lawns and flower beds.

Although the patient would meet weekly with his or her therapist in a setting more akin to the setting of the psychotherapeutic relationship, the therapist would be in relation to the patient throughout his or her attendance in the department. The rules and boundaries structuring the concrete availability and use of space, time, equipment and materials, as well as of the person of the therapist, form points of contact with the reality which psychotic processes attack.

My experience is that the rules and boundaries which form the structure of the setting can foster the experience of containment for the patient. The patient often relates to the structure, as communicated by the therapist, as if it were a persecutory, demanding object. There is a mismatch between the omnipotent demands of the 'shell-like' psychotic personality which attempts to enact its project concretely within the setting, and the availability of that which is demanded. Any and every limit on space, time, materials, or the availability of the therapist, is powerfully overruled.

Each occasion of mismatch offers a point of contact between therapist and patient, in which reality can be offered to the patient in 'bite-size' assimilable pieces. The therapist can point out as simply as possible the discrepancy between the demand and the structure representing reality, being careful to avoid falling into the persecutory role of attempting to force the patient to comply, and, rather, encouraging the patient to engage in conversation about why the structure is the way it is, what it is that is required, and what compromises might be possible.

This kind of conversation offers an encounter with the living mind and presence of the therapist, who, as such, is part of the reality which the patient so fears. In the beginning, these conversations are usually powerfully defended against, but over time they can develop. They exert a continuous invitation to the 'blob' to engage in a different experience of containment, while side-stepping the efforts of the 'shell' to turn the therapist into another part of the made up world.

A third patient, Mr C, spent his first two weeks of full-time attendance in art therapy attempting to enact an omnipotent project which I do not have time to describe. His project demanded limitless access to the setting and use of its contents, and we had many conversations of the kind I have described. In the third week of his attendance he began to relate differently to the structure, and to myself as a representative of the reality he feared so deeply. He began to ask me where various lost possessions of his were, as if I might be able to find the things he had lost. One day he added a comment:

  'I keep losing things.'

I felt this statement had great significance. The fact that he was speaking about himself as an embodied being in relation to me formed a connection between us. I felt the 'blob' had made a fleeting appearance, and there was a moment of emotional contact between us in which his distress was experienced. His words implied a wish to find and keep things, and he was beginning to relate to me as a potential finder of lost things, which suggested an experience of a possible container. At this point I was able to acknowledge his experience and to share with him the meaning which the rules and boundaries had for me.

BENIGN AND MALIGNANT REGRESSION

The structure of the art therapy setting fosters the patient's encounter with art materials. This encounter, although initially serving the purpose of the attack on reality, seems over time, by virtue of its concreteness, to grow into an area of meaning for the patient. Mr C, who initially disowned every image he made, claiming that he was dead and that gods and spirits had merely used his body to perform their acts in the mortal world, acknowledged that, whoever owned his mind and controlled his body, his body had concretely made the image of a plasticine head, which was his first action on attending art therapy. This head was periodically beaten to a pulp and reformed over the course of several years in art therapy. Over time, his relationship to the object changed.

Initially it was a 'bizarre object', experienced as alien and threatening to him. then it was equated with a girlfriend, an actual person, from whom he had separated immediately before his admission. Later it represented his own head, and I think that its concreteness as an object which had persisted over time, and over the varying relationships which he had had with it, both mental and physical, enabled him to learn from it about his continuity in relation to it. This was later expressed to me in a session:

> *'It's just the head, no neck or anything … I felt it was me as a kind of monster, dying in my sleep. It wrecked my life … It's about a crisis in my life and how I coped with it at the time.'*

Eigen (1985) suggests that the psychotic patient 'has the possibility of meaning something by noting the nothing he tries to create' (p.323). He suggests that hallucinatory experience can evolve from its point of origin into symbolising activity if the mindlessness of catastrophe is met by the mindlessness of faith. I think that the encounter with art materials can be a ground for this meeting. The act of making an image, if it is creative, offers an experience of 'benign' regression, regression in the service of ego. The very objects and materials used initially in the service of malignant regression can foster a shift in the quality of the regression itself.

I need to mention at this stage that some patients produced large quantities of visual material, and others none at all. Their engagement in art therapy was not contingent on the production of visual material. The patient's involvement with his or her image-making was treated as a private affair. The table given to the patient formed his or her inviolable territory within the relationship with the therapist, corresponding to the privacy of the core of the self from which new material may evolve.

At this point I will return to Mr A, who made the 'Shell/Blob' image. At the time of his referral to art therapy he was under a compulsory Order of the Mental Health Act, and had been diagnosed as suffering from paranoid schizophrenia. The meaning of his speech and actions was hard to understand at first and became understandable only later, after a relationship within which his experience could be communicated had developed.

To summarise in retrospect, he believed that his sexual organs had been irreparably damaged when he was 11 years old, and, shortly before admission, he began to develop the belief that his body was changing into a female body. He also believed that everyone knew about the condition of his body, and that he was a subject of ridicule by the media, who were pursuing him. He heard daily derogatory reports on the state of his body on radio and television, and read similar accounts in the newspapers.

Initially he attempted to defend against the reality I constituted by attempting to make me a part of this made up world. I was either on his side or on the side of the persecutors, and he required that I give him evidence of my allegiance by fulfilling his every demand. There were fleeting moments of contact interspersed with his demands, in which he voiced a need for 'help'. I attempted to maintain this connection by simply reiterating that I needed to keep an open mind about what kind of help would be truly useful to him until we had understood his situation, and that I hoped he would work with me on this.

He would repeatedly invite me over to his table to engage in this conversation, often with a space of only a few minutes between one conversation and another. He seemed to be inviting me to invade his private space. In order to set limits to this, I would add that this time and space was his to use privately for himself, and that we would meet together at the time of our next session. I felt it would be best if he waited until then to speak to me because I could give him my full attention. I suggested that he could write down his thoughts in between in a private notebook, which I gave to him.

Once he had begun to accept the existence of his space and had learned by repetition that I was related to this space in a particular way, and that this relationship included my separateness from it, all of which took a few days, he arrived one day with two bulging carrier bags, which he placed on the table. Laughing, he asked me for four coffee tins. I felt a strong pull of curiosity at this point. What was in the bags? Why did he want coffee tins? At the same time I recognised the importance of this transaction, in that he was testing out the validity of what we had established in our conversation. His laugh seemed to express his sense of imminent betrayal. I gave him the coffee tins.

As I went about my business, trying to contain my curiosity, he proceeded to fill the coffee tins with water, and placed the legs of his table in them. He then unpacked his bags on to the table, placing a selection of fruit, vegetables and a small collection of objects in a careful arrangement. He later told me that he had to ensure that the space would be safe from invasion by ants before he could place valuable objects within it.

I think of this as an example of a learning experience within the therapy setting. Mr A was able to use the structure to enact his project. His relation to the objects was neither truly concrete, nor truly symbolic. The objects were equated with parts of himself. He went on to paint a succession of images of the objects, of which Figures 8.3 and 8.4 are examples. These were, in my opinion, concrete attempts by Mr C to keep alive the parts of himself which he had invested in the objects. It was some time before the repetition of this motif of meaninglessness shifted to a creative involvement with visual imagery.

Figure 8.3

THERAPEUTIC APPROACH

I will now describe some principles of approach which evolved in my efforts to find a way of relating to the images produced by acutely psychotic patients in the art therapy setting in order to foster the growth of symbolisation.

I think it is important to bear in mind that the patient in a psychiatric setting has often not chosen to work on him- or herself. An important stage of work in art therapy is reached when the patient is able to relate interpersonally to the therapist to the extent necessary to choose whether or not to continue. The approach I describe refers to work that takes place before that stage is reached.

Each patient was given a folder in which two-dimensional images could be kept. The folder formed part of the weekly session with the therapist, regardless of whether it contained images or not. The patient chose what to place in the folder, and might place images outside it. Images, such as Mr C's plasticine head, could be placed out of the therapist's sight, on walls, windowsills, or in other

Figure 8.4

spaces. This allowed the image, and its potential meaning, to remain encapsulated within the setting in a different relation to the therapist.

Once the patient and the folder were in the individual therapy room, the therapist communicated as simply and as clearly as possible that this is a time and a space in which the possibility exists of sharing and trying to understand experiences together, and that the therapist is interested in the patient's images, because she thinks that they can contribute to this. However, what is shared, when it is shared, and how it is shared is the choice of the patient. All that the therapist asks of the patient is that he or she attend the session with the folder for one hour per week.

The individual session was a space in which the patient could experiment with varying experiences of connection with the therapist, and which gave the images a meaning in this context of relationship. I have found that the 'blob', which expresses itself in the patient's continuing presence in the setting, and in fleeting moments of contact of the kind I have described, often gradually accepts this invitation by the therapist to join the proceedings, and begins to employ what thinking is available to convey experience to the therapist.

Bion (1967) writes that the recovering psychotic personality's attempts to think involve the use of pre-verbal modes which have suffered splitting and projective identification. They have to be brought back by the same route as they were expelled, a kind of 'projective identification in reverse' which is a '*tour de force*' on the part of the patient (pp.61–62). Initially the effort to speak involves what he describes as an 'agglomeration' of objects, which is a precursor of the possibility of two objects coming together to form a symbol. This agglomeration can successfully convey meaning if the patient wishes to do so.

It is possible that the making of visual imagery can assist in this process of reconstituting thinking. It can give form to emotional experience, enabling the patient to develop an increasingly metaphorical language to assist him or her in the effort to convey experience. The therapist attempts to develop a conversation with the patient in which this effort is encouraged, but not demanded.

Mr A initially delivered whispered lectures to me concerning the formal aesthetic qualities of his paintings. I interrupted him to offer to write down what he was saying, in order that what he was saying about his paintings could be kept with them. This introduced an element of conversation into the sessions. I would read back what I had written and ask him if I had got it right. He would edit my words and when we had finished we attached the paper with the writing on it to his paintings.

He gradually began to play with this experience of another person, and to experiment with different ways of speaking in relation to me. He began to differentiate between statements that he described as 'stories', which he asked me to write down, and those which were addressed directly to me, and he could alter my relationship to him within the session at will. He gradually began to invest his statements with feeling, to which I could respond with nods, grunts and 'hmms', and, in time, with mirroring comments in between writing down his words and reading them back.

I tried to contain my own interest in what was meaningful to me in his images, in what he said about them, and the way he said things, as well as my own feelings of isolation and despair at feeling so unconnected with him at times, in order to allow him to explore the relationship in this way. Searles (1962, p.578) writes of this sense of isolation as an experience within the countertransference of the child who becomes schizophrenic, surrounded by others for whom her experience has no meaning.

At the same time Mr A's images became more differentiated, and he began to invest them with different qualities of meaning. He learned that they could be used to convey meanings to me. We began to develop a conversation about how he made his images, and in the course of this it emerged that he was terrified of clay and plasticine. For him the use of these materials would represent a step into the unknown. This was terrifying for him. He feared 'going mad' – having no sense of a container for an experience of this kind, and together we tried to find words to describe the quality of his terror.

One day he brought two plasticine objects into the session (Figure 8.5). He asked me to write down the following:

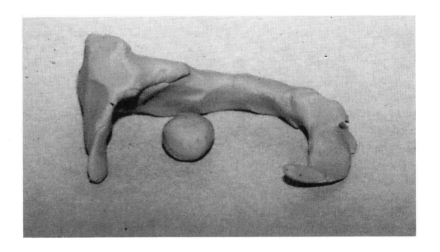

Figure 8.5

'*This was done some time ago. It is a shell like object. I did this when I was unhappy, and didn't plan what it was going to be ... It could be a sea creature ... I think the round ball goes with it, enclosed within the shell-like object like a pearl within an oyster ... The round ball and the object aren't connected and can be separated ... Maybe I have feelings about my college ... I was both happy and unhappy there ... The warmth of people. I want to meet people. I want human experience ... Recently I've felt a passion for life. I don't feel it at the moment. At the moment I feel a bit like exposed flesh. It stings. There is a lot of pain at the moment, and tiredness.*'

He went on to tell me that he had not planned what he was going to say, either. This was a new experience for him, and he had to feel ready to risk this before bringing the image in to the session, hence the delay between making the image and showing it to me. It seemed to me that he had developed sufficient faith to allow himself to think and to feel in my presence. Searles (1962) suggests that 'Awareness of emotion is the father to metaphorical thought'. As the ability to experience emotions which are defended against by defensive instability of ego boundaries increases, reliably firm ego boundaries develop, and accordingly, the thinking which they make possible.

Mr A went on to develop this capacity for play, outside and inside the sessions, and shortly afterwards the 'Shell/Blob' image emerged, as a metaphor which he was able to use as a metaphor to convey his experience to me. At this point he was able to reflect with me on his earlier experience.

When the patient acknowledges the fact of relationship between him- or herself and the therapist to the therapist, the therapist is, as it were, 'allowed' to exist without the mobilisation of psychotic defences. Therapeutic relationships of a kind which allow the therapist, at least some of the time, to exist as a living mind in the conversation, become a possibility. Accordingly, the issue of continuing therapy can be discussed because there is now 'somebody' there with whom to discuss it.

The patient can be assessed for psychotherapeutic work in which transference phenomena can be addressed by interpretation, which requires some acknowledgement of a relationship between persons in order for a therapeutic alliance to be a possibility. At this stage the patient can begin to work in analytical art psychotherapy as described by Schaverien (1992), or can be referred out of the art therapy setting for psychotherapy or analysis.

REFERENCES

Bion, W.R. (1963) *Elements of Psycho-Analysis.* London: Heinemann (republished 1984, 1989. London: Karnac).

Bion, W.R. (1967) *Second Thoughts.* London: Heinemann (Republished 1984, 1987, 1990. London: Karnac).

Bion, W.R. (1970) *Attention and Interpretation.* London: Karnac (republished 1984, 1988).

Case, C. and Dalley, T. (1992) *The Handbook of Art Therapy.* London: Routledge.

Eigen, M. (1985) 'Towards Bion's starting point: between catastrophe and faith'. *International Journal of Psycho-analysis 66,* 321–330.

Killick, K. (1987) 'Art Therapy and Schizophrenia' (unpublished M.A. thesis). University of Hertfordshire.

Killick, K. (1991) 'The practice of art therapy with patients in acute psychotic states'. *Inscape* (Winter), 2–6.

Schaverien, J. (1992) *The Revealing Image.* London: Routledge.

Searles, H.F. (1962) 'The differentiation between concrete and metaphorical thinking in the recovering schizophrenic patient'. In H.F. Searles (ed) *Collected Papers on Schizophrenia and Related Subjects.* London: Karnac (1986).

Segal, H. (1991) *Dream, Phantasy and Art.* London: Routledge.

Winnicott, D. (1965) *The Maturational Processes and the Facilitating Environment.* London: Karnac (republished 1990).

Winnicott, D. (1974) *Playing and Reality.* London: Pelican.

CHAPTER 9

Psychotic Interventions at the Arbours Crisis Centre

Joseph H. Berke

'Psychotic interventions' is an ambiguous term, but I use it deliberately. It can refer to therapeutic interventions done on behalf of individuals who are suffering or have previously suffered psychotic breakdowns, and it can refer to the actions of people, often designated as 'patients', who are going through the process of breaking down. Equally relevant, the term can point out the reaction of a human environment, the family or milieu that was supposed to be of help, but could not and did not help. The milieu is a vessel, a container which can no longer contain terrible pain, confused thinking or angry outbursts. In other words, I am considering the situation when the therapists or institution have collapsed, even if only for a temporary period: this chapter is therefore about breakdowns on the part of both parties, those needing help and those giving it; and it is about the means by which these same two sides are able to reconstitute themselves.

I shall focus on events at the Arbours Crisis Centre, a unique facility in North London established in 1973. There, three therapists and six individuals or families in acute distress live together in a large Victorian house. We call the people who seek help at the centre 'guests', both to describe their role in the house and to avoid problems of stigmatisation.

At the Centre there are three separate but interrelated and interrelating therapeutic systems: the *team*, the *group* and the *milieu*. The team consists of a guest, a resident therapist (one of the therapists who live at the Centre, the RT), a team leader (a visiting psychotherapist, the TL) and perhaps an Arbours trainee. It meets three to five times a week. The group consists of everyone who lives at the house, resident therapists and guests, and encompasses four formal house meetings per week. The milieu is the Centre as an active therapeutic environment. Perhaps active interpersonal environment is more correct, since the milieu can also be non-therapeutic or even anti-therapeutic, depending on, as we shall see, who is at the Centre and what is going on. It includes three resident therapists, six guests, nine team leaders and everyone else directly involved with the Centre. Various combinations of these therapists frequently meet with each other in order to help recognise, experience and tolerate the powerful emotional currents that flow through the house. Essentially we emphasise the role of countertransference in coping with guests who are often verbally inarticulate.[1]

In order to illustrate the diverse implications of 'psychotic interventions', I will focus on the role of the milieu as the healing or damaging agent when working with a very disturbed and disturbing person. Specifically, I want to tell the story of 'Hamid', a large man in his early twenties, whose family originally came from the Middle East. Hamid had a good intellect and did well at school. However, as he approached university age, he began to bully his parents and younger sister, and make rude sexual overtures to women both inside and outside his home.

Hamid was first admitted to hospital in his late teens because of severe aggressive outbursts. He seemed to seek out weak and vulnerable women and terrorise them. At his worst he appeared to be totally out of touch with reality and his behaviour was nearly uncontainable. He was referred to the Centre because hospitalisation did not help. After the usual medications and restraint, he remained the same incorrigible human being, but with the added burden of being diagnosed as schizophrenic.

Hamid came to the Centre for a three month period, what we call a medium-length stay. At first he was very demanding and wildly abusive. He soaked up huge amounts of food, especially milk and sugar, while refusing to sit for any meals. His great delight was to make a huge mess in the kitchen. In the house he took on the role of overbearing potentate. All the women were his playthings or prey; in return they hated him. But when confronted he would deny what he had done and shout abuse. Generally, he was extremely negative about the Centre, and usually refused to go to house meetings. But he did attend his team meetings fairly regularly.

As his stay progressed he gradually calmed down and became more sociable. He surprised everyone with a keen sense of humour and a capacity for clear thinking. People began to see him as a bad boy, rather than a mad boy. Certainly he tried everyone's patience to the limit, so much so, that on a few occasions he was asked to go home for a day or two so the house could cool down. Towards the end of his stay, Hamid showed sustained periods of sadness and could be intellectually impressive, engaging residents in long discussions about politics or philosophy. But these reflective periods were often interrupted by angry, impulsive, demanding outbursts. Hamid's accomplishments seemed in danger of being

---

1   I have discussed these three therapeutic systems and how they operate in much greater detail in my paper, 'Conjoint Therapy within a Therapeutic Milieu: The Crisis Team' (Berke 1990).

lost. He had reverted back to being chaotic and unbearable. Both the resident therapists and other guests were at their wit's end, in outrage and despair. This was a turning point. Hamid had begun his 'leaving crisis'.

What do I mean by the expression 'leaving crisis'? In a previous paper (Berke 1987), I have explained that all guests pass through five distinct crises or stages while they are at the Centre, regardless of their reasons for coming. These stages can be compared to five states of mind and greatly influence the feelings and actions of the guests while they are at the Centre. They are *arriving, settling in, settling down, leaving* and *following-up*.[2]

The fourth stage, *leaving*, invariably precipitates a fresh crisis because leaving necessarily arouses ambivalence, sadness and depressive feelings which may seem too strong to bear. To avoid the experience, many guests try to repeat their original breakdown. This was certainly the case with Hamid.

Everything seemed to blow up before his leaving date. Over the previous week he had become increasingly angry and abusive, and tempers were at boiling point among the therapists and other guests. Then, in mid-week, the house itself seemed to respond in kind, because the sinks suddenly blocked up with a black, foul-smelling liquid. The same morning we had our twice-yearly medical inspection. There was a frantic rush to get the sinks unblocked, which the RTs accomplished just before the inspector, a very pleasant, elderly doctor arrived. She had been to the Centre many times before and always enjoyed a quiet, relaxed visit. As she had entered the kitchen for a cup of tea, Hamid suddenly brushed past her, screaming: 'Get out of the way you fucking old bag.' Everyone was appalled and one of the guests, 'Katie', started to cry. Even the RTs were shaking, but the doctor was not the least fazed. She calmly commented, 'You know, it really is exciting to have a taste of real life!'

The inspection being over, the RTs began to prepare for a reception in the evening. Every other month the Arbours sponsors a public lecture. Afterwards, the lecturer and invited guests and therapists return to the Centre for refreshments and further discussion. So, having set out the food and drink in the front room, they specifically asked Hamid not to touch the stuff. Well, this was like a red rag

---

2   I have described these stages in my paper, 'Arriving, settling-in, settling-down, leaving and following-up: Stages of Stay at the Arbours Centre' (Berke 1987).

   The stages have a separate, objective existence. This has been demonstrated by the fact that they occur in other, different facilities as well as the Centre. Most notably, this paradigm has been confirmed by colleagues at the Mount Sinai Hospital in Toronto, Canada. In a paper on the intensive treatment of borderline patients they delineate stages which are practically identical to the ones I have described (Silver, Cardish and Glassman, 1987). They describe these stages as follows: one -- *Assessment* or the *Honeymoon*; two -- *Therapeutic Encirclement* or *Symptomatic*; three -- *Therapeutic Engagement* or *Working Through*; and four -- *Discharge--Liaison* or *Separation/Re-entry*. Although the Toronto group does not specify a follow-up stage, they do refer to the period 'following discharge', when patients like to return to the ward.

to a bull. Upon getting back to the Centre after the lecture, they found that he had not only eaten a lot of the food, but had been bullying the female guests.

Hamid saw the RTs and tried to be jolly: 'George, George, did you have a nice evening?' They were furious; for them, gobbling the food was the straw that broke the camel's back. Once again, Hamid had broken all boundaries, and they were left in complete chaos. All they wanted was for him to go, immediately. They called his team leader and told him what had happened, that Hamid had been warned and had to go. The RTs feared that if they backed down and he didn't leave, they would lose face and appear like Hamid's father, waffling and indecisive. Without further ado, the team leader concurred and suggested they call the father to come and collect him.

While they were about to carry this out, the RTs saw that I had just come back from the lecture and was about to sit down and talk with our visitors. Before I could do so, they pounced on me and insisted that I retreat with them to the rear consulting room to discuss Hamid. I excused myself and joined a group of very angry therapists. At this point I myself felt quite menaced, for I could see that they would not take no for an answer:

'Hamid's been on the rampage. He's eaten the food and hit another guest. He's been warned several times. He has to go.'

Nervously, I said, 'Umm, I can see that you have tried and sentenced him. It seems that I'm to act as your executioner.'

In the meantime I realised that no one was able to think. The situation was crazy. The RTs had collectively reverted to concrete, or beta, functioning.[3] Hamid had become their 'dreaded object', and as far as they were concerned, their sanity, or at least peace of mind, depended on my getting rid of him.

While all this was happening, I remembered a similar incident that had happened several years before. The Norwegian government had referred a young woman to the Centre with a long history – I would say reputation – of autism and schizophrenia. She was a huge person and very aggressive. If she had lived a thousand years previously, she could easily have been a Viking, raping and pillaging the north of England. In fact the referral was so unusual that we decided that a main motive had been simply to get her out of Norway. Anyway, Ingrid had been at the Centre for several months and had just begun to form ties with the residents settle down. One late afternoon I was called to the Centre by a nearly incoherent RT. 'Ingrid has thrown a chair at me for the last time. Either she goes or I go.'

---

3   I refer to a reversion to psychotic thinking processes, and the use of what Wilfred Bion (1977, p.6) has termed, 'beta elements'. These are indigestible bits, 'concrete sense impressions', 'influential in acting out', thought objects, 'felt to be things in themselves as if to substitute such manipulation for words or ideas'.

In fact Ingrid had also been upset by someone's leaving. so she responded with violence, the one way she knew that would destroy her nascent feelings of sadness and depression. In reality, what she had done was not much different from previous episodes, and I thought that once I came over and spoke with people, it would blow over. However, it didn't; the RT was adamant; either Ingrid left, or he did. In desperation I called my colleague, Dr Morty Schatzman, a co-founder of the Arbours, to come over and help me out. He too argued with the RT, while Ingrid was storming around in the garden, but to no avail.

Several hours passed. The atmosphere remained explosive. Morty and I realised that neither gentle persuasion nor harsh facts would work, so we told the RT to stay and said we would take Ingrid to the emergency room of a nearby hospital, the Royal Free, for a shot of Largactil and, we hoped, a bed for the night. We did not know and could not think what else to do. By then we were tired and desperate and Ingrid was still storming, so we went to the Royal Free. By the time we arrived, Ingrid had begun to calm down, but we were extremely anxious, so much so that I was prepared to do something I rarely do, revert to tranquillisers and hospitalisation.

In the emergency room Ingrid insisted that I buy her endless cups of coffee and cigarettes. 'Anything to shut her up,' I mused. 'This whole thing is nuts.' Finally the duty psychiatrist, a tiny, young Asian lady, came out for Ingrid. Quick as a wink I pounced on her, yelled a potted history and insisted on what I wanted her to do. She looked up and curtly reminded me that she was the doctor in charge and would not decide anything till she had seen the patient.

Another half-hour passed. Morty and I felt our agitation level rise to new heights. Then the doctor came out. I was just beginning to feel relieved that we could go home when I heard the hideous news: 'This person can go home. She doesn't need any medication.' 'What!' I roared. 'You can't do that. Look how upset and violent she is.'

While this was going on Ingrid came out and calmly sat on a chair, smoking a cigarette. The doctor pointed out that she was perfectly calm and did not need treatment. I was dumbfounded, but then a smile crossed my lips. The doctor and I had exchanged roles. I had called Ingrid a dangerous schizophrenic: the doctor saw her as a tired, if slightly confused, young woman. I was arguing for drugs: she was arguing against drugs. I wanted hospitalisation: she said it was not necessary. And not only had I changed roles with the doctor, I had exchanged roles with Ingrid. She was calm and quiet: I was raging like a maniac. The irony was not lost on Morty or myself. With that we began to calm down. Morty volunteered, 'Listen, it's two-thirty. I'll take Ingrid back to my house for the night. A good night's sleep will do us all good.' I readily concurred, and that is how the crisis ended. In fact, Ingrid did not go back to the Centre; she stayed as Morty's guest for a few days and then we found her a small flat of her own. She had never lived in her own flat before.

This whole episode flashed through my mind while I was trying to think how to handle Hamid and the RTs. One decision came quickly. Whatever was going to happen, I did not intend to become the knight in shining armour, the all-powerful father who provided omnipotent solutions for his regressed children. I also realised, however, that far from playing the omnipotent father, the RTs had allowed me little room to manoeuvre. They clearly wanted me to become the impotent father who had to do their bidding. Surely, this was their sadistic revenge for my having inflicted 'him' on them in the first place and for having caused them so much psychic pain.

Angrily, 'Well, what are you going to do? We can't spend another night with Hamid in the state he's in.'

Again, I was taken aback by the extreme hostility, but now I wanted to avoid appearing omnipotent or getting sucked in further.

'Well,' I said, hanging my head for effect, 'I don't know. I don't know what to do.' In reality, I was trying to buy time so that we could all begin to think. 'Let me see; you know, we do have other options. I know we can get rid of him. Indeed, that's one option. Let's see if there are any others. Right now I recall my friend Ross Speck.[4] He used to work with large families with one or more very disturbed members. He'd call them the designated patients. Could it be that is the case with Hamid? Could he be our designated patient, the carrier of all our craziness?'

There were murmurs of annoyance at my comments.

'What Ross used to do when the large family group threatened to fragment and expel a member, was to expand the group: bring in more members, distant relatives, neighbours, even relative strangers. The point was to get people who could think to join the group. Maybe we can do that by carrying the discussion to the reception. Let's ask our visitors what they would do. Let's ask everyone else in the house, too.'

There were more murmurs at this, but at least the proposal wasn't rejected out of hand.

'You know, we could also ask Hamid to join us. Perhaps he might come up with something himself.'

At that moment, as if on cue, Hamid came into the back room and looked at me somewhat plaintively.

I said, 'Hamid, I feel very sad and upset about the situation.' (I *did* feel this way, but I was also being deliberately vague.)

Hamid, who knew everyone in the house wanted him out, began to shake. He shot off to the kitchen for some milk. Then, back in the room, and before

---

4   Ross Speck and his wife, Joan Speck, worked for many years as family and network therapists in Philadelphia. (See Speck and Attneave 1973.)

anyone could comment he went up to me and exclaimed, 'Don't worry. I'll go to bed.'

With that, he started up the stairs towards his room. It was now half-past ten. Hamid had been quite disarming, and I thought it safe to suggest that we rejoin the reception. I said it would help to think; the RTs agreed.

There were about 20 people there: our speaker, a few of his friends and colleagues, a few Arbours therapists, and the rest from the Crisis Centre. Everyone seemed to want to talk at once, 'What's happening, why weren't you here, where's Hamid?'

I explained what was going on, that we had a big problem, and asked everyone for their suggestions. A few of the guests at the Centre went on the attack. Hamid had to go! 'Look, he hit me today.' 'Why should we put up with that?'

Our lecturer, Dr T, gently inquired, 'Is he on drugs?'

Somewhat flippantly, I retorted, 'Maybe we should all take some drugs, it could help us to calm down.'

The lecturer let a few guffaws pass and continued, 'You say you want him to leave. This is an unusual problem. Where I work, we usually try to get patients to stay, not to leave.'

He was quickly accosted by Katie, a thin young woman who liked to cut her arms and face in order to reduce the tensions in herself. 'How can you say that. Don't you know what I've been through?' Another resident interjected that she had not been able to sleep for days because of Hamid, and the RTs, still angry, joined in.

Dr T continued, 'You know, we could all leave. Leave him alone in the house. But then, where would the RTs go?'

An animated discussion ensued. After a few more minutes, I encouraged Dr T to add to his earlier remarks. First, he asked a few questions. Why did Hamid come to the Centre? How long for? Then Dr T presented his views about schizophrenia and schizophrenics as well as the treatments available, especially medication. People were not very interested and I could see they were shocked by all the medical psychiatric terms he deployed. Then he decided to tell a story. This was a story prefaced by the quip, 'You know, it's often easier to start again than to clean up a big mess.'

The story went: 'In Ireland there lived a mother and two boys. The boys went out one day to play by a bog. One fell in and was quickly pulled under; the other boy ran home to get his mother. She ran back to the bog and saw that her son was about to go under the quicksand. She rushed over and pushed his head under. Her other son was horrified. "Mom, why did you do that?" the mother replied, "Well, since I couldn't save him, I thought I might as well get it over with quick. Then I could start again."'

A stunned silence followed. Then Dr T added, 'In putting the boy back into the *mud*, she was really putting him back into the *mad*, into madness. Perhaps there was nothing more she could do. After all, she didn't have any drugs.'

This seemed to break the mood. I took a glass of wine, and both guests and residents started to tuck into the food and drink. Everyone seemed to be talking at once. There was a jolly, almost hypomanic atmosphere.

Midnight came and Dr T and his friends said they had to go. While I escorted them to the door, another complete change of mood took place. The residents seemed to forget Hamid and focused on Dr T: he had become the whipping boy. Katie got angry with him for advocating drugs; another accused him of being a tool of the establishment; and so on. After midnight, I had to struggle with myself to return to the meeting. I was dead tired and wanted to go home, especially since the Hamid issue was no longer pressing. It had not been settled, though, and I decided to stay as long as necessary to resolve things. In his talk, Dr T had spoken about guilt and forgiveness. I hoped that the anger and guilt which previously had pervaded the house might be replaced by a mellowing of mood and a feeling of forgiveness. Back at the meeting, I sniffed the atmosphere. The frenzied pressure to oust Hamid had gone. People were more uncertain about what to do.

Katie spoke about him, about how he had called her a whore and slag. I queried whether this image might be connected to how he saw himself. An animated discussion about Hamid and sex ensued: how perverted his ideas all seemed. Was he really angry with his sister because she was good-looking? Somehow, the phrase, 'condom soup', slipped in. 'Condom soup'? Sue, a shy black girl who usually tried not to be noticed piped up:

'At last some of the shit is out in the open. Anyway there were times when Hamid was OK with me.'

Another guest at the Centre, Ron, seemed to be falling asleep on a big pillow. But he was awake enough to remark that Hamid reminded him of how nervous he felt at times. In fact, he was usually extremely depressed. Suddenly, I realised that no one was angry with Hamid. People were chatting away about other things. However, in order not to lose the opportunity to conclude 'the problem', the point of the evening, I focused on Hamid again by asking,

'What do you think it feels like to be Hamid? What is it like to be so full of despair and fear and terror?' There was more talk. The meeting turned back to Hamid.

By now it was a quarter past one. I said, 'I think our feelings about Hamid have softened a bit. But I don't think we should just let things hang. You know, when I came over tonight after the lecture, you seemed ready to throw him out. This doesn't seem to be the issue now, but let's go over what we can do, what the options are.'

Almost as if I were reading from a prepared list of possibilities, I started, 'One … Two … Three …':

1. We can get rid of him, immediately, forever.

2. We can get rid of him in the morning after allowing him to stay overnight.

3. We can ask him to leave for the night and come back tomorrow, as we have done before.

4. We can let him stay, but set up a rota for people to stay up with him during the night.

5. We all can stay up and cancel meetings for the next day.

6. We can bring him back into the group, into the meeting right now.

7. We can follow Dr T's advice and use medication. But who should take it and how much. Should Hamid take 100mg Largactil, or the whole group?

8. We can all have a double Scotch.

At this point I interjected that when patients get agitated, their drug is Largactil, but when therapists get upset, their drug is alcohol. Many lively exchanges ensued.

Katie exclaimed, 'I'm against the use of all drugs.'

'OK, then I suggest we all take a glass of milk and honey. Let's give one to Hamid too. Then we can all go up and express our love for Hamid and hug him. I think Hamid's biggest problem is expressing and receiving affection. So, let's all give him some affection.'

Katie shouted as if speaking for the whole group, 'Joe, you give it to him first.'

I replied, 'OK, no problem, but before I do, let's all hold hands.'

In this way, I tried to open a delicate subject, the open expression of affection in and by members of the group as a whole. After all, how could we direct it to Hamid if affection remained blocked among everyone else?

Somewhat reluctantly, everyone stood up and shuffled around in order to form a circle and hold hands. Suddenly, Sonia, the RT, said, 'Let's all hug, holding hands is not enough.'

She then proceeded to hug everyone near her. I was amazed. Sonia is an affectionate, but not a very 'huggy' woman. Sue found all this very difficult and half started to run away. Sensing that she was frightened, and because she was near me, I stopped her and gave her a mild hug. At the same time I could see that the whole group had begun to exchange hugs.

Meanwhile, Ron had left for the kitchen. Like someone green with envy, he started to complain, 'Why is Hamid getting so much attention?'

George had gone to the kitchen to prepare the warm milk and honey. This is a brew which guests often take at night in place of sleeping pills. At my suggestion, and when not inappropriate, we may also add a tablespoon of fine brandy. An important part of this ritual is that the guests see that a very special brandy has been added. In this way they feel special too. The resulting drink has been good-heartedly called the 'Joe Berke special'.

Anyway, George made a point of giving Ron the milk and honey. Back in the front room Katie volunteered to take a drink to Hamid. I proposed, however, that we should ask Hamid to join the meeting. After all, all the hugs and warmth had begun *after* we had focused on helping Hamid to receive and express affection. He had, in a way, got lost, Ron's complaint notwithstanding, during all the recent exchanges of goodwill. So Katie went to invite him down. A few minutes later she returned to the meeting to let us know that he had gone to bed. It appeared that while we all very agitated, Hamid had calmed down and gone to sleep. Once again I was reminded of the story of Ingrid. While Morty and I had become increasingly agitated at the Royal Free emergency room, she had calmed down.

The group again asked me to take some milk and honey to Hamid. I agreed and went upstairs. In fact Hamid was not asleep, just lying quietly on his bed. Hamid took the drink and thanked me in a pleasant, respectful way. He was not agitated and he was not psychotic. By now it was half-past two in the morning, and it seemed that the immediate crisis had passed. No one was suggesting that Hamid had to leave that night; in fact, no one was talking about his having to leave at all. I was very tired and said good night to everyone. In turn they thanked me and allowed me to leave without feeling anxious. But, as I was later told, the evening continued.

After I left, Hamid came downstairs and joined the group of his own accord. Sonia, who previously could not bear to touch him, suggested that they all hug. Hamid demurred, but agreed to hold hands. Ron shook Hamid's hands. Then the rest of the group greeted him and made a place for him. All, including Hamid, helped to clean up. They continued to be huggy. Hamid sported a huge smile. He was amused by the group's affection for him and said playfully, 'You lot are all mad and gay.'

This statement was not a challenge. Rather, it was the harbinger of a calm and pleasant mood which pervaded the house. By the early morning everyone drifted off to bed.

It had been a good night. The group had reconstituted itself. The mad behaviour of Hamid, as well as that of the therapists and other guests, had ceased. Clearly, their psychotic anxieties and thoughts, or rather lack of thinking, had receded too. All of the residents seemed much more able to regain and contain their own feelings.

A couple of days later Hamid had his leaving meal. This is a big event for the guest who is finishing his stay as well as for the whole house. Extra food is prepared, wine is served, candles are lit: it is a real occasion. The celebration reflects work well done, on everyone's part. But completion leads to departure, so that there is usually an air of sadness too. Notably, the Centre may feel flat and empty for days afterwards.

Hamid's leaving meal was by no means certain. He had never previously stayed for dinner at any time during his stay. Yet, on the day after the lecture, when asked whether he wanted to forget the meal and leave early, he replied, 'No way. I can't leave. It's my leaving meal tomorrow.' And indeed he helped plan the dinner and stayed almost to the end. When he did leave, it was uneventful.

DISCUSSION

Both with Hamid and Ingrid, as with other guests at the Centre, psychotic regressions in thinking and behaviour can brew up very quickly. This happens particularly when individuals who are unable to cope with sadness and depression are threatened by loss. To put it another way: catastrophic reactions occur when these same people are threatened by attachment, whether by making friends, or by losing friends. Their capacity to hold depressive tensions is a very poor and primitive defence against these tensions quickly unfolding. I have used the word 'tensions' rather than anxieties. Really, we are talking about a particular state of mind, one touched by sadness, loss, frustration and so on, but unable to contain these experiences. The ensuing chaos, or regressive madness, can engulf not only the person concerned, but also everyone else in their immediate social field.

The result of our intervention with Hamid was that he formed an intense attachment to the Centre, both the guests and therapists. The actual process whereby this happened was painful and difficult. In retrospect, many of his angry outbursts had to do with his trying to reject the relationships which he was trying to establish or had already established. His final blow-up, the fury and reversion to a prior state of extremely provocative behaviour, occurred when his stay at the Centre was coming to an end and he was devastated by feelings of loss.

The situation with Ingrid was different. She was tormented by the nascent process of forming friendships. This was something she had never previously been able to accomplish. Her prior attachments consisted of a primitive symbiotic relationship with her mother or with care-givers in institutionalised care. But I think we underestimated the attachments she did form at the Centre, for, as I previously mentioned, she was clearly upset by another guest's leaving. As with Hamid, her ongoing tumult was an indication that small friendships were being established.

The massive outbursts of Hamid and Ingrid initially provoked similar responses on the part of the Centre. The resident therapists closest to them were overwhelmed by panic, rage and despair. These feelings were so powerful that they could no longer think or act as therapists. Like Hamid and Ingrid they just wanted to get rid of the threat, that is, the presence of Hamid and Ingrid, experienced as frightening monsters. These concrete experiences were the counterpart of the 'dreaded objects' which Hamid and Ingrid faced, sadness and depression. When the therapists called for help, it was not to resolve the problem, but to execute the demons.

It would appear that we acted differently in these two instances. With Hamid we were able to keep him at the Centre and I was able to 'keep my cool'. With Ingrid, however, we could not manage this, and Schatzman and I had to take her out of the Centre. Subsequently I felt overwhelmed by panic too, and could not think.

On closer consideration, the reactions of the Centre, and by that I include myself, were similar on both occasions. In both interventions we acted to expand the group. For Ingrid this included Morty and the duty psychiatrist at the Royal Free Hospital. For Hamid this included Dr T, all the guests at the Centre and all the visitors that accompanied Dr T to the reception. Then we played for time, hoping that it would have an ameliorative effect, which it did. Perhaps most significant in both interventions was that we were able to shift the focus of 'bad object' from the designated patient to another person.

The duty psychiatrist certainly became, for a brief period at least, my 'bad object', the person who refused to take my instructions and frustrated my needs. Dr T served the same function for Hamid by becoming a focus of anger for people at the Centre. They then neglected to be upset with their primary 'bad boy'.

In fact, Dr T is a highly skilled and very experienced dynamic practitioner who is very sympathetic towards the work of the Centre. He also favours psychotherapy as a basic treatment modality for psychotic patients. Certainly, it was unfair to embroil him in an emotional maelstrom: he had just come back for a quiet drink. Nonetheless, when the episode blew up, it was very important for us to involve him and for him to become part of the treatment milieu. Dr T, as did the duty psychiatrist, served commendably in the role of surrogate ego, as well as surrogate demon, and in so doing, helped us all to think again.[5]

Essentially, both disturbances were ameliorated by a therapeutic milieu which initially had been overwhelmed by chaotic currents and was later able to reconstitute itself. The result was a strictly limited breakdown, contained by the willingness of the therapists involved to suffer, and by their capacity to ask for help and regain their thinking processes. This enabled the therapists as well as Hamid, Ingrid and all the guests at the Centre to discover and rediscover their sanity and humanity.

---

5   In fact we used an array of auxillary egos: myself to the RTs, Morty to me (and the RTs), the duty psychiatrist to Morty and myself, Dr T to the centre, in order to defuse the psychotic regressions into which we had been drawn.

SUMMARY

During the course of a therapeutic intervention, both the designated patient and the therapists(s) treating this person may emotionally decompensate and revert to a psychotic state of thinking and action. This chapter discusses two such events and shows how they were ameliorated by a therapeutic milieu in which the people involved were initially overwhelmed by these psychotic regressions and were subsequently able to reconstitute themselves.

ACKNOWLEDGEMENTS

I would like to express my appreciate to Sonia Whittle, Lois Elliot and George Pearce who were the resident therapists at the Arbours Centre when Hamid was there. I am grateful to them for all the mental pain they endured and for the resilience they demonstrated during the intervention with Hamid. I am also grateful for their helping me in the writing of this paper.

I would further like to thank my colleague, Dr Morton Schatzman, for his help with Ingrid.

Finally I would like to express my appreciation to Dr T for the valuable contribution that he made during the course of the evening.

REFERENCES

Berke, J. (1987) 'Arriving, settling-in, settling-down, leaving and following-up: Stages of stay at the Arbours Centre.' In *British Journal of Medical Psychology 60*, 18–88.

Berke, J. (1990) 'Conjoint therapy within a therapeutic milieu: The Crisis Team.' In *International Journal of Therapeutic Communities 11*, 237–248.

Bion, W.R. (1977) *Learning from Experience*. Reprinted in *Seven Servants: Four Works of Wilfred R. Bion*. New York: Jason Aronson.

Silver, D., Cardish, R. and Glassman, E. (1987) 'Intensive treatment of characterologically difficult patients.' In *Psychiatric Clinic of North America 10*, 219–245.

Speck, R.V. and Attneave, C.L. (1973) *Family Networks*. New York: Pantheon Books.

CHAPTER 10

Breaking and Entering in Phantasy and Fact

Christopher Cordess

INTRODUCTION

This chapter springs from my dual interests and professional experience both as a psychoanalyst working with a range of neurotic and borderline psychotic patients, and as a forensic psychiatrist in the Health Service working in various capacities with mentally disordered, frequently psychotic offenders.

The focus of the chapter is on the phantasy of 'breaking and entering' and takes young burglars as the paradigm of the enactment of the phantasy.

In psychoanalytic terms the phantasy is that of projective identification, defined by Laplanche and Pontalis (1988) as 'a mechanism revealed in phantasies in which the subject inserts his self – in whole or in part – into the object in order to harm, possess or control it'. Rycroft (1968) includes also the denial of powerlessness in his definition: 'the process by which a person imagines himself to be inside some object external to himself…it creates the illusion of control over the object and enables the subject to deny his powerlessness over it'.

I adopt the convention of using '**ph**antasy' when referring to an unconscious phenomenon and '**f**antasy' for the conscious mental act.

EXAMPLE A

I begin by giving a (disguised) vignette of a young man with whom I have been working for three years. At the time of his offence he was 15 years old.

Peter told me that he had been at the pub with his mother, father, sister, uncle and family friends and that they had left at closing time. There was to have been a 'party' that night but it did not happen and he was disappointed. He walked home with his family and went to bed at about midnight, having drunk three pints of shandy and one pint of Guinness – in his estimation. He told me that he had drunk similar quantities on a few earlier occasions.

He says that he found himself unable to sleep, being particularly preoccupied with his relationship with his girlfriend and *her* relationship with a rival at school; he described a feeling of 'boredom'. He got up again, dressed and went walking the streets, taking a kitchen knife with him – 'in case of prowlers'. He told me that he does not normally go out carrying a knife. As he walked he found a car open and, although he cannot drive, he found the car keys and 'drove' the car a little way until it crashed into a tree. He got out and 'was going to go home', but then 'saw a house', and 'walked towards it'. He then saw a small open bathroom window and entered. He said that he did not have any clear idea in his mind of what he was about to do, nor of what he wanted. He felt confused at the time and puzzled in retrospect. Having gained entrance he 'wandered around', and at one stage defaecated on the kitchen floor. He cannot explain why he did this; he did not do any smearing, although later he told me that it had crossed his mind. He felt powerful and 'good, sort of excited but cool', and specifically said that he had no sexual excitement throughout. He put a hand into the pet fish tank and thought about killing the fish although later he doubted that he had wished to kill them. He next found a box of matches and it was only then that he thought of setting fire, which he did by lighting a match to a newspaper and then, having poured white spirit over an armchair and curtains, setting light to them. He also set fire to the carpet at the base of the stairs. He then left, initially hiding behind a bush in the garden; only then did it occur to him that there might be people in the house. He remained excited but then began to become frightened; in panic he threw stones on to the roof of the house and knocked on the door in order to waken or alert anyone who might be there. Fortunately, the family were out of the house. It was then – after a duration of whose length he had no idea – and to his great relief, that fire engines arrived and he waited and subsequently gave himself up to police at the scene: when he had done this he again felt 'calm', even 'flat'.

He is not the most articulate of young men, although he has passed 'A' Levels, but he did say with conviction and has repeated several times that in the mental state he was in whilst he was inside the house, 'anything could have happened'. He was charged and found guilty of arson. He finds it difficult to pin down his changing states of mind before, during and after the breaking and entering but he struggles to do so, feeling it to be important and significant.

This vignette illustrates certain significant features: Peter's acts are to him, to the investigating police, and to us, largely *irrational* and inexplicable in strictly conscious, rational choice terms.

He describes his mental state as one of boredom prior to getting into the car and crashing it and prior to his entry into the house. We have since understood this as a profound feeling of emptiness and of despondency, and a sense of little self-worth. Getting inside the car and the attempt to 'drive' it, although he cannot drive, appeared to be a failed prelude to the entry into the house. He felt a mixed state of strength and elation – I would say, with manic elements – when inside. He was in a state in which '...anything could happen', to use his words. There is the domestic knife that he takes with him – perhaps as a symbol of potency as well as a revenge weapon; there is an act of defaecation – perhaps a phantasy of anal expulsion of bad, possibly murderous, 'objects' as well as a physiological reaction to high arousal; there is the phantasised murder of the pet fish, which he did not carry out – perhaps, mother's babies; there is the setting fire which he had neither done before nor has he done since; there is then the sudden return to a realisation that he may have endangered the family, to a panic state as he takes back into his mind realities of the situation, and then of some attempt at rescue – at reparation.

He feels great relief when 'the authorities' arrive and he experiences 'calm' when he gives himself up to the police. He is 'contained' psychologically by their presence and his superego is thereby assuaged.

We may see the fire as a 'cleaning up' operation in phantasy – a reparation of the killing phantasies – as well as a destructive act. The common assumption is that burglars and others commit arson (firesetting) to destroy actual evidence – such as fingerprints – which may sometimes be the case. Often it may also be an acted out phantasy of destroying, of wiping out the psychological evidence, for example a murderous phantasy.

He said later, in some puzzlement, that he had taken the knife from the kitchen drawer at home and 'the reason I gave was for my protection but there was nothing or no one I needed protection from'. I understand this as a *post hoc* puzzlement about a mental state in which his murderous internal persecutors – the 'mafia gang' of his internal world, as Herbert Rosenfeld (1987) described such unconscious phantasy – were projected into his external environment and were indeed potentially grave threats. The dreams of such young men are violent, raw and barely disguised, and are frequently nightmares of being brutally destroyed – commonly of being mown down by gun-fire on their day of release from the institution.

DISCUSSION

I am mindful of the dangers of reductionism in bringing psychoanalytic thinking to bear in such an applied manner: As Elizabeth Spillius (1988, pp.223–4) has written:

'it is hardly surprising that other disciplines (other than psychoanalysis) react badly to those psychoanalysts, Kleinian and others, who invade their territory without having learned about the field from the discipline's own point of view and with what is seen as a reductive approach... One solution is to continue to work in the other field and to use analytic ideas when appropriate.'

I do work in both fields and use analytic ideas in my practice of forensic psychiatry in this applied way: however, there are always issues of the levels of dynamic understanding achievable and of the levels at which interpretations are made, or frequently only thought and not made. Commonly in such applied work, psychodynamic insights primarily help staff, and others indirectly involved, to a general understanding of the person's predicament, and thereby inform and enrich the treatment plan: it may be the case that no formal psychotherapeutic interventions are considered appropriate or they may be reserved for later in the process of management.

The law is a social construct and varies in different times and within different jurisdictions: the criminal law encompasses a range of behaviours against other people and against property – involving acts which may be destructive, violent, sexual or acquisitive in nature. Antisocial behaviour and our response to it has many aspects and involves many varied disciplines of which the psycho-analytic is but one. However, it is one which (and this underlies the thesis of this chapter) since it involves the internal world of the subject and his relation to his internal and external objects, cannot, in my view, be ignored in any account of offence behaviour which seeks to be more than partial.

Yet, in the present day, our society, and not least professionals involved in any of the wide range of disciplines which come together and overlap in the criminal justice system and the caring professions, seem, frequently, studiously to ignore – one might say, actively deny – the unconscious and its reasons which underlie and can help us understand the psychological motives of particular acts. 'Though [some of this behaviour] be madness,' to quote Polonius, yet, as I hope to show, 'there is method in it'. Media accounts of so-called 'motiveless' crimes – some of which especially defy *rational* understanding, for example, brutal and tragic murders of strangers for no apparent rational reason or motive of personal or material gain – serve to emphasise the point.

As John Rickman writes in a paper, 'The psychology of crime' (1932): 'When lawyers and intelligent laymen consider crime there is first, *surprise* that the criminal *cannot* give a *reasonable explanation* for his act. Secondly that there is such a *compulsive* element in crime, and third, that criminals often *do not* in fact *appear* to be so *aggressive* as they are commonly assumed and regarded' (p.45). That is to say that the criminal act frequently defies ordinary, every-day-sensible, common-sense understanding.

To quote Edward Glover (1960):

'Crime and common sense are refractory bed-fellows: So long as the existence of unconscious motives is disregarded we cannot learn any more about crime than an apparent common sense dictates.'

Broadly, from this psychoanalytic perspective, a delinquent or criminal act may be seen as, either, a (maladaptive) attempt to deal with, to assuage, primitive anxieties, or as a conscious or unconscious act of destructiveness, or as a combination of both. Frequently acts are repeated – since the anxieties which drive them are rarely worked through – in *fact* and not only in phantasy. The sexual perversions are the most obvious example of such a need for repetition of behaviour, sometimes to allay psychotic anxieties, but many criminal acts, including burglary, may show very similar characteristics in that they are repetitive (recidivist), gratifying, driven, based on hostility (or a defence against it), and that they effectively convert a previous experience of victimisation into a later triumphant act.

I have been consistently impressed and sometimes overwhelmed by the semi-conscious – or pre-conscious – and unconscious phantasy which is common to a number of anti-social behaviours of 'breaking and entering'. In this paper I illustrate one of its most concrete forms, the act of burglary, although sexual offending in particular frequently shares some of these breaking and entering phantasies, as noted previously by Zilboorg (1933), Glover (1944) and Limentani (1984) amongst others.

I define unconscious phantasy as the mental expression of instinctual impulses and of defence mechanisms against these impulses: unconscious phantasy in this definition underlies *all* mental processes and mental activity. The concept is therefore wide and can be misused, or overused. Since unconscious phantasy is felt by the subject to *be* reality, and not just to represent it, it is in that sense omnipotent. Equally, as an explanatory system it can be used in such a way as to omnipotently claim understanding and explanation – against which I hope I am on my guard.

The opinions I offer in this chapter are part of my experience of carrying out a research project into the mental states of the young burglar before, during and after their offence behaviour.

My sample of 'criminals' is a group of 50 adolescent burglars, 14–19 years old, seen in a young offenders' institution. The knowledge I have of them is largely observational and not analytic, in the sense that I have seen many young men once or twice only, and only three at weekly intervals (when they attend) over a period of some months, and only one over a period of three years. It seems at least likely that my sample includes a disproportionate number of unsuccessful burglars, in that these ones have all been caught. The sample and my experience may therefore be skewed towards those who burgle for reasons dictated by their particular and acute psychological needs rather than the more professional end of the burglary spectrum.

There is a difficulty in presenting such data in that knowledge about unconscious phantasy is derived from the clinical analytic situation and is communicated best by clinical experience and in supervision. It is necessarily based upon inference. However, the behavioural aspects which I will present – those of criminal acts – may be seen to be analogous to acts of play in the analysis of children from which Klein (1926, 1929) originally developed Freud's concept of unconscious phantasy. The behaviour of some delinquents – of 'forensic patients' – can represent and compellingly illustrate some common unconscious phantasies which are seen in more disguised forms – and, more or less, *remain* in phantasy rather than being *enacted* – in psychotherapeutic and psychoanalytic practice. At the time of the act the subject is frequently making use of, and is ruled by, primitive mechanisms – of splitting and of projective and introjective identification – which are the consequence of psychotic anxieties, and may indeed continue, or occur at other times, as frank and sustained psychosis. The narrative of the offence behaviour in these cases has frequently put me in mind of an account of a dream sequence: frequently the events appear to have taken place in an 'oneiroid' state of trance, in which there is a failure of symbolisation – a concretisation of the furniture of the mind with consequent enactment of the phantasy: Segal (1986) coined the term 'symbolic equation' for such states of mind.

Accordingly, I will be switching back and forth in my discussion between the phantasy and the behaviour; I shall also switch between the writings of others and my own experience. I wish to draw parallels between, on the one hand, the intense, psychotic, anxieties of the child's picture of his mother's body and later, the intense persecutory anxieties of what Klein called the combined parental figure, and his retaliatory wishes, and on the other hand, breaking and entering *behaviour* – the prototype for which is burglary, and its accompanying mental state.

I acknowledge that some burglars will be relatively integrated individuals who consciously *choose* to burgle for clearly thought out purposes of gain – much as the dominant 'rational choice' model of criminology assumes: one can call these 'professional' or careerist and my thesis has only marginal relevance for them. Frequently, however, this careerist gloss will be a cover for severe psychopathology and for the sorts of psychological motivations which I am addressing here. Such an apparently urbane young recidivist burglar chirpily described himself as having his own 'business' and never having been out of work: he gave his occupation as 'House Clearance'. It was not a bad joke but weeks later he had tried to hang himself in his cell.

My experience with delinquent adolescents, and also of some severely psychologically damaged young adults, leads me to the belief that much 'breaking and entering' behaviour can be convincingly seen as a *defensive* manoeuvre to assuage conscious feelings of boredom, of flatness, and of emptiness overlying intrapsychic experience of feelings of intense unconscious anxiety, with phantasies of envy and of revenge – with oral and anal sadistic components. In some offences what begins *consciously* as a relatively 'mindless' state – or a rationalised, relatively 'innocent', say, acquisitive one – can escalate, given certain circumstances, through a range of violent and sadistic behaviour, frequently to the horror of others including the subject's families, but frequently also to the conscious horror and bewilderment of the young offender.

The psychoanalytic perspective of crime is rich and complex – yet remains largely marginal to contemporary practice within the criminal justice system: in Forensic Psychiatry it makes an appearance frequently in a most diluted form. Psychoanalytic explanations cannot of course be sufficient or complete: they are one contribution amongst others of different but equal importance; in my view, however, they are essential ingredients if a complete 'picture' is to be drawn of the criminal act and its actor.

Donald Winnicott's view was that delinquency is so invested with secondary gain and with social reaction, adjustment and rationalisation that its core evades psychoanalytic investigation: he described how problems of management are frequently so prominent and overwhelming that pure psychoanalytic treatment is precluded (Winnicott 1953). Yet such cases demand some dynamic understanding and attempt at explanation. Before I continue and elaborate on some of the theoretical aspects, I will give an example of the fascination that a related phenomenon of the apparently inexplicable has exerted upon a writer and on generations of readers.

Deacon Brodie, a well known and apparently respectable town councillor in Edinburgh in the eighteenth Century, was discovered to be a proficient professional burglar of houses by night. He was caught in an alehouse having fled to Amsterdam after a burglary of the Edinburgh Excise office, an accomplice having turned King's evidence. Deacon Brodie provided Robert Louis Stevenson with the idea for his novel *The Strange Case of Dr Jekyll and Mr Hyde*, a fascinating account of the *almost* entire split between a good, caring reparative Dr Jekyll and the murderous dark side, Mr Hyde. There are inevitably elements of caricature but also a deep psychological truth of a state of affairs commonly seen in criminal work.

Melanie Klein in particular wrote much about the child having phantasies of getting inside the maternal 'object', the mother's body. The getting inside involves a fusion with the object and an emptying of the mind – evacuated into the object – producing a dreamy state. Although Klein first coined the term 'projective identification' it has been the work of others within the post-Kleinian development – for example, Wilfred Bion, Herbert Rosenfeld and Donald Meltzer – which has made it such a rich concept for understanding a wide range of perplexing and disturbing phenomena.

In particular Klein wrote two short and quite early papers on criminality, 'Criminal tendencies in normal children' (1927) and 'On criminality' (1934), which deserve to be far more influential than they have been. What was impressive to her (and I think to us) was how similar are some of the terrible *acts* of the criminal and the play and phantasy of the children whom she analysed.

Rooting the basis of the phantasies in the Oedipus complex she described (1927) the case of a little boy, Gerald, whose

> '...desire [was to] *penetrate* [into the adjoining parental] bedroom, [and] to blind the father, to castrate and to kill the father...Gerald had a little tiger and his great affection for this animal was partly due to the hope that it would protect him. But this tiger proved sometimes to be not only a defender but an aggressor. Gerald proposed to send it into the next room to carry out his aggressive desires on the father. This primitive part of the personality was in this case represented by the tiger, which, as I ascertained later on, was Gerald himself, but a part of him which he would have liked not to realise. Gerald also had phantasies of cutting his father and mother into pieces, these phantasies being connected with anal actions, with dirtying his father and mother with his faeces.' (p.172, my italics)

(Note the similarity with the young burglar who defaecates in the house). Klein continues,

> 'a dinner party he [Gerald] arranged after such phantasies proved to be a meal in which he and his mother were eating the father. It is difficult to illustrate how such a warm-hearted child, as this one was in particular, suffered through such phantasies, which the cultivated part of his personality strongly condemned.' (p.172)

Such phantasies, according to Klein, are developmentally ubiquitous.

A further example from Klein (1927) is directly an account of 'breaking and entering':

> 'A boy of twelve years of age who was to be sent to a reformatory was brought for analysis to me. His delinquencies were breaking open the school cupboard and a tendency to steal in general, but most breaking up things, and sexual attacks on little girls. He had no relationship to anyone but a destructive one; his boy friendships had mostly this purpose too. He had no special interests and even seemed indifferent to punishments and rewards...during this very disturbed analysis the child nevertheless did not commit any act of delinquency, but began them again during the time of the break, whereupon he was at once sent back to a reformatory, and all my attempts after my return to get him back for analysis failed.' (p.181)

It was plain that he repeated on the little girls the attacks he had suffered himself, only changing the situation in so far that now he was the aggressor. His breaking open of cupboards and taking out articles, as well as his other destructive tendencies, had the same unconscious causes and symbolic meaning as his sexual assaults. This boy, feeling overwhelmed and castrated, had to change the situation by proving to himself that he could be the aggressor himself. One important motive for these destructive tendencies was to prove to himself again and again that he was still a man, besides abreacting his hatred against his (rivalrous) sister on other objects.

In later papers she speaks of how given favourable external circumstances the healthy, reparative, resolution of these phantasies may be seen to develop in the child's play in analysis.

The post-Kleinian developments of some of these insights has been considerable and many are relevant and related to my subject matter. Donald Meltzer in his book *The Claustrum – An Investigation of Claustrophobic Phenomena* (1992), has much to say which I have found relevant and very helpful in understanding these young men: He writes that:

> 'the basic problem is one of psychic pain and the need for an object in the outside world that can contain the projection of it.' (p.38)

Of the state of mind whilst 'inside' the object – in my cases, the houses – he says:

> 'It becomes clear that the geographical confusion between the inside and the outside of the object (is also) a confusion between external and internal psychic reality.' (p.39)

That is, the state of projective (evacuative) and introjective identification is such that a state of psychosis effectively exists. Some years ago during the course of an interview with one of these young burglars I remarked that at the time of being in the house 'It's very difficult for you to know what is real and what is not', to which the young man replied with conviction that at that time surprised, but impressed, me: 'It's *all* real!'

In his analysis of children whose phantasies in his descriptions are, I think, analogous and similar to the mental states of these burglars, Meltzer (1992) writes:

> 'the utilization of the consulting room as the inside of an object is often made clear by the very mode of entry into the room, in a rush or knocking against the door jamb, or by a mode of looking about as if in a vast arena. Conversely the phantasy of having remained sequestered inside the analyst during a separation may be expressed by hiding behind the door in the waiting room or under a chair... Dreams of the patient in analysis may show the process of intrusion into the anus of the object most frequently as entering a building or vehicle, either furtively, by a back entrance, the door has wet paint, the entrance is very narrow, protective clothing must be worn, it is underground, under water, in a foreign country, or closed to the public.' (p.36)

I hope that I am making my point of the parallel discourses of common internal world events (of the unconscious mind) and of the criminal behaviours of certain offenders. One further example: one of my own psychotherapy patients had the following dream.

EXAMPLE B

'I am going down a road in a gang with my husband and with another man and woman. I think that my husband is going to accuse me of having an affair with this other man and I feel like hitting my husband.' She then decides to break into a house with the other woman. There is barbed wire and fencing – she feels very relieved when she gets into the house: the other woman disappears. She finds a cupboard of food and drink but can't touch it: Why? she wonders: it is all very curious, she is going *everywhere*. She opens a pantry door, which is neglected and is filled with half consumed and broken bottles.

Then the atmosphere changes: she realises that the house belongs to an old couple when she sees an old black bag and she feels sorry and panicky and she wants to get out. She leaves the house and walks on down the road to her grandmother's house. There are two men standing there who show her *identity* cards saying they are policemen, but the cards are just receipts, and they go in and take everything from the house.

Grandmother comes along and says she will get everything back for her but she doesn't know if grandmother can: she feels its her own fault that it was all taken'.

Without going into all the complexities I think this dream shows similarities of structure and content with the *actual* burglarious acts I have described. There is a prelude of anxiety, of accusation and of persecution: she thinks of violence but instead she gets inside a house (against much security) and goes *everywhere* – 'anything could happen'. There is food but she can't have it; there is destruction. Then her reparative, guilty, but panicky thoughts follow and she wants to get out. She does, but meets her policemen superego – who are, however, duplicit and do a similar act themselves.

DEFINITIONS

It is of interest that there is much confusion in law in definitions of burglary – of breaking and entering behaviour – as if to reflect the confusion of the mind of some burglars, as well as the multiplicity of mental states and phantasies and 'intents' which underlie such acts.

The *Oxford English Dictionary* describes burglary as 'The crime of breaking by night into a house with felonious intent'. The qualification 'by night', whilst adding some nocturnal mystery, is not now in law a requirement although it used to be so: in the popular imagination burglary is, erroneously, invariably associated with theft.

The law convincingly reflects these confusions. Burglary in law needs to be distinguished from trespass. Burglary requires an ulterior motive to the trespass, and is therefore called a crime of ulterior intent, or a 'preparatory' offence. Glanville Williams (1983, p.841), a legal authority describes six types of burglary:

1. Entry as a trespasser with intent to *steal.*

2. Entry as a trespasser with intent to *inflict grevious bodily harm.*

3. Entry as a trespasser with intent to *rape.*

4. Entry as a trespasser with intent to *do unlawful damage.*

There is then:

5. Stealing or attempting to steal *after* entry as a trespasser.

6. Inflicting or attempting to inflict grevious bodily harm *after* entry as a trespasser.

Of course the law requires intent – *mens rea* – for any serious act to be considered a crime: it needs to assume conscious 'intent' – in a legal sense – where in a psychological sense *we* may in some cases feel that the unconscious phantasies are more confused, multiple, and changing and that the most obvious and available phantasy initially was of merely 'getting inside'. Later, as the behaviour evolves, other semi-dormant phantasies become, as it were, mobilised as the action proceeds. It is for this reason that many criminal acts in which the 'breaking and entering' phantasy is central are not classified legally as burglary since, for example, they escalate to rape, violence, arson or murder but under that category of the more serious offence.

We need to keep in mind the fact that these young men are in one sense very much 'inside', in that they are locked up in prison, and frequently locked in their cells for practically all their working hours, and that this re-creates for them some of their phantasies. As Patrick Gallwey (personal communication) has pointed out, the mental life of some prisoners – the internal desolation and the manic acting out attempts to get away from this desolation – is realised, and constructed in the fabric of the prison and its cells: he quotes Jean Genet 'I think that hitherto I bore that life within me secretly and that all I needed was to be put in contact with it for it to be revealed to me from without in its reality.' Some of these offenders describe how even from childhood they had an odd feeling or preconception, dimly perceived, that they know about prison and one day would go there. They may experience relief, but may also experience feelings of claustrophobia, which may be clinically interpreted as a feeling of being imprisoned within the object (or person) of their projective identification.

I have found that – after understandable initial wariness – some of these young men verbally 'flow' in response to my invitation to tell me about themselves and how they had ended up 'inside'. Often from a dull, silently hostile, despondent and disengaged demeanour, they lighten and become enthused and sometimes excited as they related the details of their acts. They describe, for example, a variety of states of mind. One said, 'It's like excitement, but with a fear: not of getting caught. You don't know what the fear is…like an adrenalin buzz going through you: I don't think that I like it, my chest thumps and I want to shit myself... I can't think... I can't hear. There's such a thumping in my ears, I feel sweaty and paranoid.' Another said merely, 'I did it *to get in with* my group.'

The *drive* is frequently from a state of despondency and desolation, often immediately after an experience of rejection or loss: this produces a manic excitement in which the phantasy is, I think, of omnipotent access to an unfettered blissful state of pleasure, and of stealing that state. It is a phantasy and at best only partially and temporarily achieved. It is usually only later, when actually 'inside', that the destructive phantasy predominates. Often I have found myself reeling, as if invaded by the mental content of the young offender as he relates his story: often I have been made to feel sick by the rush of possibilities and the development of events and have had to take time before I could gather myself to say anything coherent and possibly helpful.

I shall give a further brief illustration:

EXAMPLE C

A 14-year-old boy described how he had an argument at night, at home, with his mother: He went out walking around his own neighbourhood and walked – I shall use his words – 'down an alley way. I saw a house and thought "that looks tasty" and I had to think how to get in: I thought the window downstairs was the best way. I get in [*his description becomes increasingly excited*]) and have a look around: I felt sweaty with excitement: I go upstairs – careful like [*rising excitement*] and go into the room where the people are sleeping [*pauses*] You've got to be out of it to do that.' He described how he went through the drawers of the bureau and bedside tables (at which point I felt a mixture of fascination and of horrified anxiety). He continued: 'I remember seeing a lady and a man sleeping there...[*he laughs nervously*] I even put my hand under the mattress.' At this point I interrupted, possibly inappropriately, but certainly ineffectively, as it turned out: 'It sounds to me as if you wanted to get into the bed.' He scoffed and cut off, looking shocked, and became critical, and rather menacing challenging me, in some confusion, 'You think I'm a fucking queer?'

In later sessions we spoke about what he would feel if *he* had the experience of someone in *his* room, with a hand under his mattress: 'I'd shit myself – if I woke up.' Again he would become excited: If challenged during such an escapade he said he would 'tie the people up'. The phantasies again are of evacuation and of utter control of others.

He estimated that he had done some thirty previous burglaries, although he had not previously been caught. He usually took something from the house – 'a momento', as he called it – which would not be of any particular worth. On several occasions he had taken a family photograph, and then thrown it away.

Robert Stoller (1976), in his book *Perversion: The Erotic Form of Hatred*, describes a severely borderline female patient and her acts of burglary (pp.163–

191). She would only enter 'homes', where there was a family, a mother and father and children: never apartments where there would, in her view, only be a man on his own or a woman. This is a common discrimination made by my adolescent burglar subjects: they too want a 'proper' home to burgle.

CODA

The fact is that few of the young men I have described will be offered psychotherapy and even fewer will take up the offers. Most will pursue recidivist careers and spend much time 'inside' within the prison system. Some break down – into psychosis – when locked up in a restricted space; some break out – explode – and smash up their cells; some accommodate. It is to be hoped that some will find their way to some or other therapeutic setting – perhaps Grendon Underwood Prison within the prison system, where they may have some help.

Where out-patient and community placement prove to be insufficient most such recidivist delinquent young men are initially best treated within a therapeutic community, a 'milieu' of some sort – a psychological as well as physical 'container' – with individual work coming later, as part of the containment. It is not for nothing that they have frequently spent their best years contained, *within* part of, for example, one of the armed services – as, say, a naval cadet – only to breakdown or to begin re-offending after leaving.

In summary, in this chapter I use my experience of a dual professional role as psychoanalyst and forensic psychiatrist to examine the mental states and behaviour of a group of adolescent burglars. I have written a parallel and intermittently connecting discourse, using examples of the descriptions of acts of burglary to illuminate the ubiquitous, mental, unconscious phantasy of breaking and entering.

It is to be hoped that such a juxtaposition of disciplines might be seen to inform them both, and to open each up to new possibilities, rather than to fall into the snare of reductionism which such applied work frequently invites.

REFERENCES

Glover, E. (1960) 'Diagnosis and treatment of pathological delinquency', Section 3. In E. Glover *The Roots of Crime: Selected Papers on Psychoanalysis,* Vol.2, 79–114. London: Imago Publishing.

Klein, M. (1926) 'The psychological principles of early analysis.' In *Love, Guilt and Reparation and Other Works.* London: Hogarth (1985).

Klein, M, (1927) 'Criminal tendencies in normal children.' In *Love, Guilt and Reparation and Other Works.* London: Hogarth (1985).

Klein, M. (1929) 'Personification in the play of children.' In *Love, Guilt and Reparation and Other Works.* London: Hogarth (1985).

Klein, M. (1934) 'On criminality.' In *Love, Guilt and Reparation and Other Works.* London: Hogarth (1985).

Laplanche, L. and Pontalis, J. (1988) *The Language of Psychoanalysis.* London: Karnac Books.

Limentani, A. (1984) 'Toward a unified conception of the origin of sexual and social deviancy in young persons.' *International Journal of Psychoanalytic Psychotherapy 10,* 383–401.

Meltzer, D. (1992) *The Claustrum – An Investigation of Claustrophobic Phenomena.* Perth: The Clunie Press. The Roland Harris Trust Library.

Rickman, J. (1932) 'The psychology of crime.' In C. Scott (ed) *Selected Contributions to Psychoanalysis.* London: Hogarth Press/Institute of Psychoanalysis.

Rosenfeld, H. (1987) *Impasse and Interpretation.* London: Routledge.

Rycroft, C. (1968) *A Critical Dictionary of Psychoanalysis.* London: Nelson.

Segal, H. (1986) 'Notes on symbol formation.' In H. Segal (ed) *The Work of Hanna Segal.* London: Free Association Books.

Spillius, E. (1988) *Melanie Klein Today, Vol 2: Mainly Practice.* London: Routledge.

Stoller, R. (1976) *Perversion: The Erotic Form of Hatred.* Hassocks, Sussex: Harvester Press.

Williams, G.L. (1983) *Textbook of Criminal Law* (2nd ed). London: Stevens.

Winnicott, D. (1953) *The Antisocial Tendency.* London: Tavistock.

Zilboorg, G. (1933) *The Psychology of the Criminal Act and Punishment.* London: Hogarth Press/Institute of Psychoanalysis.

CHAPTER 11

The Return from Mindlessness

Kenneth Sanders

My starting point is Freud's paper known as the 'Schreber case' (1912). More clearly than anywhere else, he discerns there the mind as a working structure, destroyed by psychotic illness.

We can add to this the idea that while the mind is working well, it generates feelings with a depressive colouring, such as: concern for others; accepting responsibility for actions and thoughts; regret for mistakes; a capacity to mourn; and, at a more abstract level, awareness of the transience of the human condition, of the intractability of human nature, and of our dependence on the patience and tolerance of others.

The oscillation between these feelings, which Melanie Klein (1952) called the depressive position, and a defensive retreat from them to the less painful anxieties of persecution (paranoid-schizoid position) has been one of the corner-stones of the Kleinian understanding of the functioning of the mind.

Defence against mental pain has been the foundation of psychoanalysis from the beginning: Freud's earliest concept of the 'neurosis of defence' in 1894 – a defence against sexual anxieties – was extended in the work of Abraham (1911), to the mania in manic-depressive psychoses. Manic defences were later linked to some types of splitting.

Bion's (1962) development of the idea of defence in psychosis is a defence that is radical indeed: the destruction of the structure and function of thinking itself, resulting in meaningless speech and delusional ideas. Further, the psychotic part of the personality can reverse the thinking process to manufacture lies.

'Mindlessness' is a generic term used by Meltzer (1988) for the end result of these interferences with thinking. It covers not only the psychoses but other conditions where thoughtfulness about emotional experiences is replaced by action, including the mindlessness of large groups or institutions, and psychoso-matic illness.

Underpinning all these developments is the concept of splitting and projective identification: a theory that in the dream world of internal parental objects, parts of the infantile self can be split off and projected into the interior of the internal mother with consequent confusions between self and object, which affects the individuals view of external reality.

However, a crucial distinction has special relevance to my subject. Melanie Klein's (1946) description of splitting and projective identification was of a phantasy which she perhaps saw as mainly a pathological process. A further result of Bion's (1962) concept of the mind as a container has been a second type of projective identification involved in normal development – the idea that during its period ensconced within the container of the mother, the infant mind can be nourished and taught to think.

Bion's idea was that the infant's raw emotional experience requires the assistance of a kind of digestive process, with the possibility of the process (alpha function) miscarrying (Bion 1962). In that case the infant has to dispose of the undigested emotional experience. The unassimilated is evacuated, the result is action without prior thought.

The reversal of responsibility for the aggression, so familiar in paranoia – claiming to be the victim of intrusion, not the intruder – hides another consequence. The intruded part inhabits a world which is a travesty of adult life: all grown-ups, it is assumed, are covering up their childishness, although some are more successful at this than others. It is a cynical and claustrophobic world inhabited by insincere people, and there is constant danger of being detected and thrown out.

The way back from mindlessness, therefore, will be a change from one type of projective identification to the other: from being an intruder to being a welcome guest. The change will be two-fold: in the self, and in the parental object. The burglar will abuse the house, while the guest will protect it. It will mean not only a change in the identity of the self – a more vulnerable view of the infant self – but also a different view of the world and its geography.

To demonstrate this shift in the infant character from intrusive to dependent, and from a persecutory to a thoughtful view of the world, some clinical material follows.

The analysand was an intelligent and kindly man, handicapped in his development by mental illness. He admitted to depression but privately he felt his sanity threatened by a fixed delusional idea. This distracted his attention, wasted his time, and so interfered with his emotional life that he saw no hope of being thought in the least attractive to women. It was not his appearance; it was the truth about his mental state, so carefully concealed, that was the problem.

The delusional idea was that his flat, and his personal effects were 'bugged' by the secret police. This was re-enforced by hallucinatory-like preoccupation with any slight mark or irregularity on the walls. When he first came to analysis he was wasting many hours late at night, with mounting sexual excitement, overwhelmed by compulsion to scratch and dig at these marks to find the non-existent hidden microphone.

Naturally the severity of his illness was unclear at first, but his intellectual interests were intact: he was at work, fulfilled his duties conscientiously, and was not without friends.

A start was made with a protracted struggle against the mindless preoccupation with non-existent hidden microphones. The provisional theoretical basis was that he was identified with the maternal victim of his own infantile intrusiveness. As his baby self was not equipped with a concept of a separate identity and did not in fact separate psychologically, the phenomenon could be studied in the transference.

The atmosphere was hopeful, he was keen on the analytic work and felt lucky to have found it. He experienced relief from anxiety and renewal of hope after each session. Yet as he left the consulting room, apparently he entered a world hostile to psychoanalysis. The ridiculing of its significance for him was acted out in time-wasting shopping for discounted goods. Reported conversations with friends (who knew nothing of his illness) warned him of the folly of time and money squandered on a spurious science. They offered, free of charge, an alternate therapy for his desolation: to 'get his leg over', a phrase which became emblematic of the aims of the intrusive part of his personality.

Some psychoanalytic ideas, particularly those relating to the difference between infantile, perverse, and adult sexuality, astonished him and he would exclaim in anguish that I would be shot down if I repeated them in the world in which he moved. However, the nurturing form of projective identification through the analysis was having its effect, and his capacity to remember, report and work with his dreams markedly improved. The 'shooting down' was done by the violent opposition to this from the psychotic part of his personality. He dreamed:

> 'A friend borrowed my motor scooter, and returned it with the corpse of
> his girl stuffed in the panniers. When the police stopped me they wouldn't
> listen to me, but my mother came with me to the police station.'

This combination of murderous attacks on thoughtfulness (the girl friend) by the psychotic part of his personality, alternating with hopefulness, (the mother-analysis) led to a better understanding of his fear of being thrown out of what he felt to be the elitist world of psychoanalysts (the inside of the mother's body). The analytic setting began to contain his anxieties and encouraged him to continue the struggle with the still very troublesome delusional idea. The anxiety of resisting it he described as tearing him to pieces, until he gave way and was sucked in.

About this time, his mother died, and speaking sadly, he used the expression 'the complexity of sorrow.' He was quoting Winston Smith from Orwell's *Nineteen*

Eighty-Four, who, while ruminating on his past life with his mother and sister, realises that Big Brother has criminalised feeling upset. He dreamed:

> 'I was driving by the coast trying to find my way to the Lost City of Aquarius. The road was difficult and wet and the city was out of sight beyond a headland, around which I would have to drive. But my friend told me that there were highways connecting with the city, and that I was stupid to go a long way round...'

The 'Lost City of Aquarius' had no literary or even astrological significance for him, but it seemed likely that mourning his mother was reminding him tearfully of his childhood dependence on his parents, and that being separate from his mother, he must one day lose her. In contrast, the inside world into which he was sucked – as he described it – by his delusions, was pain-free.

The cynicism attributed to his friends made him doubt the wisdom of the long way round of thought and its depressive pain. Away from the analysis, he became confused between discounting its value to him and knowing it was what he was looking for. The dream symbolised his conflict of choice: between the world of thought, the world outside the internal mother's body suckled at the fountain of knowledge of her mind/breast – the 'head' land – and the ugly, mindless 'leg over' of genital and anal intrusiveness into which he was sucked.

Another year into analysis, he reported two weekend dreams, from Saturday and Sunday:

> '...I was responsible for two very small babies, who were swaddled, tightly bound to sticks, almost finger-size or like insects. I asked John and Anne for their advice, and these little creatures began to crawl over their chests...'

I thought this was a hopeful dream: a picture of infantile vulnerability, in touch with a parental couple and on the outside of the internal mother's body, illustrating the anxiety which he describes as tearing him apart.

He associated first to the fingers, (scratching himself on the arm as he began to talk, reminiscent of the scratching at marks on the walls of his room). He recalled that as a schoolboy, dashing to catch a ball, his hand had collided with a wall, fracturing two fingers. The couple are, in external life, friends who are sympathetic to him. They seem to him to possess all he lacks: marriage, children, creative employment, inhabiting a superior world from which he is forever excluded, unless he can infiltrate it, and secretly cross the frontier between his world and theirs.

The finger-insects, as his infant self, are prominent in the sexually exciting probing and scratching when he is drawn into the delusional excitement of the bugging ('finger-size or like little insects'). Here, however, they have been prevented from damaging the object. It seems that the analytic setting (the chest wall) halts intrusion, perhaps at the cost of a fracture in his personality, yet encourages him to learn from the experience of being securely supported.

At the same session he reported his Sunday dream:

'I'm sitting at the head of a rectangular table, between Jane and Elizabeth. I fall asleep and dream [within the dream] that I've fallen asleep in an analytic session. I wake to find I'm in a hospital bed, feeling warm and snug under the blankets, aware of the cold outside. Then I wake up again, at the table, to chaos... I want to sit in Jane's seat, but Elizabeth, from the other end, ridicules me.'

Jane is a senior colleague whose good opinion he values. He thought he might have unwittingly upset her, 'as if,' he said, 'I had left an "entrail" behind me.' Elizabeth is a troubled colleague, whom, identifying with the analysis, he is trying to help.

The hospital bed repeats the swaddling theme, as with the bandaged finger. The internal mother's head/breast analysis is a warm place where his illness can be admitted and treated. But the coldness (depression) is waiting for him when he thinks about the ugliness of the 'leg over' thoughts, connected with the the 'entrail'. There is preoccupation with levels of sleep and dreaming, and confusions about inside and outside and about internal and external reality.

A year later, the same themes continue, but more insistent concerning depressive embarrassment. He dreamed:

'I was sitting next to a girl from the office, pretending to be asleep but with my hand on her thigh. She kept moving away, but I persisted in moving my fingers a little higher. She got up and walked off and I was frightened she might complain to the management that I was sexually harassing her.'

'Pretending to be asleep' leaves hope that with further understanding he can wake to full responsibility for his mind. Inside the internal mother, father is replaced by a suspicious management. Outside, via the 'headland', father is a friend, husbanding the mother's resources and guarding her against mindless intrusions.

The split between the psychotic part of his personality and the non-psychotic was indeed symbolised by a fracture. The former made him pre-occupied with the imitation, with all types of copying: photo, video, audio. Weaning becomes a euphemism for redundancy, encouragement a form of flattery, with an imitation analyst masquerading interest in an analysand pretending to be in need. The healthy part of his mind, acknowledging the analytic experience as a container for thinking, is drawn to the genuine, if painful, emotions of intimate relationships.

It became obvious in the transference that contamination by ugly thoughts of all that he valued most made him tremble with anxiety and fear to continue the struggle.

To sum up, a place where it is possible to communicate truthful emotional experiences and be supported not terrorised, is I think, for him, the 'Lost City of Aquarius'.

This checklist of dream life experiences associated with a return from mindlessness summarises the analysand's progression through analysis:

1. Being awakened, being born, a birthday.

2. Feeling little vulnerable, ill, embarrassed.

3. Receiving help from a combined object.

4. Anxiety about responsibility for a mess, i.e. depressive anxiety rather than paranoid.

5. Contact with an object that resists intrusion, e.g. a wall or locked door.

The reversal of this list, the reversal characteristic of intrusive identification, warns of return *to* mindlessness:

1. Feeling sleepy; irritated by noises disturbing sleep.

2. Megalomania; intolerance of the small or vulnerable, e.g. children, the sick and the aged.

3. Combined object separated, controlled, divorced, widowed.

4. Martyrdom in cleaning up other people's mess.

5. Intrusion through open doors followed by claustrophobia.

REFERENCES

Abraham, K. (1911) 'Notes on the psycho-analytical investigation and treatment of manic-depressive insanity and allied conditions.' In E. Joss (ed) *Selected Papers on Psycho-analysis.* London: Hogarth (1954).

Bion, W. (1962) Learning from Experience. London: Heinemann.

Freud, S. (1894) 'The neuro-psychoses of defence.' *Standard Edition,* Vol.3. London: Hogarth (1962).

Freud, S. (1912) 'Psycho-analytic notes on an autobiographical account of a case of paranoia.' *Standard Edition,* Vol.12. London: Hogarth (1958).

Klein, M. (1946) 'Notes on some schizoid mechanisms.' In *The Writings of Melanie Klein,* Vol.3. London: Hogarth (1975).

Klein, M. (1952) 'Some theoretical conclusions regarding the emotional life of the infant.' In R. Money-Kyrle (ed) *The Writings of Melanie Klein,* Vol.3. London: Hogarth Press.

Meltzer, D. (1988) 'Mindlessness: failure and reversal of alpha-function.' In *The Apprehension of Beauty.* Perthshire: Clunie Press.

CHAPTER 12

Individual Psychoanalytical Psychotherapy with Severely and Profoundly Handicapped Patients

V. Sinason

In 1977 Heaton-Ward noted that out of five International Congresses for the Scientific Study of Mental Deficiency 1300 papers were presented out of which only 40 were concerned with mental illness. At the 8th World Congress held in Dublin last year I made my own count. Out of approximately 500 papers, only ten were concerned with emotional disturbance or co-existing mental illness and only half of that ten were concerned with psychodynamic treatment.

The concept of normalisation has led to an increased awareness of the plight of many of our client-group (mental/physical handicaps plus severe psychological disturbance, autism, psychosis) and an increased motivation to improve their conditions. Not surprisingly, as all progress is double-edged, this has had its negative effects too. With growing pressure to move as many individuals as possible into the community, there has been an ambivalent attitude to mental illness and emotional disturbance. It can be hard for some community teams to accept that their clients are hallucinating or hearing voices if they have seen the long-stay psychiatric or subnormality hospitals as the 'cause' of the client's disturbance.

Some of the patients I see have challenging behaviour and it is important to emphasise that research on that subject by Oliver, Murphy and Corbett (1987) revealed that there was *no* evidence that the institutional environment caused this. Rather, the behaviour predated and often caused hospital admission. There are also handicapped individuals who were sexually and emotionally abused in their homes and who found the impersonality of large hospitals a relief. Some of these, when moved into the community, became ill because a home means being in a confined dangerous abusive space.

On the other hand, there are community or hospital workers trying to refer their clients for psychotherapy and being told that this is not a possible treatment. A. Reid (1982), whilst welcoming group therapy, commented 'the scope for individual therapy is limited. Such patients do not have the intellectual resources to benefit from in-depth psychotherapy'. However, psychoanalytical psychotherapists have to take some of the blame for the way such myths have spread. We too have clearly believed them! As a profession we have only been working continuously with this client group for ten years and there are still not more than four or five of us. Against that we need to bear in mind that in England there are only approximately 230 psychoanalysts and 200 psychoanalytical psychotherapists, a ludicrously small number if we consider the mental health needs of a country. It is not surprising, then, to find among other sobering facts the fact that the Oliver, Murphy, Corbett study revealed that of 596 self-injuring adults and children only 12 were receiving *any* psychological treatment, of which one (a patient of mine) was psychoanalytical.

Although the greater the severity of the handicap the greater the likelihood of coexisting mental illness, it is not the handicap in itself that causes the illness; rather, the burden of the handicap depletes the resources of the individual, making him more vulnerable to emotional disturbance. We can add to this the fact that the majority of our handicapped clients (Rutter *et al.* 1970) come from the lowest social class and face the greatest economic difficulty and deprivation. Buchanan and Oliver (1977) have also pointed to abuse and neglect as a primary cause of retardation and I have frequently drawn attention to that situation as well (Sinason 1986). I consider trauma to be an important key to understanding mental illness in the handicapped.

In this chapter I will show the first sessions of two patients. Both suffered from voices and hallucinations, and one was violent to herself and others. First I will provide a synopsis of the findings that come from ten years of psychoanalytic psychotherapy with this group.

1. Formal psychoanalytic psychotherapy can be used by mildly, severely and profoundly multiply handicapped patients. Verbal language is not necessary. All patients, even the hyper-active, manage the same 50 minute hour for individual therapy and one and a half hours for group therapy.

2. We find it useful to differentiate between emotional intelligence and performance intelligence. A brilliant academic might be emotionally crippled and unable to be in touch with feelings and an intellectually crippled long-stay hospital resident might be emotionally capable of facing painful truths about loss and handicap. Every patient in therapy has understood the nature and meaning of their handicap. There is no such concept as 'ignorance is bliss'. It hurts to be different.

3. The defensive ways in which someone exaggerates his handicap in order to have control of it can be more damaging than the handicap itself. For example, Don, aged 10, a boy with challenging behaviour, exaggerated his speech defect from cerebral palsy. It was so painful that his handicap was out of his control he found a way of creating his own, which was when people laughed at his voice he was really laughing at them for being the stupid ones who did not know his real voice.

4. There can be a more pathological kind of secondary handicap which I have called 'opportunist handicap' (Sinason 1986). By that I mean that wherein all the disturbed, envious and destructive aspects of the personality find a home.

5. Functioning can improve dramatically but not to normal. As Greenacre has commented, no traumatic event is ever wholly processed and some vulnerability remains, predisposing the individual to break down if the original trauma is later repeated. With out-patients, there has been the trauma of the handicap and the traumatic response of the world to it and them. We are increasingly dealing with individuals who have been sexually abused, have untreated mental illness in addition to their handicap. In some cases treatment feels more like damage limitation than cure.

6. We have noted three main stages that have to be passed for therapeutic work to be of significant value. The first deals with secondary handicap, the defence exacerbations of the primary handicap that nevertheless deplete the communication level that is possible. Handicapped voice, body posture, language, literacy can change during this period. Don, for example, began therapy speaking like this – 'I thgo tho htothpithall'. It took six months for him to show he could say 'hospital'. The second stage is a period of crying/depression. It seems to represent a proper mourning for the wasted years hidden behind secondary handicap, sorrow for the handicap itself and a terrible feeling of aloneness. This is a vulnerable period of terminating treatment; 22-year-old Eve, for example, brought a photograph of herself on a beach, all twisted and contorted, lying next to her beautiful key-worker. She cried piteously at the sight. The third stage is an improvement again in internal and external functioning. We might leave the handicap behind and deal with the psychosis.

There is an overlap between illness and severe or profound mental handicap that needs treatment. After this therapy continues as with any other client group.

MARY

Mary is 25. She is severely mentally handicapped and lives in a small hostel. She has a mother who visits her weekly. Her father died a year ago. She was referred for violence to staff and herself. There was a question of moving her because they could not manage. The social worker asked if she could come with Mary's mother. Mary's mother was very angry with the hostel and blamed them for Mary's behaviour.

So Mary came to the first meeting with her mother and her key worker and I invited them all to my room together. I introduced myself and asked if they preferred formal titles or first names. They preferred first names. (I always check, as sometimes a 20-year-old worker bringing a 50-year-old man will say 'I'm Miss Smith and this is John'.)

Mary was fat, short, had dull short hair and wore the international false-self mental handicap uniform of short white socks, ugly blouse and a pleated skirt. She sat rocking and humming and biting her hand. I then asked Mary if she knew why she was here today. 'No'. I asked her worker to say why she was here and rather embarrassedly the worker said how Mary hits herself or staff members. Mary sat still then, smiling quietly. 'My Mary is really peaceful. She doesn't hurt anyone' said mother. 'She has a really sunny nature. Look at that smile.' Mary's smile broadened. I said perhaps Mary felt she had to be happy and sunny, especially meeting me, a stranger. I asked when this violence began. 'They say six months ago', said mother, 'So don't say it was because of her father's death. She was fine for the first six months.' 'And she was not violent before then?' I asked the worker. 'No'.

Mary sat looking at me, narrowing her eyes and making her hum louder. I opened my mouth and before I started to speak Mary became silent. I said it sounded to me as if something very different happened to Mary six months ago. First there was a Mary who never hurt herself or staff and then suddenly there was a Mary who did. Mary nodded then suddenly slapped herself across her left ear.

It was a savage blow and left a red mark on the part of her fact she touched. Mother rushed to hold her hand and looked at me accusingly. Mary was sitting quietly and peacefully. Her rocking had stopped. I said she looked very peaceful now she had hurt the Mary who ·had nodded to me. She looked at me very seriously and sadly. I said that when I spoke about a Mary who never hurt herself she had listened to me so carefully but there was someone else listening; another Mary who did not like that. She nodded and then started humming loudly. Suddenly she was very quiet and jerked her head to the right. I asked her if the other Mary was talking to her. 'Yes', 'What is she saying?' I asked. 'Go 'way if I listen,' whispered Mary. 'She'll go away if you listen?' I checked. 'Yes'.

I said that made it very hard then. There was a pause. 'Does this just mean she talks to herself?' asked mother, suddenly losing her sad expression. 'Everybody talks to themselves. I do, don't I Mary'. Mary nodded and then roared with laughter, rocking up and down. She knew her mother was being stupid and it filled her with despair as well as excitement! I said yes, people did at times but there was an important difference between occasionally talking to yourself in times of stress and actually having a voice in your head. 'Hit staff! Hit staff!' shouted Mary suddenly, jumping up from her seat and just as quickly sitting quietly again as if nothing had happened. Her mother looked terrified. I asked if that was what the Mary in her head told her to do. 'Yes' she said, sitting down again. Then she looked at her key worker, flinched as if she had been hit. Her head jerked backwards again and again and curled up terrified saying 'Not me. Not me.' I said she was so frightened we would all think she was the Mary who hurt people. She was so frightened she knew we would hurt her and right now she felt we had. She nodded. Slowly she sat up in her chair again.

Mother started sobbing quietly. 'So she's mad too.' I said she had received a big shock when she heard that Mary was violent and now she had seen it and perhaps we were now beginning to understand why. Mary jumped up again and shouted 'Stupid Mary. Shut up. You'll give your dad his death'. That was different from a voice – that was the painful words and reprimands she had received stuck inside her like a record, adding to her sense of guilt. There was a painful silence in the room and all smiles had gone. I said 'poor Mary, you worry it's because you were stupid your dad died.' She sobbed and her mother held her hand.

We had four meetings all together in which it was possible to establish that the voice in her head started after her father's death. It was friendly at first and felt like a good companion filling the empty space. Then the voice started telling her she should be at home with her mother now Dad was not there. It was when her mother made clear this would not happen that the voice turned nasty and told her to hurt people.

After the first four meetings I saw her by herself for a year. The voice slowly dwindled. She started getting angry with her mother, then with me and finally was able to talk of her loss of her father and her loss of herself as a normal person.

EDWARD AGED 24

I first saw Edward when I was asked to observe him in a ward in an adult unit. Aged 24, he was mentally ill and mentally handicapped. His mother had died when he was five and he was brought up by his father. When his father died two years ago he was admitted to a short-stay unit and now to a long-stay hospital. As with many handicapped people, death produced a double loss, loss of family and loss of home.

He had autistic features and a prodigious memory for geographical detail and for train times and lines. His self-injurious behaviour, different 'voices', public anal masturbation and depression were of concern. When I saw him he sat rocking on the side of his bed, talking to himself incessantly. Every so often he would bang his head as if the words or thoughts hurt. As I walked closer I could hear that what he was saying to himself was the name of all the stations on one train line. 'He knows all of them – and British Rail too and timetables and the prices of the tickets' said the nurse. He started banging his head and moaning painfully. Suddenly it stopped. He turned to the nurse and asked in a completely normal tone 'You have to live to breathe don't you?'

Rather taken aback the nurse tried to alter that statement. 'No, it's you have to breathe to live'. 'But you have to live to breathe' he repeated. I said yes, if you killed yourself or died you would not be able to breathe. He sat still for a moment.

When I saw him for the first time on his own we were given a small staff cubicle. 'Valerie', he stated. I replied that was my name and he remembered it. 'Valerie's come from London. From Tavistock Clinic, 120 Belsize Lane. Valerie came by car along the ... or she went by ... bus to ... and then got the train from ... '. In fact he had completely accurately worked out my journey and my setting out time. I commented on this.

'Valerie' he said. I commented he was using my name to try and keep it and me in his head because once he had worked out my journey he did not know if there was any other way of being in contact with me. 'Valerie', he tried the sound again. I said he knew my name and he was satisfied that if he said it I would be concentrating on him but then he did not know how to let it go.

'Mmmm'. He started gouging his fist in his mouth. I asked if he was hungry. 'Mmm, yes. See Valerie'. Stuck his fist in his mouth again. I said he maybe felt hungry for me since he hadn't seen me for a week and would only see me two more times. He smiled and looked at me and relaxed. Then he spoke in a completely different voice. 'Stupid Edward, stupid boy, shut up, get under'. I said there was an Edward who thought Edward was stupid.

'Valerie'. I said nothing. 'Valerie. Is your clinic Finchley Road Frognal British Rail, Jubilee Line Swiss Cottage Station, Metropolitan and Jubilee Line Finchley Road station?' I said he could correctly place where I had come from because he did not feel able to place himself and me in a conversation right now.

He put a hand inside his trousers to touch his bottom and began a whispering litany. I said something had happened that had sent him away from me. Then I realised I was being a stupid coward and he was telling me something sexual but I could not bear it. As I thought this he stood up and jumped which frightened me a little. His harsh voice returned, 'Stupid Edward, get under' and then he quickly returned to train lines. I said maybe he kept travelling on train lines because if he didn't he would have to think about more painful kinds of travelling in his bottom that made him jump. He shouted 'No' and then went through an ear-piercing litany of train timetables.

On the second meeting he went through his litany of my name and my journey and when I was silent he started banging his head and moaning. I said how awful he felt when he moved from what he knew and what he could not bear to know. He looked at me intently for a moment and then started rocking and moaning again.

'Dad on top' he suddenly said. Then he began keening again even louder. 'Dad under'. I said his father was dead, was that what he meant by under? He nodded. I asked what he meant by 'on top'. I had a horrible feeling I already knew. 'Bunk beds. Dad on top. Edward under.' He started whispering and banging his head and punching the wall. I said maybe when he slept underneath he felt dead, as if her was buried under the ground. He started crying loudly. 'Dad on top.' I said maybe his dad did not just lie on top of the bed, maybe he lay on top of his body too. He nodded. 'Stupid Edward, piece of shit. Piss off. Pyjamas off. Filthy piece of shit. Get under.'

After this meeting he spent several days crying and was put on anti-depressants. Staff then thought of other comments he had made which corroborated the idea of his father abusing him, although nothing could be done now that his father was dead.

On the third meeting Edward looked white and tired. He did not say anything when I saw him. I commented how tired he looked at the memory of being under his father and now his father was under the earth and it was hard to know what to do with his feelings. He sat looking intently at me wanting me to speak. I said when his father had died he had lost his good father as well as his bad father and he had lost home.

He cried again and then stood up and assumed his harsh voice. 'Get those pyjamas off, you piece of shit. Think you're going to mess up the sheets when I am on duty. I'll give you something to mess the sheets with you arsehole.' He stood up, put his hands in his trousers and ran round the tiny room screaming and crying. I felt awful. I said it sounded to me that when his father died and he had been moved to a hospital, the one before this, or this one, a male staff member had done what his father did. He collapsed crying and whispering and returning to train maps.

Both of these extracts support Sheila Hollins' findings that the three secrets that need to be faced by the patient and the worker, and which require emotional intelligence, are handicap, sexuality and death.

A toddler I observed was hit by his mother for going near the radiator. 'No. Hot' she shouted. A week later the toddler walking near the radiator stopped himself and turned away shouting 'No. Hot' in the same tone as his mother, kicking a toy on the floor. Several months later he just did not walk near the radiator. It was possible to assume in a young child observation group that the child has processed his mother's anger and order, understood the reason for it, and dealt accordingly. We will not know if the physical shock is truly processed until the child grows up and has a child. Will he then unconsciously restrain his own toddler in the same way or will he be able to use another method?

Where conditions are adequate and there is good-enough parenting society does not notice the way in which the mini traumas of everyday life are passed on wholesale to the next generation. Where the lucky-enough child absorbs other people's comments and internalises them and develops language, the handicapped child faces greater developmental difficulty. If you cannot think and are severely handicapped then other people's words cannot get processed easily and if they are harsh or traumatic words even less so. The word then itself remains like a concrete object in the mind. Handicapped adults with a lifetime of institutionalisation have an encyclopaedia of these concrete word-weapons hurting their minds.

With these individuals I have shown the mixture of voices and hallucinations that can occur. At times the hallucination is totally the authentic undiluted trauma, at others it moves into a more florid psychosis. Jaspers (1962) did not think there was a gradual transition between a true and a pseudo-hallucination but Fish (1974) does see that transitions do occur. I wonder, too, how we can link this with the concept of disaster flashbacks. My abused patients who are not handicapped can also suddenly bring back the memory of abuse complete with smell, sound and visual image. Leff (1976) found that the perceptions of normal people undergoing sensory deprivation found it hard to distinguish between images and hallucinations and this overlapped with mental patients. If we consider the emotional deprivation and the problems in thinking handicapped people have had we can see how easy the transition is.

Think of the times the ordinary individual is driven to speak aloud and then go to T.S. Eliot's words – 'Words strain, Crack and sometimes break, under the burden' (T.S. Eliot (1936), 'Burnt Norton').

REFERENCES

Buchanan, A. and Oliver, J.E. (1977) 'Abuse and neglect as a cause of mental retardation.' *British Journal of Psychiatry 131*, 458–67.

Corbett, J. (1975) 'Aversion for the treatment of self-injurious behaviour.' *Journal of Mental Deficiency Research 19*, 79.

Fish's Clinical Psychopathology (1974) *Signs and Symptoms in Psychiatry,* ed. Max Hamilton. Bristol: Wright.

Jaspers, K. (1962) *General Psychopathology,* Manchester: Manchester University Press.

Heaton-Ward, A. (1977) 'Psychosis in mental handicap.' *British Journal of Psychiatry 130*, 525–33.

Leff, J.P. (1976) 'Perceptual phenomena and personality in sensory deprivation.' *British Journal of Psychiatry 114*, 1499.

Oliver, C. Murphy, G.H., Corbett, J.A. (1987) 'Self-Injurious Behaviour in People with mental Handicap: a total population study.' *Journal of Mental Deficiency Research* 31, 147–62.

Reid, A. (1982) *The Psychiatry of Mental Handicap*, London: Blackwell Scientific Publications.

Rutter, M. *et al.* (1970) *Education, Health and Behaviour.* London: Longman.

Sinason, V. (1986) 'Secondary mental handicap and its relationship to trauma.' *Psychoanalytic Psychotherapy 2,* 2, 131–54.

Sinason, V. (1988) 'Dolls and bears; from symbolic equation to symbol. The use of different play material for sexually abused children.' *British Journal of Psychotherapy 4,* 4.

Sinason, V. (1988) 'Smiling, swallowing, sickening and stupefying. The effect of abuse on the child.' *Psychoanalytic Psychotherapy 3,* 2, 97–111.

Sinason, V. (1990) 'Psychotherapy for abused children.' In H. Wolff, A. Bateman and D.A. Sturgeon (eds) *Handbook of Psychiatry. An Integrated Approach.* London: Duckworth.

CHAPTER 13

The Management of Projective Identification in the Treatment of a Borderline Psychotic Patient

M. Fakhry Davids

Projective identification is central to the borderline patient's mode of functioning, and the consequent impoverishment of the self diminishes the ability of such individuals to be fully involved with the activities and people central to their lives. The capacity to work may be seriously impaired and interactions with others tend to be fraught, as conflict that cannot be contained within the mind is inevitably enacted in external reality. Unlike the more overtly psychotic, the borderline patient has access to both neurotic and psychotic mechanisms. These often operate simultaneously, in treatment it is essential to engage the psychotic level of functioning – that aspect of the patient dominated by projective identification – if one is not to risk either an impasse or losing the patient (Rosenfeld 1987).

This is a demanding task because psychotic functioning leaves only limited room for the analyst to be himself. As the analyst succeeds in making meaningful contact with the patient he is subjected to rapid and powerful projections which change the patient's perception of him, forcing it back into the familial narcissistic mould (Rosenfeld 1971, 1987). The rapidity of this process makes it difficult to judge how the patient receives an interpretation. For example, an interpretation intended as a helpful attempt to understand may be perceived as, say, approval; that is, it may be felt to emanate not from a neutral analyst but from an approving admirer. It is easy for such subtle processes to evade scrutiny, yet these object relationships, which are based on projective identification, stand at the heart of the patient's pathology and must be analysed if the treatment is to progress.

Such object relationships are intensely narcissistic, but they are often invoked precisely when the patient accurately senses emotional *contact with* the analyst. This implies particular attention to the link with an external object. Moreover, the emergence of these intense psychotic defences in response to moments of emotional contact protects the patient from the anxieties that go with an awareness of dependency. In this chapter I present material from the treatment of a borderline patient that illustrates these processes. The work is in three phases; in the first two there are considerable demands on me to not put analytical understanding into words, and I trace the factors that make for a transition to the third stage where it is more possible to pursue this necessary task.

BACKGROUND

The patient, a man in his early thirties when he entered the present treatment, is the elder child of an unhappy couple. A childhood accident paralysed his mother on one side of her body, and this physical disability left a deep emotional scar in which jealousy and bitterness loom large. She married a successful professional who had thrown himself into academic and intellectual pursuits as a way of overcoming the void created by emotionally distant parents and a rigid boarding school upbringing. Their early years together were trying ones as the couple were driven by the prospect of using success in their present world as a triumph over the adversities of their respective pasts. Their priorities were a successful career for him, and a properly appointed Chelsea home, complete with family, for her.

For some eight years until the birth of his younger brother my patient was the only child to this couple – the living embodiment of one of their dreams. His own recollections of his early childhood are vague and mostly tinged with intense emotion, so that it is difficult to distinguish fact from emotionally based distortion. His earliest distinct memory is a poignant one recalled with choking emotion: in their garden he discovers for the first time that, on account of her disability, he *can* run away from his mother. On reaching the end of the garden he turns around to find that she has given up the chase, but in her eyes he glimpses the unmistakable hatred of one utterly humiliated by defeat at the hands of a mere toddler. Later, his father punishes him for this cruelty. Other memories of his early childhood involve him trying to catch up with his father in a supermarket, terrified that he would lose him, and desperate to be held by the hand, only for this longing (it was never clear whether he tried to communicate it) to be cruelly rebuffed by an insensitive father who apparently believes in children standing on their own feet from the word go. Incidents like these convinced him that while his mother was physically disabled, his father was the emotional cripple. At the beginning of his treatment he himself was very much identified with his mother in needing emotional sustenance from an unavailable father, and full of a sullen resentment on this account.

School provided a refuge of sorts. He discovered that he was bright and could use his intelligence to get what he wanted. He developed a style of being a good obedient boy who, like his father before him, shone academically. This won him the admiration and praise of teachers and parents alike, but even then he began to realise that something was wrong – he worked for an ulterior motive, and there was a desperation about *having* to shine – though he was powerless to do anything about it. Moreover, mostly it worked and he got the admiration he needed so desperately in order to survive.

Using the techniques he developed at school he went on to get a good degree from one of the finest universities in the country, but has never been able to work in his chosen profession. His wife, by contrast, is successful in an intellectually demanding profession, but this reflects an upbringing in a family unresponsive to emotional need. My patient tries to compensate for this by being a sensitive, strong and caring husband, but he cannot cope with the idea of their having the baby she so desires. I have the impression of a distinct 'babes-in-the-woods' atmosphere in their marriage.

His problems began to surface as his student days drew to an end. He was helped over a crisis (a near breakdown) in his final year by regular sessions at the student counselling centre; in retrospect he sees the counsellor as having given him the praise that was vital to sustained work. He could succeed if he felt that his efforts would so please someone else that they would think him wonderful, and hence provide the love/praise that he depended on. Once in the world of work, however, this system began to break down. There is a considerable gap between the theoretical base of his profession as taught at university and its application in day-to-day work, and in this latter sphere, a complete novice, he could not shine at the top of a class. Deprived of perceived praise, he went to pieces: he left his job, and an extended period abroad provided the complete change of scene that averted a breakdown. He returned nearly a year later, but only for the briefest of spells before walking out of his profession permanently. By the time he entered treatment with me he was driving a minibus for a nursing home.

The struggles with work finally convinced him that he had a serious problem which required help. This was difficult to accept, and his path to me was a long and tortured one with steps towards help punctuated by determined attempts to pull himself together by his own efforts. Some time ago he had seen a woman therapist for well over a year, initially fortnightly, then for extended follow-up sessions. His account of himself in that treatment was of a rather compliant patient doing his best to cooperate so that he might benefit from the help such a stance would bring. Eventually he sensed that instead of being helped, the pattern of his whole life – that of going along with people in the hope that their approval and praise would save him – was simply repeating itself within the treatment, and he became more and more angry with himself for allowing this to happen.

With this understanding of his problem, he formulated the antidote – that of leaving the therapy with a defiant determination to go it alone and find his own way. Just over a year later he realised again that this was not working and he joined a psychotherapy group. Here, in addition to the old problem of just going along with things, which he now bitterly castigated himself for, he realised that he was furious at having to battle against others in the group in order to make a space to be heard. He could not bear such deprivation, and on the advice of a friend knowledgeable about analysis had an assessment with the analyst who referred him to me.

THE ROLE OF PROJECTIVE IDENTIFICATION

Most of the background I have given above was conveyed in his first sessions, but his account lacked feeling and failed to find the emotional resonance in me that might guide a response to the material. Thus, although *I* felt sympathy for him – for instance I could imagine what it might have been like to have two parents each crippled in their own way – talking to him on this basis did not facilitate deeper contact between us. I felt kept at arms' length.

In an early session, he described the following: some years ago he had allowed his brother, then an adolescent, to spend a night with him and his wife in order to have some respite from an ongoing quarrel with their father. He decided not to inform his parents though they would expect him to, ostensibly in order to set their minds at rest, but really as proof that his loyalty to them was paramount. After dropping his brother off at the station the following morning he rang his mother, who told him that his father would be absolutely furious with him. On his way home he heard a strange noise coming from the engine of their new car, and had the thought that it was about to explode. Convinced that he was in mortal danger, he stopped the car, got out and locked the door behind him, dropped the keys down a drain and made for home. On the way a terrifying thought that his mother had committed suicide took hold in his mind: and he was immensely relieved when she answered his call from the nearest telephone.

In listening to this account, which contained the first open hint of psychotic functioning within his borderline mode of being, I was at first concerned that his level of disturbance would be uncontainable within once-weekly therapy. I felt under some pressure to understand intellectually what it all meant: what did the engine stand for, how was the explosive rage linked with the wish for an independent existence (projected into his brother), where did his father's anger fit in, how was this linked with his terror concerning a dead mother; what were the transference implications – was he afraid the new therapy might blow up? However, I was also aware that up to that point he had reacted to attempts to reach him through interpretation as though a 'correct' interpretation freed him of any anxiety; he seemed to feel 'Well, if my therapist is aware of *that* it leaves one less thing for me to worry about', so that the path to further contact was in fact closed off. This tendency seemed to parallel two aspects of the episode: that his father could not contain his own reactions to his son's growing independence; and that his own reaction to his mother's communication could not be located in his mind, but found its way into the engine as an explosive rage. Now I tried to open up a deeper investigation into the dynamics of such functioning, and said that he wanted me to know that he had an enormous rage inside, but was uncertain whether I could tolerate it.

I must have expected my patient to be relieved that I recognised the explosive rage as internal, for I was quite taken aback by the violence of his response. He took my use of the term 'enormous' to be a complaint at the extent of his rage, and became quite paranoid, attacking me for expecting him to hide it, submit to me and agree meekly with what I said. In the moment I spoke he had experienced me as the very embodiment of all those in his past who had taken for granted that he would accommodate himself solely to *their* desires, ignoring *his* inner state. This provoked a merciless barrage, full of defiant rage, that did not abate until the session ended: he had had enough of that sort of treatment and would never submit to it again. Lost in this rage, I could not reach him: for instance, I put it to him that he heard my interpretation as a complaint; or later, that he seemed to react as if I was pushing nasty thoughts into him; but every such attempt to remedy the situation simply provoked him afresh. The damage had been done.

The patient clearly was not in a state of mind to take things further, but I myself reflected a good deal on what had happened. Initially I had reeled from the shock of his sudden, vicious attack – it was in stark contrast to the composed gentleman of the previous sessions – but after detailed consideration of my countertransference I eventually understood that he had found the fact of my having made an interpretation, in itself, so provocative.

My interpretation links the psychotic episode with a specific need of me, implying that he needs my help. I believe the interpretation reached a sane part of the patient in which his treatment is accurately perceived as a central relationship in his life, but the anxiety engendered by this recognition is unbearable due to his difficulties with dependency. His inner equilibrium depends on denying his own neediness by projecting it into his object. In the transference I *was* the needy part of him: at the beginning of a treatment I clearly lacked information about him, and he was in a position to fulfil that need. This projective identification allowed considerable room for manoeuvre, and transference interpretations, even ones that appeared to suggest he needed something from me, could be heard as evidence that I had obtained the material I needed and was therefore happily working away. As *interpretations* they did not touch him; they were simply proof that between us a familiar defensive order was in place.

The understanding of how much he relied on projective identification to get by brought perspective to the material I had thus far obtained. One can appreciate that there is a part of him that desires to get on – variously, in the toddler who tries to get away, in the sojourn abroad after his first near-breakdown, in his not asking his parents for permission to keep his brother, in his brother who stays away (as he himself never could), or in his father who lets go of his hand in the supermarket – but this is based on splitting. Each scenario contains an abandoned, hopelessly dependent part of him projected into someone left behind in a bad/mad state, and this deprives him of a supportive object essential for real growth.

In the absence of a containing internal object, the only tools he has to manage anxiety are the primitive ones of splitting and projective identification. As a result of such projection his object becomes more and more frightening and correspondingly less suitable as a container. In the session, his relationship with an uncontaining object was reflected in my countertransference worry about containment, and the pressure I felt to make intellectual links. Projective identification depletes the ego of its resources, hence he could not distinguish between the engine, which now contained his explosive feelings, and his mother, the primary internal container who he fears has died because of a projection.

My interpretation was an accurate response to his need to be understood, which I think he glimpsed for just a moment, and then immediately 'saw' it challenged an entire mode of being based on projective identification. His response is to re-establish his equilibrium by insisting that I am making a complaint, not an interpretation. But this leaves him without an object that can help him bear the anxieties associated with dependency, and he is then forced to expel violently all associated 'concerns' (not yet experienced as such, e.g. that I might not be up to the job) in an unrelenting barrage, leaving no room for thought. In turn, he 'fears' that this violent projection into me (of indigestible beta elements, see Bion 1963) will lead to a cycle of retaliation that will end in his rejection. He cannot bear this fear, and transforms it into a mad conviction that the feared event has already happened: 'You have rejected me' is the only fragment of this complex sequence that enters awareness, and to which his outburst is an apparent response. If it has already happened then of course he has survived it, and there is no intense anxiety or fear to be faced. In this way, I become a mother crippled by projection, and although full of an enraged bitterness, resentment and complaint, he is at least alive to tell the tale.

This solution to the problems of dependency that stem from a momentary experience of being properly attended to is an elegant but psychotic one. On the basis of hearing just one word, 'enormous', he omnisciently *knows* an entire string of meanings in my mind. It also involves a denial of reality – psychic reality, in that anxiety is obliterated, and external reality, in that its link with a containing object in the transference is lost – and this destruction of links with reality means that steps to ameliorate the situation are not possible. Without knowing one's inner state, and what in the external world has brought it about, primitive disturbance cannot be transformed into troubling thoughts, which is the path to sanity (Bion 1963). All that remains in awareness is a sense of an unknown menace within the treatment.

In the next session I discovered that the attack on me was itself denied, including any possibility that it could have touched me. Apparently, being a therapist confers an impenetrable shield affording omnipotent protection. But this creates a new fear: an impenetrable me would be unable to receive any projection, and the unbearable matter would be stuck in him. When I took up his denial of the attack the intense anxieties mobilised necessitated further desperate defensive manoeuvres whose dimensions emerged clearly in the first phase of treatment.

TREATMENT

The above formulation has been central in my work with this patient. Three phases are discernible in the treatment to date, based on his stance towards me, and correspondingly, towards his inner world. Each presented characteristic demands from the point of view of containing and managing projective identification.

Phase One

This phase lasted approximately eighteen months and began to acquire its particular character following the above sessions. For most of this period he had twice weekly sessions.

In response to the situation outlined above, he split the therapist with a capacity to understand him into two: an idealised me, subsequently identified with the physical aspects of the treatment – the times, the sessions themselves, the therapy, the room etc. – and a denigrated me, identified with the person in the sessions with him, into whom all his unwanted and despised aspects were projected – I was angry and determined to get him, full of complaints, unthinking and incomprehensible, needy etc. – and who in turn was out to get him. Murderous projection would beget murderous attack.

Based on this split, a paranoid transference situation took shape in which he became convinced that I was intent on pushing innocuous-sounding understandings into him with the aim of taking over his mind and making him my possession for life, in revenge for the attack I insisted he had carried out on me. He perceived virtually every kind of bad motive in me, and the priority was to keep me at bay. In his desperation to protect himself sessions were kept to a minimum, and he resolved to give me as little as possible, and not to take anything directly from me. This was a torture because he was intensely hungry for understanding and felt cruelly tantalised by interpretations that appeared to make sense. However, he remained convinced that were he to take anything in he would, in the fullness of time, discover that he had lost his *self* to my beguiling reasonableness in just such an unsuspecting moment; his mind would have been taken over.

He managed by preparing in advance every topic he was prepared to discuss, and paid meticulous attention to the sessions as they unfolded, betraying little reaction. Later, on his own and safe, he would carefully weigh the contents of our meetings, and anything he retained as a result would of course feel like his own – the lion's share of making sense of my cryptic utterances had been done by him. He was extremely sensitive to my introducing ideas other than those he mentioned – for instance, my speaking of a transference version of something – and this would be rejected as a deft slipping in of my own agenda: 'Mr Davids is taking me round the houses again. "Come, follow me, down this path and you'll be saved!"' he would mock. Of course he would have nothing to do with such nonsense, although, months later, a faintly recognisable thought of mine might appear as one of those things he had worked out for himself.

A sadistic pathological organisation (Steiner 1987) thus enshrined splitting and projective identification as his solution. The vulnerable, needy patient was desperately attached to his actual sessions – an idealised couple – while the wary, combative patient present in the room was locked in a sadistic battle with his therapist – a bad couple locked in hatred. The focus now shifted to a desperate battle for control, in which I was felt to bar his way to the goodness of his sessions – his right – while he was determined to change the pattern of his life by standing up to me instead of simply giving in to injustice. He did so, more in sorrow than anger, because he had no choice, and the blame for bringing it about was mine. I could have been sympathetic and understanding, but chose to interpret and reach a troubled him. Moreover, he was convinced that I would be determined to distort this fact and shift that blame on to him by any means possible, a preoccupation that coloured the whole of phase one.

When one considers the whole situation as outlined here it is possible to have sympathy for him. However, the reality of his life, recreated in the sessions, was so broken up and devoid of these connecting strands that it proved futile to try to contact the needy him. I was confronted with a split situation in which there was no longer any awareness of such a being, only an idealised core and a belligerent shield. He was dominated by a narcissistic insistence that his perception of the situation was not one view, but the only true reflection of reality. By the time he heard a comment of mine it would already have been distorted to prove his version. For instance, if there was a sharp or firm edge to what I said, I was attacking him. If I presented an understanding in a reasonable tone, I was simply trying to seduce my way into the idealised core, thus trying to take him over and deny his separate existence. Safety lay in organising himself and being prepared for every eventuality. Internally, the vulnerable aspect of himself was concealed beneath a hard combative shield, which afforded omnipotent protection and rendered a nurturing relationship in the external world superfluous. He fought desperately to keep this shield in place, a fight that consumed all his energy, and, in addition, gave him considerable satisfaction. As a result, however, the vulnerable and needy patient was repeatedly left out of the real discourse in sessions.

Given his experience of my interventions as either violent or seductive, I gradually learnt that any formulation of his problem had to be kept alive only in my own mind. My task was not to put understandings/thoughts to him but to confine myself to creating the minimal conditions under which the therapy might provide containment. One central issue was the frequency of sessions: the referrer thought he needed five; initially he was adamant he would have only one. This opened the area of how important it was for him to feel in control, and in this arena some room for manoeuvre became possible.

Perhaps because of my attention to the setting, he sensed an area where grievances against me might be legitimate. He seized this opportunity with both hands and watched the times of sessions like a hawk. I came to anticipate that even a fraction of a minute's lateness on my part would mean serious trouble. For some sullen months an atmosphere of bitter resentment prevailed, until it emerged that in his mind I was robbing him of a minute at the beginning of sessions. I fetched him from the waiting room at the beginning of his time, but by the time he had got up from his chair, followed me, closed the door and settled down in the consulting room ready to begin, a full minute would have elapsed. I felt under enormous pressure to give in to him – partly, I think, because of the mauling I had received in the session I reported earlier, and partly bcause of the apparent reasonableness of the demand – but realised that he was recreating in the transference an experience of a depriving object. This helped me to stand firm on the parameters of his sessions, without explaining the rationale to him, and to interpret his hatred and its displacement into the issue of control – he never left sessions on time, I had to wait for my money, I was kept out of his life, etc. – as well as the consequences of this.

Reporting the material of these difficult months could give the impression that once I understood, the work was uncomfortable but straightforward. This was not the case. In my countertransference I was deeply affected, and my functioning interfered with, by this man. To be subjected to the sort of tyrannical control – no movement, mental or physical, is tolerated except with his express permission – stirs up tremendous hatred which I recognised only slowly and painfully. One tired morning I turned off the alarm clock only to be woken an hour later by a triumphantly furious patient at the other end of the telephone line. For a moment I detected relief that I was there, then he calmly informed me of the facts: it was 8.20; I had a patient at 8.00; he had been worried, what happened? In my guilt I rushed over and with only ten minutes remaining offered an alternative time, which he accepted, but nevertheless proceeded to abuse and tyrannise me with demands for an explanation. He had to know what happened, otherwise how would he know whether he could trust me in future? The abuse only stopped when I pointed out that now that I had put a foot out of line he was gleefully torturing me. Instantly the tables were turned, and he felt outraged and bitter at being wrongly accused as the villain when he was clearly the victim.

Incidents such as these slowly alerted me to the immense hatred he evoked in me, and this made me realise what a vicious person lurked in him. I saw that this hatred at being so controlled, whose intensity I had denied until I acted it out by going back to sleep that morning, was a projection of his intense hatred at being dependent on the treatment. Of course, I could not put this to him, and the focus of the work was on what happened to that hatred in me. I believe that focusing on his experience of my hatred in the here and now, identifying what provokes it and how he accommodates himself to it without identifying it as his projection, and of course the survival of a stable therapy setting, gave him an experience of a minimally containing object. Paradoxically, by slowly and painstakingly interpreting how, following his attacks, he hears whatever I say as a counterattack which he must then respond to in kind, he has the experience of someone who can think, rather than simply resort to action in order to get rid of intense bad feeling. Of course, this makes him fleetingly aware of me as an object on which he might be dependent, and starts the whole cycle again. By bringing all of this to light, without resorting to explanation, he had the repeated experience that hatred can be survived.

Phase Two

This phase lasted nearly a year during which my patient's functioning in the more demanding part-time job he had acquired broke down. This led to him being hospitalised for a spell of in-patient psychiatric treatment following detailed work on his terror of losing his therapy were he to break down. I initiated the referral and throughout he was able to attend his three weekly sessions with me; soon after discharge he began coming for a fourth, then a fifth session.

As a result of the detailed work of the previous stage the patient began to sense minimally containing qualities in me. The repeated testing of my patience, and the consequent experience of me as consistently and reliably available within the confines undertaken, but able to stand up to the tyrannical control he tried to exercise – evidence in his eyes of a capacity to survive destructive attack – allowed him to have this experience. This development, in turn, allowed a more realistic perception of his relationship with his mother. The masochistic identi-fication with her – in which his own hatred of her limitations is projected into a hostile father to whom they both submit – gave way to a recognition of how damaged both she is, and he had been, by the cosy collusion between them. He began to build an alliance with his father who agreed to help with the increased cost of his treatment.

The material in the sessions now changed. Whereas my exclusion from his outside life had been almost total, he now tried to recruit me as an ally. He became aware of the importance to him of one of his colleagues. He had little to do with this woman, who sat behind him, but when she was away he began to realise how much he relied on her benevolent presence, usually just taken for granted, to be able to function at work. This led to the detailed description of how he always relied on an anticipated glow of praise from parents and teachers in order to fight the accumulated obstacles that came at him whenever he tried to work. It was a fight for life itself. Praise, he said, was as vital to him as sunshine is to plants – it was both the motive for work, and the reward for triumph over work.

I understood the descriptions of his changing relationship with his father, and the relationship with the colleague, to point to the emergence in the transference of a therapist felt as quietly supportive of him, my resources placed at his disposal. In someone as ill as my patient this development was bound to pose problems, and he responded by idealising his relationship with me. Nevertheless, for a time this changed perception of his relationship with me allowed some beneficial work to take place.

Material from his outside life, as opposed to the total transference focus of the first phase, made it possible to explore the dimensions of his dependent relationships with people at work; how he needed them, what he wanted, what the consequences of gratification and frustration were, etc. By separating out his impulses, thoughts and feelings, a measure of separation of his inner world from the world of interaction was achieved. It became possible, for instance, to say that the 'glow' of praise might express the need to be kept in mind, sensed as vital to the survival of an infant within, sensed as vital to survival.

I avoided linking this material with his dependency in the transference, since I felt this would plunge us back into the turbulence of the first phase; I was also relieved to have some respite from that torrid time. However, one line of work in the transference did become possible. When he described the details of his need for his colleague I sometimes felt a strong impulse to refer immediately to his dependence on me. It dawned on me that I felt sidelined and saw that this recreated in the transference a mother who had to face that she had limitations. (At a deeper level, of course, it is the infant who has to face that it is not the only thing in its mother's life, as it once may have believed.) My countertransference impulse to get in there was clearly just what he feared – an object who could not keep out. This difficulty with exclusion – a projection of his own problem – could be analysed in me, and allowed a deepening of the work on his paranoia. When I described this situation I was actually experienced as critical and demanding redress, but analyst-oriented interpretation (Steiner 1993) gradually helped him to distinguish his perception from what I actually said.

For the first time it became possible to map out the contours of his aggression following its projection. At work, without the protection of his benevolent colleague, he was exposed to extremely hostile and destructive forces tied up in 'work' tasks themselves. He described vividly how, when she was away, he would become totally incapacitated. As he approached the task on his desk, the letters on the page in front of him would come at him and scramble up his mind, creating confusion and disorder. He would not know where he was or how far he had got with even the simplest task, and would pour every ounce of energy into a desperate effort of will to regain control. Of course, little real work could proceed and 'work' became a dire struggle with an out-of-control, unruly monster, that preoccupied him totally, eventually leaving him depleted, distraught and full of impotent rage. Again, while I understood that the hostility was his own, much understanding of its nature – what were its motives, how did it work, etc. – could proceed as long as I did not make this link explicit.

As I indicated, all of this took place within an idealised transference. Of course, while he did what he could to keep hostility away from his treatment, the increasing recognition of need meant that my limited availability stung him more acutely. This, in turn, increased the splitting, so that he felt more and more got at in his work, while believing that I am the mother he felt he never had.

The change in the transference was paralleled by changes in his outside life. Contract work during these Thatcherite years paid handsomely and he and his wife were able to leave behind their incurably damp flat for a much more spacious home, in need of only minor work. There was unspoken hope too in the idea that here they might have space for the baby his wife longed for. A kitten was taken in, I thought as a sort of trial run. Then the recession set in, and he summarily lost one of his contract days, with no guarantee that the same might not happen to the other two as well. With my help in clarifying how much he needed his work to be a place that he could just take for granted, he got a glimpse of the idealised longing that lay beneath his reasonable demand for at least some warning before being made redundant. Within a matter of days he had confronted his employer, and summarily resigned when the latter would not back down. By contrast, his relationship with me was now totally idealised. Now that he felt I understood him he acted as if I would concretely provide for his every need, and he would need no one else. His entire days were spent either in their new home, doing the odd jobs that needed him, or in coming to his sessions. He was all mine to look after; but soon the physical, mindless tasks themselves began to torment him as his contract work had earlier.

I had to bear in mind that behind the desperate splitting that left him with such a broken up world lay a terror of integration. Schematically, one could think of this as evoking a phantasy of a catastrophic intercourse between the parents (Money-Kyrle 1968; Britton 1989) that leaves both crippled. However, interpreting that he could not tolerate integration was unhelpful, as it was perceived as doing the very thing I was describing, i.e., forcing an integration of observation and thinking, to which he reacted as though something violent was happening inside his mind: all he had understood up to that point was being smashed up. If he were properly understood I would appreciate that he could understand very little. At this point his capacity to think had to reside in me.

He became more aware of how crippled he was, how little he could cope with, and once verbalised, the demand for round-the-clock care was unstoppable. Being surrounded by continuous work on the new home seemed a partial solution, but as I have indicated the tasks themselves became the neglected, desperate, hungry, demanding, and angry infant, and persecuted him. Showing him this process made it worse, for he expected, quite literally, that I would take that infant in and provide the care consistent with looking after an actual baby. Of course, this idealised version of care denied all that I had done for him within the confines of the limited therapy, and was based on a split in which all the chronic problems were left behind – in the flat, in his mother, etc. – while this would be a new beginning, the reparative experience to make good all past deprivation. Moreover, any attempt on my part to describe this in words was felt as an attack: while I seduced him into believing that I understood a needy infant in him, I really meant that it was his fault if there was something infantile in the patient who could not, rather than would not, cope with being an adult. I was accusing him of being responsible for it all. I expected, quite madly, that mere words would magically heal him.

He was breaking down, and the omnipotent combative patient now took over. While it was I who had raised the possibility of psychiatric help, this now became *his* idea, his crusade, and I was constantly badgered to get on with it, to report on progress, discuss options with him, etc. He was the therapist, who relied on a rather recalcitrant me who had to be cajoled into letting go. In the midst of this it was quite difficult to be clear as to my own judgment on the issue; it became important to counter my own omnipotence and avail myself of consultations with senior colleagues. This made me realise how lonely this work had been as I had to keep so much in my mind that could not be part of the shared work of the sessions, as is possible with a less disturbed patient. I arranged regular supervision.

Phase Three

At the time of writing, this phase has lasted approximately eighteen months. His hospitalisation gave me some peace of mind; it provided greater freedom within his therapy, as it released me from the worry that, were I to take up certain issues directly with him, he might break down. In a concrete way, the claustrophobic relationship between us was broken, and it was more possible to imagine that he had the equivalent of two parents in his treatment. The family parallel seemed to hold, too, in the different types of relationships hospital made possible – senior and junior doctors, nurses, occupational therapists, other patients, etc. This makes for greater safety; for example, he could play off one against the other and not feel that his entire world would crumble were someone to turn against him.

In line with his idealised expectations the patient hoped, of course, that the hospital would cure him. This brought the struggle with dependency on his therapy to the fore. After some considerable acting out of this struggle, the thought sunk in that, for better or worse, this was where treatment would have to happen. The hospital could contain but not treat. The frequency of sessions increased first to four, then to five, and he began to use the couch. Of course, none of these transitions was smooth, but as a result of them I felt that a containing structure was now in place. This enabled me to address more directly issues at the heart of his pathology, which I knew would elicit violent reactions beyond his control, but which had to be analysed in the here-and-now of the sessions rather than simply understood by me. Given his level of disturbance, this task could only be tackled in the knowledge that psychiatric backup was in place.

I shall end my account of his treatment by describing one session, and giving an excerpt from a second, to show the sort of work, based on the understanding of his use of projective identification, that now became possible. I shall also give an indication of my own responses to his material to show how much more possible it was for me to think in his sessions.

The first is a Tuesday session – the first of his week – from the time he was still in hospital. The previous week he learnt that I had been to see the consultant psychiatrist, and was furious that I did not give him a full report of that meeting.

As he enters he hands me his cheque, and I notice that for the first time he crossed it with the words 'A/C Payee only'. Later I think this must refer to a direct link that he wants between just the two of us, which excludes any possible third party. He looks at me, and I realise there has been a directness of eye contact since his admission. He reports that he has given thought to what I raised on Friday concerning what made him go into hospital. I notice that he is in a reasonable state of mind and seems to have retained a link with Friday's session, but there is no reference to the fact that there has been a weekend.

He describes in some detail that he simply wanted others to take responsibility for him – he'd had enough of trying to get by on his own, of looking after himself. By giving himself over to the hospital he was freed of the terrible threat that if he doesn't look after himself he will not only go to pieces but be blamed for it. Well, it worked: he had the space where he felt he could just be himself without having to take any responsibility. For six days he had that space, then his wife, who up to that point had been sympathetic, became difficult because she had no one to talk to at home. He is very aware of feeling responsible for her, and this makes it complicated now. I inquire whether she has been seen at the hospital. No, he says, not in her own right, although they would be willing to offer joint sessions, which he does not think will be helpful. She has, of course, seen the social worker who interviews relatives. But the doctors think it is not right to see her since it is really he who is their patient. He will have to see: but the main issue that concerns him is who is going to look after him. I have in mind Friday's theme about how he cannot bear to wait, and say it is interesting that he was able to hang on all this time, but once I had spoken to Dr J (the psychiatrist) he couldn't wait any longer, and had to hand himself over straight away. Having spoken, my mind moves onto how controlling he had become, how I was made to feel like an errant child who had not done what I had been told, etc. I wonder whether this is his solution to feeling terribly left out, but realise I had to process these thoughts more before putting them to him.

It could be, he responds, he's not thought of it like that. This is an awkward moment, when I suddenly wonder whether, in all my thinking the last few minutes, I am actually giving in to an idealised longing for just the right interpretation.

This is followed by an interchange, the details of which I have forgotten, in which I speak of his sense that what I offer is terribly limited. There is a pause for some moments, then he says that at the time he was very angry with me because had to wait such a very long time when his wish to hand himself over felt terribly urgent. On top of that I never tell him when I plan to meet Dr J though I know it is important to him, like the other day. He had thought that when he made a fuss of it in the sessions I didn't want to know... I had seemed annoyed that he was making more demands of me. Then the day after I'd gone and he raised it here I seemed annoyed again. He told his wife about this, and that he just can't take responsibility for himself any more, someone else should, and I should do at least some of it.

There is another pause during which I think again of how he cannot bear Dr J and me getting together, and say: the moment there is a link between Dr J and me, his hatred of the me who doesn't provide all he needs seems to come into play. I thought this is expressed in him not being willing, for another moment, to do anything for himself. As if he were saying to me, with great resentment: 'Now you can do what you should have done all along.'

After another short pause, in which he appears to be considering my comment, he says doesn't feel he hates me at the moment, but it is just that he has been very angry that I don't look after him properly. I keep him waiting for things that are essential in his care, such as speaking to the hospital and putting them in the picture. It must be right that he should have two parents who talk to each other – me and the hospital jointly responsible for him; he can see that he might hate my not contacting them, and not keeping him in the picture when I eventually do. He pauses, and I become worried that this conversation is all too sensible, and that the real patient has been projected into his wife, who is not going to get the help she needs. I am also aware that if I put this to him, he will immediately feel left out, i.e., that *his* concerns in the session are being ignored while I indulge *my* theories. Remembering that there are two different persons inside him – the pseudo-mature gentleman and the violent psychotic – makes me realise that the hospital patient appears not to be present in the session: I have the pseudo-mature one. I see that the patient is free of the problem of how to get these two parts of him to live together – that problem is being lived out between Dr J and myself; moreover when we do meet, something violent happens, hence the attempts to reassert control. I see his violent hatred of being excluded as at the root of this, but am aware of his sensitivity to feeling blamed when I locate aggression directly in him.

I interpret that he feels it important for the team and me to have a link, but in the moment that we do, he feels terribly excluded. Then he gets totally inside his place at the hospital, but worries that I might feel left out. (When he returns, therefore, he has to be conciliatory and sensible.) Following this interpretation I temporarily lose my memory of what I said.

He says he has no trouble whatsoever talking to the nurses and knowing they exclude him by talking about him among themselves. I realise I have reached him only intellectually; I say he has a compromise in which they can, provided Dr J and I don't. There is a longish silence, eventually broken by him complaining that I seem unwilling to accept his version that he needs some control, that he needs to know what steps I am taking, what has been discussed. It is the fact of my withholding information from him that makes him feel so unsafe. There is a shorter silence. It makes sense to him this way, he says, and explains the urgency of both Dr J and I taking him seriously and talking to each other. But the pace of it is very slow for him; he's sure that the two of us have lots of other things to do, it's just a normal pace, but for him it is an eternity just to sit out there and wait until we eventually get around to it. The only way, then, is to get a handle on things, to get some control, as I would say. I see that he has shifted the focus back into his more rational approach, not allowing what I said to penetrate. The patient is being kept away; I feel the atmosphere is too cosy here, work is being evaded, and wonder whether the earlier gaps in my recall were an attack on my functioning.

I try a more direct approach: although he senses it is important for me to have a relationship with someone other than himself, when I do so it is intolerable, and stirs up immense hatred and resentment (expressed by the attack on my independent thinking in the session). He is quiet for a few minutes, then asks how would I give him a picture of that? (Meaning: make a story that I can hold on to, and I very nearly did!) I say: I must explain; there is little chance of our developing a picture together. This pushes him into a different frame of mind – still reasonable but with an edge of irritation in his voice he explains that is because when he hears something new from me he is wary that I might be confused, since I am always throwing bright new ideas at him. I see that something has taken place very quickly: he felt I understood – a picture exists – but immediately feels excluded by the thinking process that has produced the understanding, then wants to be right inside it. However, when I do not give in to the demand to include him, hate that cannot be felt is projected into my mind, leaving it in a confused state. That leaves him worried and angry that he is in the hands of a confused analyst, thus he resorts to subtle control. I therefore say that when he senses I have a picture of my own about him, which I do not let him into, he cannot bear it, and wants to be inside. However, as he is left on the outside his perception of me changes from one who has a picture to one whose mind is mangled, but is desperately trying to cover his tracks. He is silent for a moment, looks at his watch and realises that the end is upon us. He says that he will be coming tomorrow, but is not sure of the next day, we shall have to discuss it. I take it that the interpretation reached him, but there is also a part of him that wants no truck with it at all. However, there is no time to put this to him.

In this session I think the patient was more available for analysis. It is possible to see how he projects the disturbance into his wife at the outset, and creates a pseudo-mature atmosphere between us, which I collude with for a time. (It is such a relief to have a less stormy session with a patient like him.) However, I try hard to regain control, and this alerts me to the fact there are transactions in the transference that are alive, but are not being addressed. When I do pursue his exclusion by me, it eventually becomes possible to pinpoint the early Oedipal exclusion between us, and the consequences of the projection into me of his hatred, which creates a confused object. This was sufficiently precisely located to enable further sustained work.

I shall now present an excerpt from another session, some months later, when the theme of my excluding him had been worked on for some time, and his aggression is more to the fore. The direct awareness of my cruelty in shutting him out had been too much for him, and he had stormed from his Friday session, shoes in hand, a minute before the end in order to prevent me 'pushing him out', nearly taking the door off its hinges in the process.

He begins by describing the enormous effort of looking after himself out there as mining a tunnel in which he has to prepare the entire path for himself, requiring a tremendous mental effort. Then he falls silent for a long period, in which my mind goes all over the place, and I cannot keep hold of anything at all. Eventually I think he is boring his way into my mind, leaving no space for independent thought; he lets out a loud 'Phew!', and after a moment I inquire, 'What?' He gets irritated, demanding to know what do I mean 'what?' he's waiting for me to say something more and I am just tormenting him with my silence, keeping him hanging on.

I interpret the pressure for idealised contact in the here and now: I do something horrible by pushing him out, but now that he is here, I should let him in and surround him with the constant sound of my words; that is the only way to even things between us. After a pause he says well, he is aware that he could have said more at the beginning; there are many things he is been thinking since he was last here, but he is just not prepared to. That would send completely the wrong signals and he is not going to go soft on me like that.

I respond that when he senses the possibility of a meeting with me, of something softer, that is the moment he chooses for his revenge: then I am to remain the shut out one (thinking that in the process the needy patient is shut out). He is quiet for a while, seems resentful at what I said, then says he hates what I do to him, and he is not going to say more than me. Why should he? And allow me to sit here, watch and play games with him? No! I think it is worse than I thought; that in the moment he has a softer impulse, he no longer feels in a benign presence, but all the aggression has already been projected into me, so that I am concretely experienced as superior, mocking his need, and cruelly controlling. He continues: he comes here and accepts the responsibility for starting his sessions, despite everything. He started, didn't he? But then the ball is in *my* bloody court. Then I have to speak. *He's* not going to have any of *my* games he says defiantly, but smugly.

He stuck to his guns in the remainder of this session, and the familiar accusation–counter-accusation scenario ensued. However, it was possible to spell out how, motivated by revenge, he cruelly attacks the possibility of a coming together. He insists that the only way to put right exclusion is for me to let him burrow his way in and thus to avoid all awareness that he and I are separate individuals. The sound of my voice would be a womb that surrounds him, and by its very presence apologise for shutting him out. If he belongs in a womb he should never have been shut out in the first place. When, instead of giving in to this idealised wish, I interpret it, he feels the game is up, and only hostility and a bitter struggle over who will have the last word remains. A paranoid situation prevails, but can now be analysed.

The major difference between this phase and the previous two is that there is now a way of putting all of this in words, of witnessing how within a session there is some softening, and then watching how the actual shutting out in the session is handled. It is possible to follow how my renewed exclusion of him in the process of thinking about him stirs up hostility once more. Often I find it difficult to think, only afterwards realising what has actually gone on – intense attacks on my functioning is very much a lived reality.

I have presented this material because I think it shows how much more possible it is to get hold of the tremendous difficulties he has in being dependent on someone else – who has a life of their own, but perhaps more importantly, a mind of their own. It is clear that this stirs up tremendously destructive forces in his mind, and I am not sure to what extent it will be possible for him to use the treatment to put things right. This leaves a question of why dependency is so difficult for him. He has a definitive answer to that – because he happened to have a depriving object – whereas I sometimes wonder, particularly when his hatred in the sessions is at its most intense, whether it is based on being unable use something good if it does not belong to him. In this view, a disabled mother is not the cause of, but the solution to, his fundamental problem.

ACKNOWLEDGEMENT

I would like to thank Mrs Ruth Riesenberg Malcolm whose meticulous supervision has helped me to understand this patient's pathology and to pursue the treatment along the lines indicated in this paper.

REFERENCES

Bion, W. (1963) *Elements of Psycho-Analysis*. London: Heinemann. (Reprinted by Maresfield Reprints, London, 1984.)

Britton, R. (1989). 'The missing link.' In J. Steiner (ed) *The Oedipus Complex Today: Clinical Implications*. London: Karnac.

Money-Kyrle, R. (1968) 'Cognitive development.' *International Journal of Psycho-Analysis 49*. Reprinted in D. Meltzer (ed) *The Collected Papers of Roger Money-Kyrle*. Strath Tay: Clunie Press, 1978.

Rosenfeld, H. (1971) 'A clinical approach to the psychoanalytical theory of the life and death instincts: an investigation into the aggressive aspects of narcissism.' *International Journal of Psycho-Analysis 52*, 169–78.

Rosenfeld, H. (1987) *Impasse and Interpretation*. London and New York: Tavistock.

Searles, H. (1986) *My Work with Borderline Patients*. Northvale, NJ: Jason Aronson.

Steiner, J. (1987) 'The interplay between pathological organisations and the paranoid-schizoid and depressive positions.' *International Journal of Psycho-Analysis 68*, 69–80.

Steiner, J. (1993) *Psychic Retreats: Pathological Organisations in Psychotic, Neurotic and Borderline Patients*. London: Routledge.

List of Contributors

Eleanore Armstrong-Perlman, MA, TQAP, is a psychoanalytic psychotherapist in private practice.

Dr Peter Barham, CPsychol, AFBPsP, is Founder and Adviser to the Hamlet Trust and Visiting Senior Lecturer in Mental Health at Goldsmiths' College, London. His publications include *Schizophrenia and Human Value* and (with Robert Hayward) *Relocating Madness*.

Dr David Bell is a member of the British Psycho-analytical Society and Consultant and Clinical Tutor at the Cassel Hospital, Richmond, Surrey. He will shortly be moving to take up a post as Consultant to the Adult Department at the Tavistock Clinic.

Dr Joseph Berke is Co-founder and Director of the Arbours Association and the Arbours Crisis Centre. His most recent work is *Sanctuary: The Arbours Experience of Alternative Community Care* (edited with C. Masoliva and T. Ryan). He is currently working on a book entitled *Psychoanalysis and Kabbalah* (with S. Schneider).

Dr Christopher Cordess has been consultant Forensic Psychiatrist with the North West Thames Forensic Psychiatry Service, St Bernard's Hospital, London, since 1987. He is an associate member of the British Psycho-analytic Society.

Fakhry Davids practised and taught in clinical psychology before pursuing further training in psychoanalysis and psychoanalytic psychotherapy. He is a Member of the Tavistock Society of Psychotherapists and Associate Member of the British Psycho-analytical Society. He is in full-time private practice.

Jane Ellwood is Principal Child Psychotherapist at the Department of Child and Family Psychiatry, Yorkhill NHS Trust, Glasgow.

Dr Arthur Hyatt Williams is a medical psychoanalyst and was Head of the Adolescent Department at the Tavistock Clinic. Now retired, he is in private practice and travels widely teaching and lecturing, with a particular interest in forensic psychotherapy.

Dr Murray Jackson is a psychiatrist and psychoanalyst, formerly a consultant at King's College Hospital and the Maudsley Hospital. Since retirement he has taught extensively in Scandinavia and is co-author of *Unimaginable Storms: A Search for Meaning in Psychosis*.

Katherine Killick, MA, RAth, is a clinical trainee at the Society of Analytical Psychology, working in a private art therapy and psychotherapy practice in St Albans. She was formerly Senior Art Therapist and Manager of the art therapy service at North West Hertfordshire District Health Authority.

Richard Marshall was Consultant Clinical Psychologist, Nottingham Healthcare NHS Trust. He died in April 1995, shortly before the publication of this book.

Kenneth Sanders, MD, came to psychoanalysis from general practice and has written of his experiences in two books, *A Matter of Interest* (1985) and *Nine Lives* (1991) (Clunie Press). He is a training analyst for the child psychotherapy course at the Tavistock Clinic and teaches in Italy.

Valerie Sinason is Consultant Child Psychotherapist at the Tavistock Clinic, London.

Robert M. Young is a psychotherapist in private practice. He is Visiting Professor at the Centre for Psychotherapeutic Studies, University of Sheffield, Editor of the journal *Free Associations* and author of *Mental Space* and *Whatever Happened to Human Nature* (Process Press).

Subject Index

References in italic indicate figures.

Author Index